"Bureaucracy is the bane of the SENCO's life, leading to burnout; Jean Gross' essential book helps SENCOs to streamline their activities whilst meeting the statutory requirements of the role, enabling them to fulfil the needs of students at the source – the classroom."

– **Abigail Hawkins**, Director of SENDCOSolutions/
SENsible SENCO

Beating Bureaucracy in Special Educational Needs

Are you overwhelmed by the amount of paperwork that SEND generates in your school? Would you like to spend more time improving the quality of teaching and learning for pupils with SEN or disabilities? If so, this is an essential book for you.

Beating Bureaucracy in Special Educational Needs shows how schools can tackle SEND bureaucracy by reducing the need for provision that is 'additional to or different from' that available to all pupils, through developing inclusive environments, curricula and teaching. This means placing fewer children on SEND registers and focusing SEND Code of Practice procedures squarely on those pupils with more complex needs.

Fully revised and updated, the fourth edition of this bestselling, practical text demonstrates what can be achieved, with new case studies describing schools with outstanding SEND provision, inclusive teaching and successful partnerships with parents. The book also explores how SENCOs can effectively reduce their workloads by making the most of technology and by distributing responsibility to class and subject teachers and middle and senior leaders, rather than operating as a lone voice. A toolkit of ready-to-use proformas, also available as an online resource, includes

- a model policy to give to Ofsted;
- information for parents, including the facts on 'Velcro' 1–1 support in the classroom;
- strategy sheets for all the main types of SEND;
- provision maps and proformas to help you plan, monitor and evaluate your provision.

Full of helpful and achievable strategies, this book is an essential resource for school leaders, SENCOs and anyone undertaking national SENCO qualifications. It shows how to put responsibility for supporting children with additional needs firmly back where it belongs and will help you – in the words of one SENCO – 'get your life back'.

Jean Gross, CBE, is a national expert on special needs, formerly holding the role of England's Communication Champion for children.

nasen

Helping Everyone Achieve

nasen is a professional membership association that supports all those who work with or care for children and young people with special and additional educational needs. Members include SENCOs, school leaders, governors/trustees, teachers, teaching assistants, support workers, other educationalists, students and families.

nasen supports its members through policy documents, peer-reviewed academic journals, its membership magazine *nasen Connect*, publications, professional development courses, regional networks and newsletters. Its website contains more current information such as responses to government consultations.

nasen's published documents are held in very high regard both in the UK and internationally.

For a full list of titles see: www.routledge.com/nasen-spotlight/book-series/FULNASEN

Other titles published in association with the National Association for Special Educational Needs (nasen):

Inclusive and Accessible Science for Students with Additional or Special Needs: How to Teach Science Effectively to Diverse Learners in Secondary Schools
Jane Essex
2023/pb: 978-0-367-76627-6

True Partnerships in SEND: Working Together to Give Children, Families and Professionals a Voice
Heather Green and Becky Edwards
2023/pb: 978-0-367-54494-2

Teaching Reading to All Learners Including those with Complex Needs
Sarah Moseley
2023/pb: 978-1-032-11475-0

The SENCO Survival Guide: The Nuts and Bolts of Everything You Need to Know, 3ed
Sylvia Edwards
2023/pb: 978-1-032-21947-9

Cultural Inclusion for Young People with SEND: Practical Strategies for Meaningful Inclusion in Arts and Culture
Paul Morrow
2023/pb: 978-0-367-64123-8

Providing Relationships and Sex Education for Special Learners
Paul Bray
2021/pb: 978-1-138-48747-5

Inclusion: A Principled Guide for School Leaders
Nicola Crossley and Des Hewitt
2021/pb: 978-0-367-34528-0

Leading on Inclusion: The Role of the SENCO
Mhairi Beaton, Geraldene Codina and Julie Wharton
2021/pb: 978-0-367-42050-5

Beating Bureaucracy in Special Educational Needs

Helping SENCOs Maintain a Work/Life Balance

Fourth edition

Jean Gross

Routledge
Taylor & Francis Group
LONDON AND NEW YORK

Designed cover image: © Photolibrary/Getty

Fourth edition published 2023
by Routledge
4 Park Square, Milton Park, Abingdon, Oxon, OX14 4RN

and by Routledge
605 Third Avenue, New York, NY 10158

Routledge is an imprint of the Taylor & Francis Group, an informa business

First edition published by Routledge 2008

Second edition published by Routledge 2013

Third edition published by Routledge 2015

British Library Cataloguing-in-Publication Data
A catalogue record for this book is available from the British Library

Library of Congress Cataloging-in-Publication Data
Names: Gross, Jean, author.
Title: Beating bureaucracy : helping SENCOs maintain a work/life balance / Jean Gross.
Description: Fourth edition. | Abingdon, Oxon ; New York, NY : Routledge, 2023. | Series: Nasen spotlight | Includes bibliographical references and index.
Identifiers: LCCN 2022061208 (print) | LCCN 2022061209 (ebook) | ISBN 9781032322384 (hardback) | ISBN 9781032322391 (paperback) | ISBN 9781003313526 (ebook)
Subjects: LCSH: Special education—Great Britain. | Special education teachers—Job stress—Great Britain. | Classroom management—Great Britain.
Classification: LCC LC3986.G7 G757 2023 (print) | LCC LC3986.G7 (ebook) | DDC 371.90941—dc23/eng/20230313
LC record available at https://lccn.loc.gov/2022061208
LC ebook record available at https://lccn.loc.gov/2022061209

ISBN: 978-1-032-32238-4 (hbk)
ISBN: 978-1-032-32239-1 (pbk)
ISBN: 978-1-003-31352-6 (ebk)

DOI: 10.4324/9781003313526

Typeset in Sabon
by Apex CoVantage, LLC

Access the Instructor and Student Resources: www.routledge.com/cw/gross

For all the dedicated SENCOs
who have tried so hard, over the past twenty years,
to make the unworkable work.

Contents

Acknowledgements

I am grateful to the SENCOs who provided the new case studies in this book, and to their schools: Becky Ashley at Tetney Primary, Elizabeth Barneveld at Houldsworth Valley Academy, Marie Beale at Whitefield Primary, Jen Beaton at Castle Manor Academy, Margaret Relf at Anglesey Primary Academy, Thomas Tillier at Aylesford School, Karen Truelove at Cathedral School, Toni Quinn at Porters Grange Primary and Rhian Williams at Henley Bank High School. The SEN Support Team at Southend Borough Council also deserve my thanks.

I am indebted to George Ellis, Director of Education SEND at the Unity Schools Partnership, for her insights into the current Multi-Academy Trust SEND landscape, and to Dr Tim Coulson, Unity's Chief Executive, whose commitment to SEND is an inspiration and example to all.

Thanks also go to those who provided case study material for previous editions: staff at Grays Infant and Nursery School, Torriano Primary and St James' Primary in Gorton. Also to Sheffield local authority for permission to use their intervention planning outlines and data collection sheet, to Amanda Corcoran for her ideas on monitoring the quality of interventions and to the former Globetown Action Zone for their examples of differentiated lesson planning.

I am particularly grateful to Abigail Hawkins of SENDCOSolutions, not only for helping me understand new developments in technology and locating case study contributors but also for the tireless support she gives to SENCOS everywhere, through her SENsible SENCO network sessions, Facebook group and website.

Finally, my thanks go to the generous photographers who provided the copyright-free *Unsplash* images I have used in illustrations for this book.

Preface

I wrote the first edition of this book in 2008, at a time when schools were awash with SEND paperwork, especially Individual Education Plans, overwhelming SENCOs and preventing them from doing their real job – helping class and subject teachers adapt their teaching and classroom environments to meet children's many and varied needs.

So what has changed since then? Two things make me feel hopeful that we can make progress to reduce the bureaucracy so often involved in SEND.

The first is the improvements to classroom teaching that mean learners who struggle can more easily succeed in lessons without the need to have separate plans written for them. Modelling, breaking tasks down into smaller chunks, repeated return to the same content to aid recall, dual coding – these science-driven techniques are music to the ears of those who have promoted such strategies for children with SEND for many years.

The second thing that makes me hopeful is the power of technology – assistive technology, which when well used can enable those who can't easily read print to hear it read to them, or those who struggle with writing to dictate to a tablet. IT systems, moreover, that automate the communication of information for staff, so that a teacher can, at a click of a button, pull up all they need to know about a pupil with SEND, and the SENCO quickly and easily pull off reports and data that allow them to provide evidence for Education, Health and Care Plan (EHCP) assessments, information for governors and evaluations of interventions.

Yet all is not yet hunky-dory in beating bureaucracy. Some local authorities still demand that every child with SEND has an IEP or Individual Support Plan (ISP). Some schools still believe they have to develop such plans in order to comply with SEND Code of Practice. Other schools spend a long time producing documents, such as Passports or Profiles, that sit in a drawer or in a file on a computer but don't actually influence what happens to the child in school. Person-centred planning, which gives back to students the ownership of goals and targets, and empowers them to communicate what they need to their teachers, has made only slow progress in many schools.

There is still a big job to do to give schools confidence that they can introduce simple systems to meet SEND, and document what really needs to be documented, in manageable ways. I hope this fourth edition of my book will help them do that.

1 The SEN paperchase

At its peak, the identification of SEN by mainstream primary school teachers ran at one in five of all children. Mainstream secondary schools identified an even higher number. This meant a huge and unsustainable workload for Special Educational Needs Coordinators (SENCOs). A SENCO in one large city secondary school, for example, estimated that her department circulated over 6,000 Individual Education Plan (IEP) sheets every term – one in each subject for 400 pupils, 20 per cent of the school's roll.

This is an extreme example, but it reflects a problem that every teacher who picks up this book will recognise. The problem is the oppressive weight of administration and paperwork generated by a well-intentioned aim that every child with special educational needs or a disability (SEND) will have an individual plan describing their needs, and how the needs will be met – each individual plan then generating its own cycle of review dates, discussions and meetings.

After an initial decrease in the percentage of children identified with SEND following the government's 2014 SEND review, numbers are on the rise again. The number of pupils on SEN Support has risen every year since 2016 and currently stands at 12.2% of all children. The number of Education, Health and Care Plans (EHCPs) has also risen steeply, increasing by 10% between January 2021 and January 2022 and doubling since 2015.

So now we have another SEND Review, driven by the rise in EHCP numbers and the associated cost pressures, with another push to improve the quality and impact of provision at the SEN Support stage in the graduated approach. If this is to succeed, schools will need to find new ways of helping children with SEND to make progress – without at the same time generating more paperwork and further overburdening SENCOs. This is the theme of this book.

It shows how schools can successfully put responsibility for supporting children with most types of additional need firmly back where it belongs – with class and subject teachers. It describes how to use existing systems for class and subject teacher target-setting, recording and planning, rather than time-consuming, bureaucratic and separate SEND systems, to ensure that all children who find learning difficult can succeed.

DOI: 10.4324/9781003313526-1

The difficulty for SENCOs

Most SENCOs feel they have inadequate non-contact time to carry out their role. The most recent national SENCO workforce survey (Boddison *et al.*, 2020) found that primary phase SENCOs have on average 2.15 days protected time per week, but around a third report having less than 1.5 days. Less than one in five report that they have sufficient time to ensure that children at SEN Support are able to access the provision they need.

Secondary SENCOs have on average 2.32 days per week for their role, and 28% have less than 1.5 days per week. Given the size of most secondary schools, it has been estimated that 70% of secondary SENCOs are not given enough time to do their job effectively (Boddison *et al.*, 2020).

This means that they are carrying a heavy workload and are often unable to maintain any sort of work/life balance. It also means that they have little, if any, time to do the job they would like to be doing – helping teachers plan their lessons with the needs of children with SEND in mind, supporting the work that teaching assistants (TAs) do with individuals and groups, evaluating practice so as to improve the provision that children receive or teaching children directly. Seventy-eight percent of primary SENCOs and 63% of secondary SENCOs say that administration takes up most of their allocated time. In the words of one SENCO I interviewed for this book, 'too much time is spent on paperwork; the 'expert' is locked away', unable to deploy their expertise effectively.

The problems of excessive bureaucracy are not confined to SENCOs. On average, a teacher in Year 5 (the peak year for SEN numbers) might, in a class of 33, be operating individual plans for seven to eight children. In schools serving areas of high social deprivation, the numbers will be very much higher, sometimes as many as half the class. Each child might have around four targets on their plan. That makes at minimum between 28 and 32 different targets that the teacher is meant to remember. This is clearly an impossibility.

And if the teacher cannot remember what the targets are, how can they possibly use them in any meaningful way to guide their teaching or the child's learning? This is the real emperor's new clothes of the individual-plan system: the fact, rarely commented on, that teachers (like all human beings) have a useful working memory span of no more than seven to eight items, and that if this is exceeded by overuse of any form of individual plan, those plans are likely to become static documents with little impact on progress.

Some schools, however, have found a way out of this maze of paperwork. They have focused on what SEND provision really means – in law, a learning difficulty or disability that calls for 'special provision, that is, provision that is additional to or different from the provision normally made available'. Then they have sought to increase the range of 'normally available' provision so that fewer children require additionality. They have also used provision mapping and helped class and subject teachers set and monitor targets for children with SEND within the everyday feedback systems they use for all children.

> When I took over as SENCO a lot of children had a Personal Plan for SEND but the target in Year 5 was almost always 1–1 reading sessions once a week . . . that should be **normal**. So now we don't need all those plans.
>
> Primary SENCO

This book is about sharing the practice of these schools. It represents an attempt to liberate SENCOs and class teachers from an excessive workload, whilst at the same time protecting the rights of children to the best possible inclusive teaching and learning.

> We need to move on from IEPs. . . . I investigated how long it takes to write them; we are spending tens and thousands of pounds on that kind of paperwork . . . parents up and down the land would rather the school was inclusive and that teachers were making a difference in lessons rather than that they had a piece of paper that was written once and nobody necessarily comes back to it.
>
> Hannah Maloney, SENCO and SEND researcher (2022)

Why all this paperwork?

The rewards for schools for producing a high volume of paperwork around SEND are many, enough to outweigh the negative impact on work/life balance and quality of provision.

For example, in secondary schools, a school's low Progress 8 value-added measure may be interpreted more favourably if the school has identified large numbers of pupils as having SEND.

The individual plan, a visible indicator of what teachers should be doing to meet SEND, easy to get hold of (in both literal and metaphorical senses) by Ofsted inspectors whose expertise in SEND might be limited, continues to receive heavy emphasis in some inspections. One SENCO recently reported that inspectors asked to see all 30 learning plans for children with SEND; during the inspection, they then interviewed children to see if the child felt the plan was used in practice, and looked for evidence in the classroom that the plan was being implemented. A recent Ofsted research report 'Supporting SEND' (2021) was critical of schools where pupils did not have written support plans, saying that 'this meant that the graduated approach was not in place', and suggesting that this affected parents' opportunities to influence provision for their child.

Funding mechanisms in some local authorities encourage schools to focus on paperwork. 'Chasing the EHCP' is the approach many schools take in order to meet parental expectations, with the EHCP seen as a magical solution to meet need. EHCP assessments are only granted if the school can supply copies of multiple individual plans demonstrating the provision that has been made over a period of time. Once EHCP funding has been agreed, the only way to keep it often seems to be to prove, through voluminous records, that the child is still struggling despite being well supported.

The rewards for plentiful, elegantly executed individual plans can be great; the SENCO's credibility, and often his or her 'earning power' for the school, can stand or fall on IEP/Individual Support Plan performance.

Nevertheless, there are a number of trends which have the potential to reduce some of the bureaucracy associated with SEND. The large majority of schools understand that high-quality inclusive classroom teaching is the best way to raise standards for learners with SEND, rather than paperwork. Officially, Ofsted's primary focus in inspections is not looking at individual education or support plans, as such, but at teaching and learning within the classroom.

Equally, technology, via the opportunities to store and share information about pupils presented by management information systems, has fundamentally changed the way teachers can build knowledge about individual pupils' needs into their planning. And finally, we have seen the growth of provision mapping. First developed by my colleague Ann Berger in Bristol schools, and later incorporated into materials I wrote for the government's National Strategies, it provides a simple way of recording the extra interventions that the school provides in each year group. A teacher or SENCO can highlight on the provision map the interventions that a particular child receives, and use this, together with personal targets set by the class or subject teacher, as an alternative to writing separate individual plans.

What is stopping schools from reducing bureaucracy?

Government after government has clarified that individual plans for children with SEND are not and have never been a statutory requirement.

In 2011, for example, the DfE made explicit their view that IEPs had had their day:

> We know that parents value the use of non-statutory Individual Education Plans (IEPs), which are recommended by the Code of Practice. In the period since 2001, when the Code was last revised and published, we know that many schools have developed new approaches to planning, reviewing and tracking the progress of all pupils that have enabled them to achieve what IEPs aimed to do without many of the associated bureaucratic burdens. These approaches have included new ways of tracking pupil progress, involving pupils in setting their own targets, engaging regularly and effectively with parents, and using individual profiles and provision mapping.
>
> In order to reduce bureaucratic burdens on schools, in reviewing and updating the Code of Practice, we will remove advice on using IEPs and encourage schools to explore the ways in which these and other new approaches can be used to enable pupils with SEN to develop, progress and fulfil their potential.
>
> *Support and aspiration: a new approach to special educational needs and disability* (DfE, 2011)

The 2014 SEND Code of Practice fulfilled this promise. It makes no mention of IEPs, leaving it up to schools to decide what paperwork to use and referring only to meetings with parents and pupils where 'a record of the outcomes, action and support agreed through the discussion should be kept and shared with all the appropriate school staff. This record should be given to the pupil's parents.'

And yet despite these new freedoms, many schools have stuck to the safety of the known, changing only the name of their IEPs to Individual Support Plans (ISPs), Passports or Profiles. There seem to be a number of factors behind this:

- Pressure from class teachers, who believe that maintaining an individual plan for a child will mean that the child gets support, usually in the form of a teaching assistant
- Concerns about parents' reactions if a formal written planning process or the linked push for EHCPs are not used
- A historical belief that the quality and quantity of paperwork is the key to attracting and retaining funding
- Bureaucratic procedures in some local authorities, such as encouraging schools to provide provision maps as well as, rather than instead of, individual support plans. Whether or not schools persist with such plans has been found to be highly dependent on local authority advice, which varies greatly across the country (Ellis *et al.*, 2012)
- A belief that individual support plans make a difference to pupil outcomes

Do individual support plans make a difference?

All the paperwork involved in SEND would be worthwhile if we knew that it was actually making a real difference to children. But is there any evidence of this?

Schools tend to think there is, because they see children achieving the small-steps targets set for them on their individual plans. There is a circularity, however, in school self-evaluation systems claiming proudly that children are achieving the targets set on their plans when the targets are required from the start to be specific, measurable, *achievable*, realistic and time-constrained. Achievable targets may not be sufficiently stretching; in their 2010 review, Ofsted noted that 'the challenge represented by the targets in individual education plans was highly variable . . . using these targets to judge whether children or young people were making good progress was extremely subjective'.

There is an issue too in whether the achievement of a series of these achievable targets actually aggregates, over time, into improved attainment or personal and social skills. National data, as we will see later, suggest that the procedures of the SEN Code have not, so far, led to these improved outcomes.

Schools have historically embarked on the paperwork involved in SEN for one main reason – the quest for additional resources. And yet those resources, once painfully achieved, may in fact make little difference to the child's progress. Pinney (2004) analysed a wide range of national statistics and found no link between the numbers of what were then Statements (now EHCPs) maintained by local authorities and the results achieved by their pupils with SEN. A series of key national reports (Ofsted, 2004, 2006, 2010, 2021) have all made clear that the provision of additional resources to pupils with low or high incidence SEND – such as teaching assistant support – does not ensure good quality intervention or adequate pupil progress. Substantial research from the Institute of Education (Blatchford *et al*., 2012) even concludes that the more teaching assistant (TA) support pupils receive, the less progress they make – a finding that holds even after controlling for SEN status, prior attainment and other factors that might explain the relationship.

The lack of any link between established SEND systems and improved attainment is most evident for pupils with literacy and numeracy difficulties – the most common type of SEN. Year on year, around one in ten boys leave primary school with the reading skills of an average seven-year-old, unable to read the simplest of secondary school texts. All will, at some point, have been on the SEN register and no doubt have had any number of individual plans with literacy as their prime targets. All those targets, written by thousands of schools on millions of plans – 'Will learn to read first 50 high-frequency words', 'Will be able to read CVC words' – appear to have had little impact. All the training provided to teachers on how to write SMART targets, how to select appropriate strategies to achieve them and how to measure and document the outcomes, appears to have made no difference at all to the numbers of children failing to learn to read.

A similarly static national picture applies to the overall attainment and progress of pupils with SEND, where the gap between children with SEND and their peers has not decreased in recent years. Nor do the procedures of the SEN Code appear to have had much effect on reducing the frequency of behaviour difficulties. Exclusions did not reduce over the period when more and more children were placed on individual education or behaviour plans because of behavioural, emotional or social difficulties. Being identified as having SEND does not appear to afford particular protection to such pupils; the Timpson Review of school exclusions (2019) found that children with SEND accounted for 46% of all permanent exclusions and 44.9% of fixed period exclusions.

The only area where it is possible that the SEN Code's procedures have made a difference may be personal and life skills. But here we have no evidence either way, since we have as yet no agreed means of assessing and recording children's development in these areas, nor definitions of what would constitute an average, above average or below average rate of progress. What we do know about the well-being of pupils with SEND is not encouraging; in the autumn of 2020, pupils with an EHCP had a persistent absence rate of 25.6%, and for those on SEN Support, it was 19.3%. This compared to 11.1% for those with no identified SEND. Research on the cohort of children born in 2000 has found that those with SEN are twice as likely as other children to be persistently bullied (Chatzitheochari *et al.*, 2014) and more recent research (Anti-Bullying Alliance, 2021) found that 36% of pupils with SEND experience frequent bullying compared to 25% of those without SEND.

In sum, the evidence that all the work schools put into implementing assessment and planning systems for learners with SEND is effective is slender, to say the least. And in schools where it has proved possible to bring about significant reductions in the numbers of children failing to achieve basic literacy, numeracy or social, emotional and behavioural skills, this has not been through having more children on the SEN register, or more and better individual plans. Instead, these gains have been produced by changing the way groups and classes of children have been taught, using the kinds of inclusive classroom teaching strategies and evidence-based additional interventions described later on in this book.

The problem with the individual model

Much SEND practice rests on the identification of individual children's difficulties and the targeting of resources to address their perceived problems. Many writers have commented on the inadequacies of this individual model. Their argument has been that it shifts responsibility away from what schools as institutions might do to better meet the needs of all learners, towards a model that seeks to prop up the child identified as different (and by implication deficient) in accessing an otherwise undifferentiated curriculum through the provision of additional individual adult support.

An example comes from the illuminating story told by David Moore, HMI, who observed a secondary class being taught about the workings of the spinning jenny. The worksheets used were difficult, and the TA who was supporting one young man (herself with a physics degree) had to go and ask the teacher what she meant. 'Don't get worried', the boy said to the TA, 'I never do'. When HMI asked him why he never got worried, he replied, 'Cos she's always here to do the work for me, in't she?'

A model based on the identification of individual children's difficulties thus often prevents teachers from making adaptations to the way they teach. It may also serve to lower expectations for what children with SEND can achieve. For example, Shifrer (2013) demonstrated that teachers and parents hold lower educational expectations for high school students labeled with a learning disability than for similarly achieving and behaving students without this label.

Cathryn Knight (2021) compared children diagnosed with dyslexia with a non-dyslexic group matched on ability, socioeconomic class, levels of parental education and income, gender and age. She found that teachers and parents of children labelled with dyslexia, and the children themselves, held lower beliefs about their ability in English and maths than their matched peers without this label. They were also significantly less likely to say that they would go to university.

Another interesting study (Tymms and Merrell, 2006) compared the progress of children who had been formally identified through screening procedures as having SEN (in this case, ADHD) with those who also had ADHD symptoms but where the child's class teacher was not told of this, nor SEN procedures invoked. The teachers of this second group were simply provided with general information about how to teach inattentive and hyperactive children. The teachers in the first group were provided with both this information and the names of children identified through screening.

Providing information on teaching strategies was helpful; children in the second group had more positive attitudes towards school and reading, and showed improved behaviour, when compared with children in schools not given the teaching information. But formally identifying children as having ADHD was not helpful; the researchers found a significant negative effect on the reading and mathematics attainment of children who had been identified, when compared with children not identified. They suggest that this is because once children are labelled, teachers focus more on keeping them happy and calm rather than pushing them to attain. Equally, it might mean that teachers relinquished more of the care of the children to additional adults, rather than working directly with them themselves.

What this research and anecdote suggest is that over-reliance on identifying SEN and invoking the associated procedures can sometimes mean that the teacher who is responsible for the child's learning may do less to adapt his or her curriculum delivery than if the child were not identified. This has been a direct consequence of the individual model of SEN and of the way in which targets for change have been located with the child and not with the teacher.

The problem with IEP/ISP targets

To understand the problem with targets on individual plans, we need to understand who they belong to. Targets *do* work: we have only to look at increases in the number of children achieving nationally expected standards in English and maths at the end of Key Stage 2, and five good GCSEs, to see this. Most education professionals have, by now, experienced for themselves the powerful (if uncomfortable) effects of working towards a target for which they felt personally accountable, and which was clear, measurable and time-constrained.

The targets we have all as individuals experienced, however, have one thing in common: for them to work, we needed to know what they were, and to be constantly reminded of them, frequently monitored on them and recognised if we achieved them. Yet if we undertake the exercise of asking children with SEND what their individual targets are, we often find that they have no idea. The targets may have been made up by the SENCO sitting at home with her paperwork, or they may have been spawned by an IT program. Even if the child was involved originally in agreeing targets, the chances are that no one has reminded him or her of them since.

There are other problems with targets as well as the problem of confused ownership. Individual-child targets have a habit of replacing meaningful hopes and dreams with what can be readily measured. The drive to get SMART has meant, at worst, a generation of children (and of the adults around them) who believe that staying in their seat for five minutes, not tearing up their work or packing their bag before school in the morning, will magically make them be able to concentrate, to believe in themselves or be well organised. We tend to forget that teachers and children still need this broader sense of where they meaningfully want to get to in the end.

Effective interventions for children with SEND, moreover, are often far too complex to reduce to a few SMART targets. The exceptionally effective Reading Recovery literacy intervention provides half an hour of daily one-to-one teaching for a period of 12 to 20 weeks. Each day, the highly trained Reading Recovery teacher assesses the child's knowledge and skills. Each day, the teacher plans what he or she will teach on the basis of this assessment. The teaching on any one day might include a new grapheme-phoneme link, a way of breaking a word into chunks, how to use phrasing and expression when reading aloud, a way of forming a letter, how to hold a sentence of increasing length in the mind while writing it, how to write an irregular but common word quickly and fluently. How could all this be expressed in a small number of termly SMART targets?

Consider another effective intervention, this time for children with social and emotional difficulties – placement in a nurture group. Such a placement involves around two terms in a small group of around 12 children, working all day every day in a family-like environment to learn the basics of how to relate to others, to share, to concentrate, to listen, to talk. Again, how can all this essential and ever-changing learning be described in a limited number of targets?

And what would be added to either the nurture group provision, or the Reading Recovery teaching, by writing an individual plan for the children taking part? In both cases, we have a skilled teacher who is constantly developing, monitoring and reviewing targets for what he or she wants the child to achieve. In both cases, the teacher may well articulate for the child what they need to focus on: 'Today, I want to see you. . . . ', 'What I'm looking for when you read this book is that you. . . . '. But the teacher will not waste precious teaching time on writing half-termly or termly paper plans for every child worked with.

The importance of talking

IEPs/ISPs were never intended to be 'just bits of paper', recording measurable but over-simple and often meaningless targets in the absence of ownership or involvement of the person potentially most willing and able to put in the energy needed to achieve them – the child him- or herself.

Before the paperchase began in earnest, when there were fewer individual plans and those there were had a less bureaucratic purpose, the plan was just the written record of a much more important human process. This process was about *talking*. It brought together the people most concerned about the child's progress (parent/carer, teacher and child) at a meeting where the purpose was to share information, clarify the broad objectives for the child's progress, remind everyone of the child's strengths and arrive collaboratively at some priority targets to which all present could subscribe and all contribute.

Properly done, this kind of meeting – including deciding who will do what to help the child reach the priority targets – takes up to an hour. To be effective, it needs to be followed by frequent monitoring of the agreed actions, and frequent monitoring of progress, in a way that keeps the targets alive for the child. There must be a review date set not so far away that participants can forget that they will at that date be held to account for the success or failure of the joint enterprise – more than a term will be too long, and less would be better.

From this it is clear that in schools where high numbers of children are identified as having SEND, it will be challenging to implement the talking model of individual planning successfully. This is why a potentially energising, effective idea, admirable in its intent, has degenerated into a paper exercise. In these circumstances, it is important to consider whether it is worth doing routinely at all, or whether there might not be other, better ways of planning that will maximise the achievement of pupils with SEND.

Schools may decide they need to focus the full, teacher-dependent planning process on only those children who need a fresh, concerted, home-school impetus to move them on, and those with the most complex needs. These schools will adopt simpler systems for meeting the wider range of additional needs.

In doing so, they will go back to first principles and consider what essential functions the SEN bureaucracy was meant to achieve, so as to decide how those functions might be met in different and less paper-driven ways. In this book, we will take each of these functions in turn and describe ways of fulfilling them that are manageable, effective and non-bureaucratic.

But first let us look at two case studies of schools that have chosen to 'do SEN differently' and less bureaucratically.

CASE STUDY

Tetney Primary School: an IEP-free zone

At Tetney Primary School in Lincolnshire, an inclusive curriculum and environment for all has reduced the need for provision that is 'additional to and different from' that available to all children – and therefore the number of children who need individual SEND paperwork. Where additional and different provision is required, simple systems are in place to plan and record it.

Curriculum

The school's curriculum has been designed to support those with difficulties in learning.

In maths, for example, recall learning from the White Rose curriculum has been added to the Effective Maths scheme the school uses: all learning is in very small steps, with overlearning (practising newly acquired skills beyond the point of initial mastery) built in. Same-day intervention forms part of the mastery approach.

Some pupils work on maths topics one or more years behind the class as a whole, but the topics and methods are the same for all. Differentiation would be by the size of the numbers the pupils work with, for example.

In English, the school's Power of Reading approach is heavily oracy-based, giving all pupils a chance to engage and contribute, even if their literacy levels are low.

Interventions

The school provides a range of interventions that do not have to be accessed via SEND identification systems. Termly class pupil progress meetings, and detailed assessments available to schools who subscribe to the school improvement PiXL Club, are used to identify children in need of additional interventions.

At the end of any unit of work, teachers will identify gaps and use PiXL 'therapies' (carefully planned catch-up learning activities) for children who need them.

One intervention used by the school is tutoring. A teacher who runs her own company comes in each afternoon to work on gaps in learning identified by class teachers. She liaises with the class teacher after each session and holds a summary meeting with the teacher and SENCO after each six-week block of tutoring.

Training

Training for staff has been central to creating high-quality inclusive teaching and environments, with CPD on trauma-informed practice, and restorative approaches proving especially effective. All staff, for example, have been trained to run restorative circles with their classes when there have been problems. This has prevented poor behaviour being repeated, thus reducing the numbers of children who otherwise might have been identified as having SEMH.

The SEN register

Numbers on the SEN register are low. Provision for children is categorised into the 'Waves': Wave 1 is high-quality inclusive teaching, Wave 2 additional small group interventions/catch-up programmes, managed by the class teacher and taking place in the classroom, and Wave 3 the stage where the SENCO and/or outside agencies are involved. Only children at Wave 3 who continue to struggle despite this involvement go on the SEN register.

The paperwork

Paperwork is kept to a minimum. Each class teacher enters the names of children in their class who are receiving provision at Waves 1, 2 or 3 on a whole-school provision map (Table 1.1), each half term. Colour coding is used – red for children with cognition and learning needs, blue for those with communication and interaction needs, green for SEMH and brown for sensory and/or physical needs. Those on the SEND register are highlighted in bold.

Every fortnight there is a 'welfare check' with the SENCO, where teachers can discuss any child for whom the provision they are making is not working. For children on the SEND register, the SENCO does a regular formal review to explore what is working, what is not working and what might need to change.

	Quality first teaching			
Wave 1	**Cognition and learning** Differentiated curriculum Differentiated delivery Differentiated outcome Increased visual aids Visual timetables Use of writing frames ICT/tablet devices to support Use of concrete materials Concrete – pictorial – abstract Guided Group work	**Communication and interaction** Flexible teaching arrangements Structured school and class routines Differentiated curriculum delivery Differentiated outputs Increased visual aids Visual timetables Use of symbols Gestures and signals	**Behavioural, social and emotional** Whole school and class reward system Whole school/class rules Whole school policy for behaviour Circle time as part of Jigsaw Buddy system Well-being breaks Jigsaw	**Sensory and/or physical** Flexible teaching arrangements Teacher awareness of S&P Impairment Fiddle toys Workstation space Golden Mile
	Small group interventions/catch-up programmes			
Wave 2	**Cognition and learning** Additional RWI High frequency word activities – precision teaching/ATTACK 3 in 3 In-class support from TA Individualised reading support daily Guided Group work	**Communication and interaction** First Call Time to Talk Repeating back accurately	**Social, emotional and mental health** Small group circle time Circle of friends Time to talk	**Sensory and/or physical** Brain break exercises (daily, x5 min) Fine motor skills practice Gross motor skills programme Coloured paper or overlays

	Reception	Year 1	Year 2	Year 3	Year 4	Year 5	Year 6
	Individualised, targeted support for pupils with SEND						
Wave 3	**Cognition and learning** Working with adult outside of class in small group Working memory training	**Communication and interaction** Speech and language therapy work Autism Outreach Team Makaton Personal Visual organiser ICT – Writing with Symbols programme		**Social, emotional and mental health** Counselling Individual reward system Home–school record (daily) Peer mentoring (as appropriate) ELSA		**Sensory and/or physical** Individual support in class during PE and lunchtime Physiotherapy programme Occupational therapy programme Access to laptop	
	Reception	Year 1	Year 2	Year 3	Year 4	Year 5	Year 6

Table 1.1 Tetney Primary whole school provision map summer 2022

In addition to the provision map, all vulnerable children (those affected by trauma, looked after children, severely disabled children) have a One Page Profile detailing their likes, dislikes, what they need and (in a separate box) why they need it – for example, that an autistic boy needs to be allowed to keep his coat on because he sees it as his protection. Another box is used to identify triggers that might spark behaviour issues; for one child whose parents had been drug abusers, this was flashing lights and sirens, which she associated with bad things about to happen. The purpose of these Profiles is to ensure that teachers understand the child's needs. Becky will stand with them until they have read and signed the Profile to show that they do.

IEPs or ISPs have not been used since Becky became SENCO. Class teachers were delighted not to have to fill them in anymore and happy to work with the three-wave provision map system instead. Becky had noticed that most IEPs had three targets, usually one for English, one for maths and one for another issue. To be SMART, the targets had very small steps – for example, 'Put finger spaces between words in my work'. Once this was achieved, children had to wait for the IEP review (usually termly) for their next target. The IEPs were not live documents influencing teaching and learning.

Now pupils' targets are part of marking their work as next steps in learning rather than written into individual plans. Everyday systems are used to review progress against targets. In maths, for example, a highlighting system is used at each end-of-unit assessment to indicate greater depth (blue), expected (green), needs more work on this (yellow) for specific aspects of the unit. Recap is then used. Review of progress is built-in: teachers and leaders can look through pupils' subsequent work to see if there are questions that they are now getting right, where they were on 'yellow' before.

Targets related to SEMH needs are set with children by the school's ELSA, who provides Wave 3 support to children in the school's nurture room. Such targets are always shared with other staff so that they too are 'live', frequently changed and actually able to influence practice.

Working with parents

Becky runs a coffee morning for parents every four weeks, where parents can come if they have any concerns they want to discuss. Another session every four weeks focuses on the subject curriculum. There is also a monthly coffee morning with the headteacher. All this means that parents have regular contact with school and many opportunities to talk about what is on their mind.

In Becky's time as SENCO, only one parent (a SENCO herself) has requested an IEP for their child. A conversation soon convinced her of the benefits of the alternative, IEP-free system.

Working with the local authority

By the time a child has been through several cycles of Wave 3 provision, there will be multiple outside agencies involved, all supporting the need to move to EHCP assessment.

In her applications, Becky submits copies of a modified provision map with other children's names deleted and each school year broken down into terms, to show the provision the child has had over time. Alongside this she submits an Excel spreadsheet showing the cost of the provision to the school budget, demonstrating that it exceeds the notional £6,000 that is required before any top-up funding kicks in.

These systems are effective and acceptable to the local authority. Currently, the school has a near-perfect success rate in applying for EHCPs.

Reasonable adjustments at Castle Manor Academy

Jen Beaton, SENCO and Assistant Headteacher at Castle Manor Academy in Suffolk, has made it a priority to ensure that in her school 'SEND is part of the narrative, not a bolt-on.' SEND is built into leadership roles, with SEND data, for example, always part of the number-crunching that is done for heads of year and team leaders. Jen sits on the senior leadership team. SEND development is part of the school improvement plan; Jen not only reviews action on this element regularly but also can see what is planned for in other areas (such as teaching and learning), where she might need to prompt further thinking about SEND.

The key to effective provision for SEND, Jen believes, is a high-quality inclusive teaching offer for all pupils. Despite relatively high levels of disadvantage, only around 13% of the school's population are on SEN Support, with 5.6% having EHCPs, many of these for children in the school's special provision for cognition and learning needs.

Jen finds the term 'reasonable adjustments' useful, asking staff, for example, 'Is it a reasonable adjustment for a child to type in your lesson rather than use a pen?' If so, that child does not need to go on the SEN register because the adjustment is routinely being made.

Other examples would be reading pens, now being rolled out as part of normal classroom provision, so pupils can have print read aloud to them. Adjusting seating plans is also a reasonable adjustment used in the school. Staff don't automatically sit children with SEND at the front; a student might ask for this ('I find it hard to concentrate, so can I sit near the front?'), but equally they might prefer to be near the door because of anxiety, or at the back of the room if they worry about the judgement of peers. The student can always express their preferences.

As well as adjusting where they sit, teachers might routinely make special efforts to build their relationship with the pupil or give them special roles in the classroom.

In general, children only go on the SEN register where external support is involved. A child with ASD might not be on the register if their progress is good; similarly, a child with hemiplegia who simply needs PE staff to make reasonable adjustments would not be regarded as having SEN.

The paperwork

Where a child is on the SEN register at SEND Support, they receive a 'K' code on the school's Go4Schools management information system, or a 'E' code if they have an EHCP. The codes appear on seating plans and class lists, and this is a trigger for staff to go to a desktop SEND folder to find the 'Support and success plan' for the student. Care plans for medical needs are in the same folder, as well as a medical folder, thus, Jen notes, 'reducing the number of staff click needs.'

The support and success plans are open documents to which staff can add strategies they have successfully used with the student. They have a 'Review' space at the end, and if any member of staff meets with the child's parent or carer, they can note that discussion there. There is contact with parents at least three or four times a year, sometimes through the SENCO, sometimes through the achievement leads (Heads of Year) or well-being lead.

Jen's communication with subject staff is often face-to-face; at twice-weekly briefings for staff, she or other leaders can say, 'Can I just have five minutes to talk about x student, please?'

Much target-setting is built into regular subject teaching. Go4Schools prompts staff to write what's working well for each child with an EHCP that they teach, and what the next small step in their subject is and to review progress against these steps. All this information goes to parents.

Children have a generous amount of tutor group time, so form tutors know their children really well. Jen cites a tutor with a student on the autistic spectrum who she 'really gets'. This means that many problems don't even need to come to the SENCO or lead to paperwork; they are resolved by those who know the students best.

Tutors and other staff only come to the SENCO when they feel stuck. They do not have to fill in a referral form – 'they can just ping an email to ask if they can talk to me about a child.'

Shared responsibility

Responsibility for students who are in any way struggling is distributed rather than being the sole responsibility of the SENCO. The safeguarding lead, deputy safeguarding lead, achievement leader, assistant head for behaviour and values, headteacher, vulnerable children's officer and SENCO all hold a caseload. If achievement leaders or subject teachers notice that a student is not doing well, Jen will ask what has happened in response – for example, whether anyone has talked with the student's parents. Jen sits on the safeguarding group so is able to cross-check whether safeguarding issues could be the cause of the problem. 'So many SENCOs don't see the whole of the child's life', she notes. Jen is also the reading lead for the school and is currently working on screening and tracking progress, which is very helpful in terms of SEND such as dyslexia.

Additional interventions

The school provides a wide range of interventions for any child who needs them: for example, phonic gap work, Lexia, maths tutoring, the Herts for Learning reading fluency project. Interventions are delivered by subject staff – tutors, English teachers, an achievement leader delivering an adapted Lego Therapy programme with a small group of Year 9s. There is also a strong well-being offer for all, with two ELSA-trained support staff trained in the 'Language for Behaviour and Emotions' approach, and an external Mental Health in Schools team. The wide range of normally available provision reduces the need to identify children as having SEND when their needs are simply catch-up or support with social and emotional learning. Where children do have SEND, Jen's role is to connect them with the right provision. She has, for example, made sure they are appropriately prioritised for tutoring funded through COVID catch-up money and that they receive tutoring from teachers rather than TAs.

Working with parents

Following the principle of weaving SEND into everything the school does, and everyone's roles, Jen helps parents and carers to talk to the right people – 'If it's a friendship problem, they go to the form tutor, if it's how to help children reach maths targets via homework they need to go to the maths teacher.' SEND review meetings are scheduled on a case-by-case basis; some parents like a half termly meeting, others prefer contact by email.

CPD for staff

CPD is prioritised: 'the best thing we can do is invest in staff so they can all be awesome teachers for SEN', says Jen. One thing that has been very helpful is the short weekly teaching and learning briefings the school has introduced. Based on Rosenshine's principles of instruction, Doug Lemov's *Teach Like a Champion* and Tom Sherrington's *Teaching WalkThrus*, these sessions have helped staff develop their skills in scaffolding and chunking learning, which has been very helpful in relation to SEND. Other influential CPD that Jen cites has been training in trauma-informed approaches.

KEY PRINCIPLES

Key take-aways for SENCOs

- If you are finding your workload very heavy, and that most of your time is spent on SEND bureaucracy and administration, you are not alone
- Time spent managing large numbers of individual pupil plans may not pay off
- You may have more impact if you focus on helping colleagues develop inclusive teaching so that fewer children need provision that is additional to or different from that available to their peers
- You can then, for that smaller number of pupils with more complex SEND, implement the Code of Practice procedures as they were originally intended, with regular face-to-face meetings involving pupils, parents and teachers

Key questions for the wider school leadership team

- Does your SENCO spend most of their time on administration? If so, are there more efficient ways of managing this?
- How far do the case studies in this chapter represent practice in your school? Are there any changes you would like to make?

2 Doing SEN differently

The case studies: common features

What can we learn from the schools, described in the previous chapter, who have chosen to 'do SEN differently' and less bureaucratically?

They share two key features:

- Avoiding over-identifying pupils as having SEN
- Using ordinary systems for all pupils rather than separate SEND systems

Avoiding over-identification

Currently, 16.5% of all pupils are identified as having SEN, the highest figure since the 2014 SEND reforms. As many as four in ten children are considered to have such needs at some stage in their educational journey (Hutchinson, 2021).

The reasons for identifying children as having SEN are interesting Can it really be, for example, that one in four ten-year-old boys have SEN? This is what their teachers think, according to official figures (DfE, 2022). Or are these children simply not on track for success in end of key stage tests, with the SEN label used to provide an explanation? Can it be right that summer-born children are many times more likely to be on SEN registers than those born in autumn or winter – with nearly half of summer born boys identified as having SEN at some point during their primary career (Campbell, 2021)? Or is this, too, an artefact of accountability pressures in the system?

> There is a structural creation of SEND within the context of the wider school and policy environment. Rigid prescriptive 'expectations' not suitable for relatively younger children result in many of these children being denoted with SEND.
>
> (Campbell, 2021)

DOI: 10.4324/9781003313526-2

We know why over-identification happens. Pressure to achieve ever higher standards encourages teachers to attribute the lack of success of some children to within-child deficits; children can have extra time in their end of key stage tests if they have an EHCP, schools are concerned about pupils not coping when they transfer to secondary school, secondary progress data looks better if SEN numbers are high and so on.

But, as the *Lamb Inquiry* (2009) reminded schools, 'Being behind your peers in learning does not of itself mean that a pupil has SEN'. Ofsted (2010) also notes that it is important to avoid over-identification of SEN occurring because 'the standard offer of education or care is insufficiently adapted for frequently found needs', or because 'such identification is the only way in which parents and schools can gain access to support from a range of in-house or external providers.'

It is important to remember that there is a distinction to be made between pupils with SEN and pupils who have 'a learning need, but not necessarily a special educational need' (DfE and DH, 2014). Schools can ensure that pupils who have learning needs and have fallen behind can access 'catch-up' intervention programmes. They do not have to identify them as having SEN to do so.

> One primary school sent us 36 children, **all** on the SEN register – I think just because they had an intervention in Year 1.
>
> Thomas Tillier, Assistant SENCO Aylesford School

Nor, of course, do children who are disabled necessarily have a special educational need. A child who uses a wheelchair does not have special educational needs if their school has ramps rather than steps and they have no difficulties with learning. This is generally understood. But what about children with dyslexia – do they really have to have special educational needs when the technology that can translate speech to print and vice versa is freely available, as it is now if they are allowed to use their mobile phone in school?

It is always worth reflecting on the medical and social models of understanding disability, which can be applied to a wide range of educational 'difficulties' (Table 2.1). Whether something represents a difficulty or not, or the extent to which

Medical model: The problem is the child	Social model: the problem is the environment
Confined to a wheelchair	Not enough lifts, stairs, ramps
Has ADHD	Young children expected to sit still for long periods
Can't read	Lak of texts at the right reading level, or audiobooks or print to speech technology
Suffers from dyslexia	Totally print-based curriculum
Poor receptive language	Techers often give long and incomprehensible instructions
Slow learner	Lesson pace too fast

Table 2.1 Medical and social models

it represents a difficulty, depends entirely on whether the situation or environment is enabling or disabling. A child on the autistic spectrum, for example, may function well under conditions of calm and quiet and less well under conditions of high sensory stimulation.

> Take social skills. If you watch the dialogue in Autcraft, the autism-friendly server version of Minecraft, you will experience positive, polite and co-operative interaction. The autistic players are focusing on something they love in an environment they feel comfortable in, and all of a sudden, social skills don't seem to be so 'impaired'.
>
> Debby Elley, mother of two autistic boys (2020)

By describing a child as 'special needs' there is a risk that we absolve ourselves from the responsibility to provide enabling environments, and reinforce the notions of purely within-child or within-family explanations of learning difficulty. These within-child and family explanations are still prevalent in schools. It may have been shown that school factors can have much more influence than home background factors on the amount of progress children make in reading, writing and maths, but teachers still find it very hard to get away from the idea that learning problems reside primarily in children's individual characteristics and those of their families.

So some schools still do over-identify SEN. For example, one put all its Reception children taking part in the Nuffield Early Language Programme (NELI) on the SEN register. Other SENCOs still feel they should put all children who have special access arrangements in exams on the register, even though the guidance is absolutely clear that this is not necessary or appropriate.

Factors like these help explain the enormous variability in the proportion of children identified with SEND in different schools. An influential report by the Education Policy Institute (Hutchinson, 2021) highlighted this starkly, finding that 'which primary school a child attends makes more difference to their chances of being identified with SEND than anything about them as an individual, their experiences or what local authority they live in.' Differences between school were more important than differences between individual children (such as their attainment at five, their gender, ethnicity and even their levels of disadvantage); between-school differences accounted for 69% of all variation in numbers on SEND Support, and 67% for those with EHCPs. Neighbourhood deprivation and low attainment at five did of course increase the odds of a child being identified as having SEND, but just as important was the school's historical SEND rate and (curiously) the school having an Ofsted grade that was outstanding or less than good.

The report describes the identification of SEND as a lottery. It also suggests there may be some unfairness in the system: while all children living in disadvantaged neighbourhoods had substantially higher odds of being identified with SEND, this effect was greatest for the least disadvantaged children within those neighbourhoods. Even within a system that is heavily weighted towards disadvantage, these patterns suggest some capture of resources by the middle class. In other words, schools are more likely to put better-off children on the SEN register, perhaps because of pressure from parents.

Who should be identified as having SEND?

Part of the reason for variability is that there are no clear criteria for when a child should be identified as at SEN Support (although some local authorities provide guidance). The current SEND review has suggested that a framework of national expectations be introduced to help solve the problem. We shall have to wait and see how that turns out.

Fundamentally, SEND is in the eye of the beholder rather than being an absolute. Blogger Nicole Dempsey expresses this well (Dempsey, 2021):

> The current approach is based on the fairly arbitrary notion of there being distinct SEND and non-SEND learners . . . it forces a dichotomy that I think simply does not exist. The abilities and needs of our students

> exist on a vast and always evolving matrix of spikes and troughs, clusters and gaps, that cannot be usefully polarised or made linear. . . . Of course, I know there are students who have needs that are met through additional and different to our standard offer, but that distinction is made on the limitations of our offer, not – as we behave like it is – the 'deviation from norm' of the child.

Ultimately, Nicole goes on to say, the line between SEND and non-SEND depends on the scope of the school's universal offer as much as it does on the needs of the children. In this book I advocate that SENCOs and other leaders do all they can to bolster that universal offer, restricting the formal identification of SEN to children requiring more individualised and specialist provision, and so reduce the numbers identified as having SEN to a relatively low percentage of their roll.

> A lot of children would be on the SEN register elsewhere but in this school they aren't, because the teachers are used to working with a range, from top end to the children new to this country.
>
> Toni Quinn, SENCO at Porters Grange Primary in Southend

Deciding not to put a child on the SEN register does not mean failing to understand all the factors that may be influencing a child's learning or behaviour, so that staff can respond appropriately – failing to assess a child with behaviour problems, for example, to identify potential underlying speech, language and communication needs. It does not mean ignoring neurodiversity or failing to recognise autism or dyslexia. Early identification of learning and development needs and prompt action is vital; it is just that this has got mixed up in our minds with placing children on the SEN register and the consequent invocation of the full-blown graduated, bureaucratic approach.

Children do not have to be on a SEN register to have their needs understood so that staff know what might work for them. Nor do they have to be on the SEN register to have reasonable adjustments made.

Take this example from a SEND leader I interviewed for this book:

> I have three dyslexic children. The middle one is not on the SEN register. He is making sure he gets the green paper he needs to write on . . . he is making sure he gets the right exam arrangements. If it's something they can do independently, then they don't need to be on a register.

Not all parents find the SEND label helpful, either. One mother, writing on Twitter, noted that when her child was identified as having SEND, his school put in a range of out-of-class interventions and strategies such as fidget toys, but in the end all that was needed was to seat him at the back of the room, ignore his wriggling and give him more autonomy in his work.

Using ordinary systems

We need to decouple the identification of need from the bureaucracy associated with placing children on SEN registers. Having done this, it is a sensible idea to learn from the case study schools described in Chapter 1 and as far as possible use *the ordinary systems used for all pupils* to establish targets for pupils with SEND, to track their progress and to communicate progress to parents and carers, rather than set up separate paper trails.

This has benefits beyond reducing bureaucracy. It conforms to the requirements of the 2014 SEND Code of Practice in locating much of the responsibility with the class or subject teachers – those who are in greatest contact with the pupil and therefore have the greatest influence on their learning – rather than with the SENCO or learning support department. It means that teachers keep pupils' targets and the strategies required to meet them in their minds because they are embedded in planning tools and records that are in daily use. It makes a reality of the well-known statement that 'every teacher is a teacher of SEN'.

It is not, however, what happens in the majority of schools. It is more common to find processes that place a whole group of children outside of schools' regular systems for setting expectations, monitoring progress and reviewing and adapting curriculum, organisation and teaching methods. One SENCO told me how staff in her school talk to her about those with SEND as 'your children' (to which she smartly replies, 'My children don't go to this school'). Another very experienced secondary SENCO, Rhian Williams, spoke to me about persisting 'misconceptions that SEND is the responsibility of the SEND team . . . a belief that SEND is overly complex. . . . TAs still attached to children like Velcro. . . . It's like the 2014 reforms never happened.'

Abandoning separate SEND systems, however, also carries distinct risks. At the extreme, it could mean that the particular needs of pupils with SEND get lost – that teachers are unaware of them, that no special efforts are made to teach them in the ways they learn best, that additional provision is not made for them and that parents are left in the dark about what the school is doing to help their child. The aim of this book is to show how these pitfalls can be avoided. It will describe how we can 'do SEND differently', whilst never losing track of the essential purposes of all SEND legislation and guidance – protecting the rights of a minority group of children to have their needs identified and met.

The role of the SENCO

Many SENCOs feel concerned that their expertise and knowledge will not be used if the planning for pupils with SEND is handed over to class and subject teachers. This need not be the case.

What is suggested in this book, and already in place in many schools, is a *universal* system for identifying individual needs and acting on them. In this system we can envisage SEND practice as simply bringing to bear on these universal systems a particular expertise in SEND, provided by the SENCO and outside agencies. This represents an intensification of existing systems rather than using separate ones, and locates action within everyday classroom teaching and learning rather than a parallel universe of separate SEND record-keeping and review.

This idea of progressive intensification was expressed by the House of Commons Education and Skills Select Committee in its 2006 report on SEN:

> To achieve real progress in terms of early intervention the Government needs to change the premise on which SEN is provided to one in which literally every child matters. This would mean a radically new approach to SEN provision where a system of assessment of learning and intervention takes place for every child on a spectrum of provision that can be geared up for children that require high levels of support.

It is in this 'gearing up' that the SENCO has a vital role, applying their particular knowledge of SEN and disabilities so as to scale up existing systems in place for all children.

Let us look at one example to see how that might work in practice. The example chosen relates to the interaction between routine whole-school processes for identifying children who may need a boost to their learning, and the identification and assessment of needs element of the SEN procedures.

There will always be children who come to school with needs that have already been identified – children with developmental disorders or impairments evident before they started school, or children who move from an early years setting to school, or from primary to secondary school, with an existing history of receiving SEND provision. For many children, however, special educational needs are identified in the course of a key stage, usually as a result of expressions of concern by teachers or parents/carers. Current good practice in whole-school assessment and tracking, however, offers a more systematic route to identifying children who may require extra help in one form or another. In these systems, class or subject teachers track all pupils' progress using ongoing assessment supplemented by discrete assessment tasks and tests, and review each child's progress regularly.

Pupil progress reviews, held two to three times a year, consider data on prior and current attainment, attendance and behaviour and effectively identify any pupil who is not on track to make the amount of progress expected over a key stage. In a primary school, this review might be the trigger for the class teacher to discuss what extra steps could be taken to accelerate the child's progress with the SENCO, EAL lead or the person who leads on behaviour or well-being. In the secondary school, the information on pupils who are struggling should ideally be fed to the year leader, whose role is to identify pupils causing concern in a number of subjects because of effort/behaviour, academic progress or attendance. The year leader in turn works with other middle managers to determine what interventions might be needed to support the pupil – some of which might come under the aegis of the SENCO.

Much guidance is available to support class and subject teachers in how to track and assess pupil attainment levels so as to identify pupils who are experiencing difficulties. The SENCO's role can usefully be to 'coach' subject teachers and class teachers so that they are able to assess against the performance descriptors, mastery statements or skills ladder points at which pupils with SEN or disabilities may be working. Upper Key Stage 2 staff will need help in recognising, for example, the key indicators of progress in age-related expectations from Year 1 to Year 2, or Year 2 to Year 3, not just from Year 4 to Year 5 or Year 6. Subject teachers and primary teachers will also need the SENCO's active involvement in assessing against the pre-key stage standards and the engagement model that has replaced 'P levels'.

SENCOs can also support colleagues' assessment skills by providing training, modelling and coaching on child – adult conferences, aimed at obtaining 'a window into the child's mind' and acquiring a deeper and shared understanding of what it is that holds the pupil back and what can help them as a learner.

Children with enduring learning difficulties and with the social, emotional and mental health difficulties we might class as 'true' SEN, however, will need more in-depth assessment. SENCOs have a crucial role in contributing specialist expertise to assessment that seeks to establish not only that a given pupil is not trying hard, behaving well or making progress but also *why*. Such an assessment might involve one or more of classroom observation, use of questionnaires, standardised tests, analysis of children's work, analysis of underlying perceptual, motor or memory skills or gathering information from parents/carers. A range of tools a SENCO can use are suggested in *Special Educational Needs in the Primary School* (Gross, 2002) and *Who really has special educational needs?* (Gross, 2013). An hour spent on this kind of assessment will make more difference than many hours spent on organising IEP/ISPs.

EXAMPLE

At Henley Bank secondary school, SENCO Rhian Williams has used her specialist expertise to help staff unpick what might previously have been called moderate learning difficulties (MLD). Any pupil with a standardised score below 90 on a group reading test will be assessed by her team using a range of tools from GL Assessment, including the RAPID dyslexia screening tool. Assessments will identify problems with recall and processing information. Where a child has processing difficulties, the speech and language therapist commissioned for two days a week by the school will do a full assessment to identify any language difficulties or social communication needs.

At Whitefield Primary in Liverpool, high-quality teaching supports all learners. Against his background, staff are good at flagging up children who are really struggling. SENCO Marie Beale then suggests in-depth assessment to better understand these children's needs. The school uses the WellComm tool for language needs, the Strengths and Difficulties Questionnaire (SDQ) for behaviour and well-being, the assessments within the NumberStacks intervention programme for maths, and those within the software the school uses for literacy. Potential safeguarding concerns are explored through half-termly use of questions based on the 'three houses' approach: in the first 'house' children record their worries, in the second the good things in their life, and in the third they write or draw what they think needs to happen. One of the school's HLTAs formerly worked for the ADHD Foundation and has therapy qualifications; she can 'rustle up a sensory profile' for children where sensory processing may be an issue underlying behaviour and learning needs.

> I try to unpick the child's needs, especially if they have been identified as having MLD. One child had an EHCP for MLD and SEMH, but when I assessed him it was clear he is dyslexic. We put the right interventions in place and he is now only 15 months behind in reading, not the 39 months he was before.
>
> Margaret Relf, SENCO at Anglesey Primary

The question of diagnosis

The aim of effective assessment is to identify the child's strengths so that they can be helped to draw on them, and barriers to learning so that plans can be made to overcome them. It is a moot point whether assessment also needs to attach a diagnostic label to the child or not. In some cases, formally identifying individuals and making special plans for them appears to hinder their progress rather than help, as we saw in Chapter 1.

Nor are diagnostic labels always fairly applied. A longitudinal study looking at children born at the millennium (Knight and Crick, 2021) found that socio-economic class and parental income were significant predictors of being identified as having dyslexia by a teacher at age 11. If parents had a managerial or professional job, the chances of the dyslexia label being applied were greater than they were for less affluent poor readers.

On the other hand, there is evidence that labels such as dyslexia and autism (Gross, 1994; Papps and Dyson, 2004) are actively helpful because they help adults to respond in more effective ways to behaviours they would otherwise construe as evidence of 'laziness', 'bad behaviour' and so on. There is evidence that where neurodiversity is recognised and understood, children benefit socially and emotionally. One study (Oredipe *et al.*, 2022), for example, found that college students who learned they were autistic when they were young felt happier about their lives than those diagnosed when they were older.

Diagnostic labels can help children and young people connect with others with similar characteristics and experiences, to whom they can relate. It can also help them understand their strengths:

A strengths-based approach

Dyslexia does not just mean difficulties with literacy. Dyslexic people have strengths in problem-solving and focusing on the wider picture. It is no coincidence that around 40% of top earning CEOs are said to be dyslexic, with research (Fitzgibbon and O'Connor, 2002) finding that dyslexic entrepreneurs were reported as excellent at oral communication, delegation and creative and spatial awareness tasks.

ADHD can be a strength when a task requires a creative point of view, where intense physical or mental energy is helpful or where a degree of risk-taking is involved.

Autism involves a range of 'superpowers', from attention to detail to deep focus, a methodological approach and the ability to retain facts.

So diagnostic labels can sometimes be helpful – but what is important is that assessment systems in schools don't rest on waiting on a 'diagnosis', a medical model that often only means sitting on a waiting list. Teachers should accurately and promptly identify a child's difficulties but also their strengths, steering the child, family and school staff away from notions of deficit towards the idea of difference. This is a key role for the SENCO.

Functions that SEN procedures were meant to fulfil

To ensure that in moving towards universal systems we still protect the rights of children with special needs or disabilities, and their parents, we need first to reflect on the objectives that effective SEND processes should seek to meet.

These include

- identification – ensuring that children's needs are identified as a result of expressions of concern by teachers or parent/carers;
- assessment – ensuring that some assessment takes place, to better understand the barriers to learning and how they might be overcome;
- communication – making sure that all relevant staff and outside agencies know what the child's needs are and what should be done or has been done to support them;
- identifying priorities and setting targets for learning or behaviour;

- identifying strategies, in the classroom and elsewhere, to help the child achieve targets;
- reviewing progress and celebrating success;
- engaging parents and carers – agreeing priorities and targets with them, making sure they have a say in and know what is being done to help their child and to what effect, suggesting ways in which they can support their child's progress;
- engaging children and young people themselves in decisions about priorities and plans;
- coordinating the actions to be taken by the school and outside agencies;
- informing decisions about the allocation of resources – extra adult time and/or physical resources;
- supporting transition – making sure that information about the child's needs is passed on as they move from one class or setting to another.

Other less intrinsically useful but necessary functions of the SEND systems are those of accountability and referral:

- Proving to parents, tribunals, Ofsted and the local authority that the school is meeting pupils' needs effectively
- Demonstrating a need for additional resources (the involvement of outside agencies, extra funding) by showing that the school has done all it reasonably can before seeking outside help

Let us now take each of these functions in turn and consider ways of fulfilling them that are manageable, effective and non-bureaucratic, using case studies from schools I interviewed for this book.

Identification and assessment

The schools I spoke to when writing this book used sophisticated *pupil tracking* (moderated by sensible teacher and parent judgement) to identify children causing concern. They all then kept some sort of record of pupils flagged up in this way.

Ideally, their pupil tracking systems could be supplemented by routine screening to identify children who may on the face of it be making adequate progress yet are not fulfilling their potential or are not secure in their well-being. These will be children who have special needs of a more subtle, less obvious kind. The SENCO might, for example, ask year group teams once a year to look through checklists of indicators of dyslexia, autistic spectrum disorder, dyspraxia, language difficulties and minor sensory impairment (Gross, 2013) and consider whether any of the children in their care show evidence of these potential special needs. Or the school might use computerised screening systems.

EXAMPLE

Anglesey Primary school in Staffordshire screens all its children using Speech Link and Language Link to identify children with SLCN; the children it flags as 'red' are referred to the speech and language therapy service, but for those flagged as amber there is a range of school-based provision based on the profiles generated by the computerised screening. Groups of children with similar gaps in their comprehension can be pulled together for intervention using the strategies suggested by the screening programme.

Communicating needs

One of the prime functions that IEPs/individual support plans were meant to fulfil was that of communication, for example:

- making sure that staff teaching a child were aware of their needs, targets and the strategies to be used;
- making sure that parents/carers were involved and were updated regularly on the child's progress;
- making sure that if the child failed to make progress, information on what had been done to help them would be available for outside agencies and the local authority;
- making sure that if the child moved, information would follow them to a new placement.

In practice, the volume of individual plans that many schools maintain has made it impossible to use them as an effective communication tool. All too often they languish on the laptop of the primary class teacher, or in the folders of the learning support department in secondary schools, brought out only when accountability – in the shape of Ofsted or IEP/ISP review dates – looms. Parental involvement in many schools is reduced to token status, with the class teacher or SENCO pursuing a parent in the playground to ask them to sign an individual plan in which they have had no part, simply so that it can be forwarded to the local authority to prove the case for additional resources. Paperwork is passed on to other schools if the pupil moves, but does not always tell them what they need to know and know quickly – what are this child's strengths and difficulties, what works for them in the classroom and what additional provision they require.

There are, however, simple and more effective ways in which the communication function of the individual plan can be met that do not require volumes of paper.

EXAMPLE

At Henley Bank secondary school, students with SEND work with an adult to create a simple Pupil Passport recorded using Tes Provision Map (previously known as Edukey) software. Parents get an email with their own log-in so they can see their child's Passport. Tes Provision Map links to the SIMS management information system, so staff can enter, for example, 'Y9, pupils I teach, filter by class, filter by SEND' and see the relevant Passports. Pupils play a leading role in getting their own needs understood and met; they sometimes come to the SENCO Rhian Williams to say, for example, 'I don't think teachers have read my Pupil Passport for a while . . . can you send it out again?'

Rhian's team will also monitor what is happening for a child, and if, for example, they are frequently being sent to an isolation room, she will email the Passport to staff with a 'Read Request'.

Even with the simple system for accessing information, Rhian finds that subject staff

> can't keep all the Pupil Passports in their heads for a class they teach, so I do the key take-aways of what a particular condition or need is, what it looks like in lessons, some top tips, a link to more information and then at the bottom the initials of children with that condition in each year group.

An example of one of these 'SEND snapshots' can be found in Table 2.2.

SEND focus – cognition and learning	
Key takeaway	Having a SEND makes life altogether that little bit harder. Most students will struggle to listen and read at the same time (different things), process information as quickly as we do, remember what they've read/heard as well as be able to follow instructions. Be mindful of cognitive overload. What do they need to know now? What information will help them understand? What information is going to muddle their thoughts? If it will – don't say it/show it.
Further reading/ research	What does this look like in the classroom? – Chapter on SEND Carl Hendrick and Robert Macpherson
What does this look like in a lesson?	**Think Powerpoint slides** – keep information to a minimum – if **it's important for them, then print it** (ensuring that their print out matches what is on the board); if it's not important, don't add it. LO's are NOT needed on every slide. What else just 'muddies the water?' If it does, remove it. **Visuals** – pictures portray ideas so much easier – however, make them relevant to the students **Demos** – Chunk – watch this, then do, come back, watch this, then do – Visualisers are available (Ask Mr Phelps) **Chunk, chunk and then chunk some more** – teacher talk, texts, tasks **Pace** – slow it down. How quickly you talk, what you expect from them

Year 7 Names of children	Year 8 Names of children	Year 9 Names of children	Year 10 Names of children	Year 11 Names of children
What works for SEND works for all				

Table 2.2 SEND snapshot

Other schools suggest strategies for individual pupils in each class a subject teacher will work with by creating pupil profiles that are short enough to fit into one cell of a spreadsheet. They then sort the profiles into class sets electronically.

EXAMPLE

Boyle, Isaac. Needs to fidget to stay focused – will have a piece of Blu-Tack to fiddle with in lessons. Praise him for asking for clarification if he hasn't understood something. Warn him in advance if you are going to call on him for an answer. Give him opportunities for closely monitored pair work with an appropriate peer. He can be sent 'with a message' to the SEND office if his behaviour is not acceptable.

Morris, Joanne. Excellent at art. Plays for school netball team. Learning difficulties. Reads at level of an eight-year-old. Numeracy similar. Needs a buddy reader, short instructions, writing frames, learning linked to everyday real experiences. Can get very upset/difficult when falls out with friends – show understanding and ask her if it would help to go and talk to Miss Perry.

And why not make information about pupils really engaging? Some schools support pupils in making Pupil Passports in the form of PowerPoint presentations. There are helpful blank templates at www.communicationpassports.org.uk/Creating-Passports/Templates/.

Then there is film. A secondary SENCO in Bristol took a video camera out and interviewed Year 6 pupils with SEND who were due to come to his school. He asked them what helped them learn and what got in the way of their learning. A hearing-impaired child with good lip-reading skills described how 'I can't manage when two people talk at once,' and 'It's really bad when the teacher talks when they are writing on the board 'cos I can't see what they are saying.'

Shown to all subject staff who were to teach the incoming Year 7, these short films were far more powerful in changing teacher behaviour than any number of written communications.

Identifying priorities and setting targets

As the case study schools in Chapter 1 illustrate, setting individual targets is now commonplace for primary class teachers and secondary subject teachers. These do not need separate paperwork; they are found where they can make a difference to everyday learning, in pupils' books and end-of-unit assessments, in school management information systems, on working walls.

Systems like these can meet the purposes of effective SEND systems and remove the need for separate ISPs/IEPs, as long as progress against targets is systematically recorded and parents are kept informed.

Where more effort may be needed for children with SEND is in making sure that the right priorities have been established for the child's learning, even before targets are set. These priorities may not always be in the core academic subjects. Underpinning areas such as language development or social and emotional learning may be more important. This, though, is not just a SEND issue – teachers have to judge priorities carefully for many children, including those going through a difficult time at home, those learning English as an additional language and so on. Schools will be good at setting the right priorities to the extent that they have robust systems for gathering information on all their pupils, listening to parents/carers and listening to children and young people themselves.

Planning strategies to meet needs and reach targets

The SENCOs in our case study schools all spend considerable time on staff development so that teachers have a good sense of how to make their everyday teaching as inclusive as they can. On top of this, they provide class and subject teachers with suggested strategies for individual pupils. Sometimes these will be in Pupil Passports, framed in the child's own language. In other schools, they can be found on classroom walls (Figure 2.1). In secondary schools, they will be on the school's management

To encourage positive behaviour in this class we try to:

- Repeat instructions three times
- Use children's names
- Say 'I feel sad when …'

Strategies to support TB

- Ignore as much low level attention seeking as possible
- Attend to him doing the right thing using descriptive praise
- Two areas of focus:
  - Doing what an adult says
  - Kind hands and feet (no hurting)

Rewards:

Figure 2.1 Posters to remind staff of inclusive strategies

information system, accessible from the teacher's class register or mark book at the click of a button.

Essentially, the role of the SENCO and their team in schools like these has switched from manager of plans and meeting dates to acting as a consultant to colleagues on what works in helping children and young people overcome barriers to learning.

The other way in which schools can record the strategies used to help pupils meet targets is through provision maps. These set out the additional provision made in each year group under the broad areas of literacy, mathematics, language, motor skills and social/emotional development. A map highlighted with the provision a particular pupil receives, together with guidance for staff on strategies to use in everyday class teaching, fulfils the 'planning strategies' function of an effective SEND system effectively in a time-saving way, obviating the need to keep writing the same descriptions of provision over and over again on separate individual targets.

Reviewing progress and celebrating success

Once strategies have been planned, monitoring progress is readily achieved through the excellent whole-school tracking systems in place in almost all schools. These schools now also have a means of *evaluating* progress that was never available under the IEP system, through provision maps which enable them to use simple baseline measures before an intervention is put in, and repeat these at the end of the intervention. These may be measures of reading or spelling age, standardised scores on a language or maths test, measures of social and emotional competence or simply teacher-assessed curriculum mastery. The measures allow not only for the progress of individuals to be evaluated (and shared with parents) but also for evaluation of the overall impact of the intervention on a number of pupils.

EXAMPLE

At Henley Bank secondary, the SENCO taps into data from the 'Pupil Attitudes to Self and School '(PASS) online survey, which is routinely used each year with all pupils. The data helps her identify pupils who are struggling but also provides an impact measure to help her evaluate the school's SEND provision; last year she found that in Year 7 the progress on PASS over time was greater for pupils with SEND than those without.

Children who experience barriers to their learning often need more effort put into the celebration of success than do their peers. IEP review meetings sometimes provided for this. To make sure this celebration function is not lost, schools can flag up some children for extra 'noticing'. This may be by asking staff to send good news home – to make a note in a pupil's planner or send a quick text message home when the pupil has met a target, however small. It may be more frequent meetings between a pupil and a tutor or mentor to review what has been achieved. Home-school diaries and good news postcards can also be used, along with assemblies, class plenaries and so on.

Engaging parents and carers

A prime function of any effective SEND system must be to provide parents and carers with guaranteed involvement in the school's efforts to meet their child's needs and a way of challenging the school if these efforts are insubstantial. In practice, this function has been poorly fulfilled by bureaucratic systems.

In contrast, the relatively paper-free systems in the schools I spoke to when writing this book are partnered by conspicuous efforts to engage parents and carers. This is achieved in different ways at each school. What characterises them all is informality and ease of access. Extra time is given at parents' evenings where children have additional needs, or the school has drop-in sessions and identifies a key link person for parents to speak to whenever they need to. The additional provision that can be made for their child can be made clear to parents through a provision map that describes different interventions and provision and what entry levels entitle a child to access that provision.

Individual plans and reviews were also meant to enlist the help of parents in supporting their child's learning at home and provide them with guidance on how best to go about this. Again, as we will see in Chapter 10, they rarely achieved this. What does seem to be both successful and time-efficient, however, is practice where parents are involved in workshops and support groups that are explicitly aimed at empowering them to provide the best possible home support.

> As a result of COVID we were having the same conversations over and over again, so we did a workshop on 'helping your anxious child' for twenty parents.
>
> SENCO, Henley Bank High School

EXAMPLE

At Houldsworth Valley Primary, staff take time to build relationships with parents, beginning with a Teddy Bears' Picnic before children start in Reception. There are family reading cafes, fun and interactive sessions to help parents support their children's reading ('Come into the story café and have a cake'). Parents are involved with the school's allotments scheme; every teacher phones two parents a week to 'say something lovely.' Class DoJo is used to engage families, with pictures posted of events and work in class and individual online reports including new words learned, reading age, reading fluency and a measure of reading progress. School nurses employed by the Unity Schools Partnership (of which the school is part) offer drop-in sessions for parents; the school might send out a Parent Mail message such as 'Annie's in on Wednesday, if you'd like to speak to her about anything.'

Coordinating the actions to be taken by the school and outside agencies

Where a number of agencies are involved with a pupil, there is a need for a system that coordinates and records their work. Some schools may wish to continue using individual plans where several different agencies are involved with a pupil. Equally effective, however, in recording who is going to do what (and when) can be a simple note of actions agreed in multi-agency meetings. And to keep an overall perspective of which agencies and personnel have been involved over time, the SENCO can add a column labelled 'external agency involvement' to the school's provision map and write in the agencies involved when pulling off a copy and highlighting provision that an individual pupil receives. Alternatively, the agency involvement can be recorded on the cumulative overview/record of progress that will be described in Chapter 4.

Informing decisions about the allocation of resources

The SEN system is meant to make sure schools allocate resources according to pupil need, basing decisions on staged procedures (the graduated approach) in which progressively more resources are allocated as pupils move from SEN Support to an EHCP. The theory is that if the resources deployed to deliver actions in individual support/education plans have not been successful in helping the pupil progress, more resources are needed. In practice, the staged system often serves only to distort efficient management of time and money. It drives much of the excess paperwork schools undertake as they seek to document in detail what has been done at each stage so as to make a case for a move to the next. It assumes that if resource allocation was unsuccessful, then the *child* must have needs greater than those resources could support. It does not prompt schools to consider whether they had deployed resources effectively in the first place. Nor does it lead to equity. Several pieces of research have now shown (Gross, 1996; Pinney, 2004) that resources tend to be skewed towards those children whose parents are most able to articulate the case for extra help.

Planning resource allocation in school on the basis of individual SEN support plans is also problematic in that it can sometimes drive models of allocating TA time to individual children for in-class support – a model we know to be ineffective. It separates the 'SEN budget' from the overall school budget and from other budget lines designed to help children who have fallen behind in their learning – such as the Pupil Premium and COVID catch-up funding – which often need to be targeted at the same children. As we will see in Chapter 8, there are ways of bringing separate budgets together to plan an overall school provision map whilst still maintaining accountability for each discrete budget. The allocation of resources can then be based on an overall data-based audit of present and upcoming need in each year group in the school rather than on individual SEND plans. On the basis of this analysis, provision can be planned proactively, at the start of the year, then regularly adjusted through pupil tracking systems that quickly identify pupils who are not making the expected progress.

Supporting transition

Another purpose of good SEND systems is to secure the effective exchange of information at times of transition for pupils – moving from one class to another, or from one school to another. The schools I interviewed have not found that the transfer of copies of individual paper plans at primary-secondary transition is useful. Instead, they allocate time for primary and secondary staff to meet, or explicitly ask for information on the strategies that worked in the primary school. Supporting the child to make their own One Page Profile or Pupil Passport to give to their new teachers works well. Another useful idea for primary schools is an end-of-year staff meeting, where staff team up in pairs (Year R with Year 1 etc.) and go through class lists, discussing particular children's needs, what has worked for them in the past, what triggers to avoid and any other useful information. The pair record a profile for each child discussed and photocopy it there and then for the SENCO and the teacher whose class the child will be joining.

> When we've identified a few children needing additional transition work we have the secondary SEN and Pastoral team and the Year Group leader come in and meet me, classroom staff and the children . . . it works better than passing on lots of stuff on paper.
>
> Toni Quinn, SENCO at Porters Green Primary

Proving that the school is meeting pupils' needs effectively or demonstrating a need for additional resources

This is the big worry for many schools. How, without drawers full of IEP/ISPs and fat pupil files containing dusty records of what is often years of SEND support, can a school show Ofsted that their practice is good, convince a SEN Tribunal that they have acted appropriately, request the involvement of outside agencies or compile evidence so as to request an EHCP?

Let us look first at Ofsted. In a recent inspection, the SENCO was asked to select a number of children's individual plans so that they could talk to these children, observe the provision made for them in class and talk to their teachers. At another, the SENCO was asked for records of meetings with parents and the planning that went with them. At another, the focus was on how the SENCO could show the overall impact of the school's SEN provision on pupil progress.

On the face of it, some of these inspectors could be seen to be asking for paperwork. But they asked for it not so as to tick a 'paperwork-in-order box' but so as to explore particular issues and hypotheses. The issues and hypotheses will have emerged from the school's data profile, from any self-evaluation the school may have done and from first-hand evidence during the inspection.

In the school where the SENCO was asked to select individual children's plans, Ofsted would be looking at their key general concerns about children with SEND not accessing the curriculum because they are spending too much time out of the classroom with TAs, and at whether class or subject teachers are actually adapting their teaching to meet children's needs.

In the school where documentation of meetings with parents was the apparent focus, the inspectors may have picked up from parents' questionnaires broader issues about parental involvement and satisfaction and decided to explore whether these issues extended to parents of pupils with SEND.

In the school where the SENCO was asked how she could show the impact of the school's provision, the inspectors might have been testing a hypothesis about leadership and management, having noted an absence of any data analysis relating to the progress of lower-attaining pupils and any evaluation of the impact of the school's interventions for pupils with additional needs.

In all cases, Ofsted was not interested in compliance with procedures. Their interest was in outcomes – pupils' academic and personal development and in what the school was or was not doing to help pupils achieve these outcomes. In some cases, they did look for evidence in paper records of individual pupils. But the paperwork was not the point.

As schools come to use many different systems for SEN records, and indeed for measuring and tracking all pupils' progress, inspectors will need schools' help in knowing where to find evidence in order to check out hypotheses. It is up to the school to point them in the right direction. The SENCO can do this by writing a single sheet, part of their SEN or Inclusion Policy and the 'School Offer' that they post on the school's website, which describes how the needs of children with SEND are met – the systems for identification, assessment, setting targets, identifying strategies, working with parents/carers, involving pupils and so on. The sheet will make clear for which children the school uses some form of individual plan (for example, those with the most complex needs, or where outside agencies are involved) and for whom it uses alternative means of planning. It will give the rationale for the systems that are in use so that the reader understands the benefits that result from reduced bureaucracy and increased class/subject teacher involvement.

An example of such a policy statement is provided in the toolkit section of this book. Suitably adapted, this information sheet can be given to inspectors so that they will know where they need to look in order to test out the effectiveness of the school's work with pupils who have SEND. In the first example earlier, they would of course need to be given individual plans for children, but in a beating bureaucracy school, these would only exist for children with complex needs, children who are 'stuck' despite everyone's best efforts and/or children with external agency involvement.

For this and the other examples, Ofsted could be pointed to these sources of information:

Access to the curriculum for children with SEND	→	Curriculum maps that demonstrate a carefully planned, sequenced inclusive curriculum
Parental involvement and satisfaction	→	Notes of meetings with parents. Results of a survey undertaken by the SENCO as part of SEN self-evaluation
The impact of the school's provision	→	Data analysis showing the curricular progress made by all the pupils with SEND over a key stage. Evaluations of interventions on provision map

All of these would provide fruitful ground for testing of inspectorial hypotheses while at the same time demonstrating that this is a school that has thought carefully about how to develop truly effective systems for supporting pupils with additional needs.

Another big fear for schools, which often drives unnecessary bureaucracy, is the fear of being called to account by parents through tribunals or the courts. As the Implementation Review Group of headteachers put it, 'Too often we are driven by what appears to be the overriding concern of protection from litigation' (Independent Review Unit, 2006). But, just as for Ofsted, similar 'evidence' (this time solely at the individual pupil level) can easily be pulled together from existing sources to demonstrate what has been done to support a pupil. At tribunals, the focus is likely to be on the provision map and evidence of strategies used by class or subject teachers as the questions will usually be about what provision the school can make available, and whether this is sufficient. Similar issues will be of interest in any court procedures.

Finally, in relation to outside agencies, it is not difficult to provide succinct information about the child's needs and what has been done so far to meet them through

- pupil Passports or One Page Profiles;
- pupil tracking records showing academic progress and progress in personal development;
- highlighted provision maps showing the provision made over time.

If further 'proof' is needed, for example, when requesting high-needs funding or an EHCP assessment, then notes of meetings with the pupil and/or parents, screenshots of information and strategies provided to subject teachers and spreadsheets showing the cost of this provision can also be appended. Again, you may need to include your information sheet on how you manage SEND in your school so that the agency or local authority administrators will understand that you have not just forgotten to enclose 'copies of the last three individual plans' or whatever else their own bureaucracy asks for but are providing the same information in a different way.

Beating bureaucracy: the essential kit

A simple set of systems will allow you both to provide information to others who ask for it, and at the same time manage SEND effectively internally. We can call this the essential bureaucracy-busting kit. It is illustrated in the toolkit section of this book and should include

- a note in your SEND policy on how you fulfil essential SEND functions without over-reliance on individual plans;
- a register of pupils with SEND – with numbers kept to a minimum by placing on the register only those children for whom high-quality inclusive teaching and normally available additional interventions have not proved sufficient;
- a provision map to show what additional provision you are making in each year group;
- a pupil-led way of communicating needs to all who work with them, such as a Pupil Passport or One Page Profile;
- strategy sheets for the main types of SEND, to highlight and give to staff;
- a way of adapting curriculum planning;
- a way of tracking pupil progress and engaging regularly with parents/carers.

The *register* is needed so that you can complete your pupil census (PLASC), identify the percentage of your roll with SEND and make links to the range of data the school holds on each pupil. Without a register, you cannot define the group whose progress you will want, as SENCO, to evaluate and compare with that of pupils not on the SEN register. The simplest way of keeping a register is to use an existing information management system, recording a 'Yes' in SEN Support or EHCP columns and the type of SEN in another column. You can then print your register, if you need to, using the filtering function.

The *provision map*, described in Chapter 8, is fundamentally a planning tool for you but also, when copied, dated and highlighted to show the provision received by an individual child, serves as a record of what the school has done to provide support.

The *Pupil Passport or One Page Profile* is the way that staff know about individual pupils' strengths and barriers to learning and what helps them best.

Strategy sheets give handy hints on strategies for specific types of SEND (dyslexia, autism, speech and language difficulties, ADHD and so on). They can be copied, highlighted as appropriate for the individual pupil and given or made available electronically to staff who work with the child.

A *system for adapting curriculum planning* is the way that staff translate information from personal profiles and strategy sheets into learning and teaching in the classroom.

Engaging with parents/carers can be through written reports and through meetings. For children with SEND, there will need to be additional agenda items, over and above those used in standard parents' meetings, plus a brief record of the key points of discussion at meetings, and any actions agreed.

KEY PRINCIPLES

Key take-aways for SENCOs

- Schools which succeed in reducing bureaucracy avoid over-identifying pupils as having SEND
- Such schools try to use ordinary school systems to establish targets for pupils with SEND, track their progress and communicate with parents/carers, rather than separate SEND systems
- SENCO expertise can be brought to bear to enhance rather than replace these whole-school systems

Key questions for the wider school leadership team

- How and why are pupils identified as having SEND in your school?
- Are some pupils felt to have SEND just because they have fallen behind in their learning?
- How much of the SEND activity and paperwork in your school is driven by worries about Ofsted, litigation or by the search for additional funding? How much is driven by meeting pupils' needs?

3 Setting targets and monitoring progress

The 2014 Code of Practice (DfE and DH, 2014) notes that where pupils are on SEN Support, 'teachers should use appropriate assessment to set targets which are deliberately ambitious'. EHCPs should specify 'the outcomes sought for the child or the young person. This should include outcomes for adult life. The EHC plan should also identify the arrangements for the setting of shorter term targets by the early years provider, school, college or other education or training provider'.

In this chapter we will look at how such target-setting (and even more important, target-getting) can be embedded within whole-school systems rather than make extra work for SENCOs and teachers.

Most schools use some form of whole-school system for setting targets for what each child should achieve at the end of a key stage, supported by targets for each school year or term.

These are numerical targets. They can be motivating for pupils with SEND. To know what you are aiming for is helpful, if combined with knowledge of what it is you need to do in order to reach that level. And that is the essential next step – turning the numerical target into *curricular* targets.

An example from one school is wall displays of 'learning ladders' showing the steps children need to take on the way to achieving at or above age-related expectations. Children attach their names to the step they are on; arrows show them the next step. In one class, for example, a display backed with paper to look like a brick wall had the following steps:

Step 1 To use connectives to improve my sentences.

Step 2 To use connectives and pronouns to improve my sentences.

Step 3 To use a range of interesting connectives to join ideas together and to start new paragraphs.

Step 4 To vary sentence length and word order, to keep the reader interested.

Step 5 To use a variety of sentence openings in my writing, e.g. verbs, adjectives, connectives.

DOI: 10.4324/9781003313526-3

Curricular targets, phrased in 'I can . . . ' terms, describe what it is the pupil has to learn next. They often define *key* pieces of learning that children will work on over about half a term; they are broader than lesson objectives, which are specific to the particular content of a given lesson. They may stem from a whole-school or subject improvement priority.

For example (Figure 3.1), a secondary school might analyse its pupils' results and decide that a priority is to improve enquiry skills in science. This whole-school curricular target is then 'layered' into age-related targets so that each year group has its own curricular targets. In Year 7, the target might be 'Pupils can plan their own investigation'. This is then layered further into medium-term curricular targets for each half term or unit of work. An example might be 'In investigation pupils are able to identify the key variables that they can and cannot control'. In pupil-speak, this becomes a group or pupil target, 'I will focus on planning my own investigation, say what I think will happen, what will change and what I will measure'.

How might this be relevant to a pupil with SEND? If the pupil has significant difficulties in cognition and learning, the target might be adapted so as to focus on the skill of prediction (a useful, cross-curricular learning-to-learn skill that the teacher knows will be relevant to the pupil's progress in a wide range of social and learning situations). Over a series of lessons, the pupil's target might then be 'I will tell my teacher or a friend what I think will happen in our investigation'.

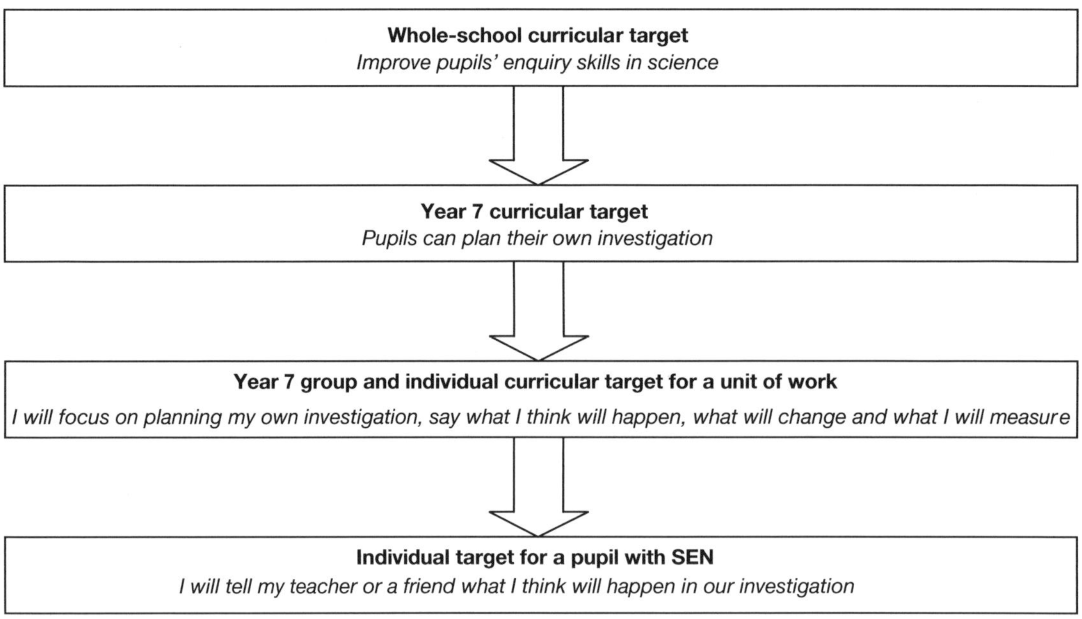

FIGURE 3.1 Layered curricular target for science

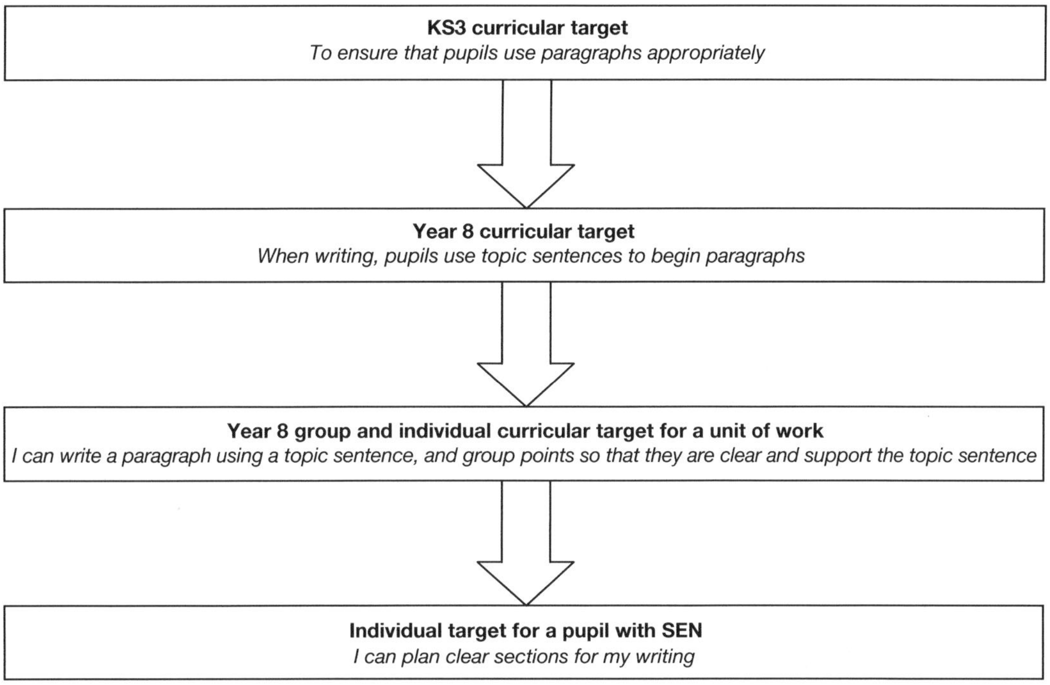

FIGURE 3.2 Layered curricular target for English

In English (Figure 3.2), a Key Stage 3 target to ensure that pupils use paragraphs appropriately might 'layer' back to a Year 8 target, 'When writing, pupils use topic sentences to begin paragraphs', and a group target, 'I can write a paragraph using a topic sentence, and group points so that they are clear and support the topic sentence'. For a pupil with significant learning difficulties, the *individual* target might be 'I can plan clear sections for my writing', something expected of the average Year 2 pupil.

In the primary school, when working on measurement for length the overall curricular target for a Year 2 class might be 'To estimate, measure and compare lengths using standard units'. For a child with significant learning difficulties the personalised target might be 'I can compare the lengths of two ribbons or necklaces' (Figure 3.3).

Most schools now use some type of ladders of curriculum content or skills pupils must master over time, for formative assessment purposes and to replace levels. Variously called hierarchies of expectations, progression objectives, progress ladders, milestones or grids of 'I can' statements, and often linked to software, they provide a rich source of curricular targets for pupils with SEN. For primary maths, the Ready to Progress exemplifications from the National Centre for Excellence in the Teaching of Mathematics (NCETM) are a good example of what is useful for pupils with learning difficulties, highlighting the essential learning within the national curriculum.

Curricular targets need not be confined to the core subjects. They can also embrace social and emotional learning. For example (Figure 3.4), a school might decide on a

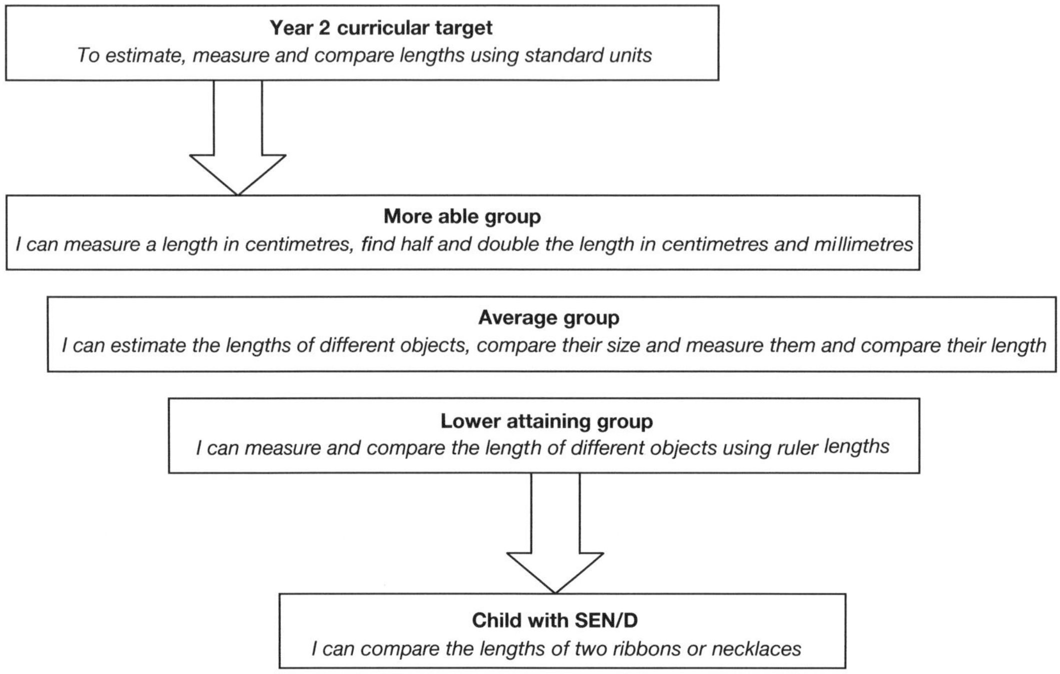

Figure 3.3 Layered curricular target for measurement

whole-school target that children will work well together in groups. Using the Social and Emotional Aspects of Learning (SEAL) materials (DfES, 2005a, available at www.sealcommunity.org), they might then set layered targets for each year group. In Year 6, the target might be 'When working in a group I can tell others if I agree/don't agree with them and why, and listen to others' views, thinking about what they have said'. But some children might not yet have secured earlier learning and have a personal target taken from Year R, 'I can take turns in a group, and share'.

Using layered-back curricular targets for pupils with additional needs has the great advantage of keeping the targets within the realm of the class or subject teacher.

The targets are linked closely to the work of the class as a whole and will be addressed through the teacher's regular classroom planning. They have a much better chance, therefore, of guiding teaching and learning than the computer-generated, filing-cabinet targets that characterise too many individual support plans.

Expecting class and subject teachers to use curricular targets which include children who are performing well below age-related expectations is the key to a reduction in the SENCO's workload. It is also the key to better progress for children who experience barriers to their learning.

Curricular targets set by the class or subject teacher also have disadvantages, however. While they may be highly relevant to the direction the whole school, class or group is taking, they may not be particularly relevant to the unique and pressing needs of the

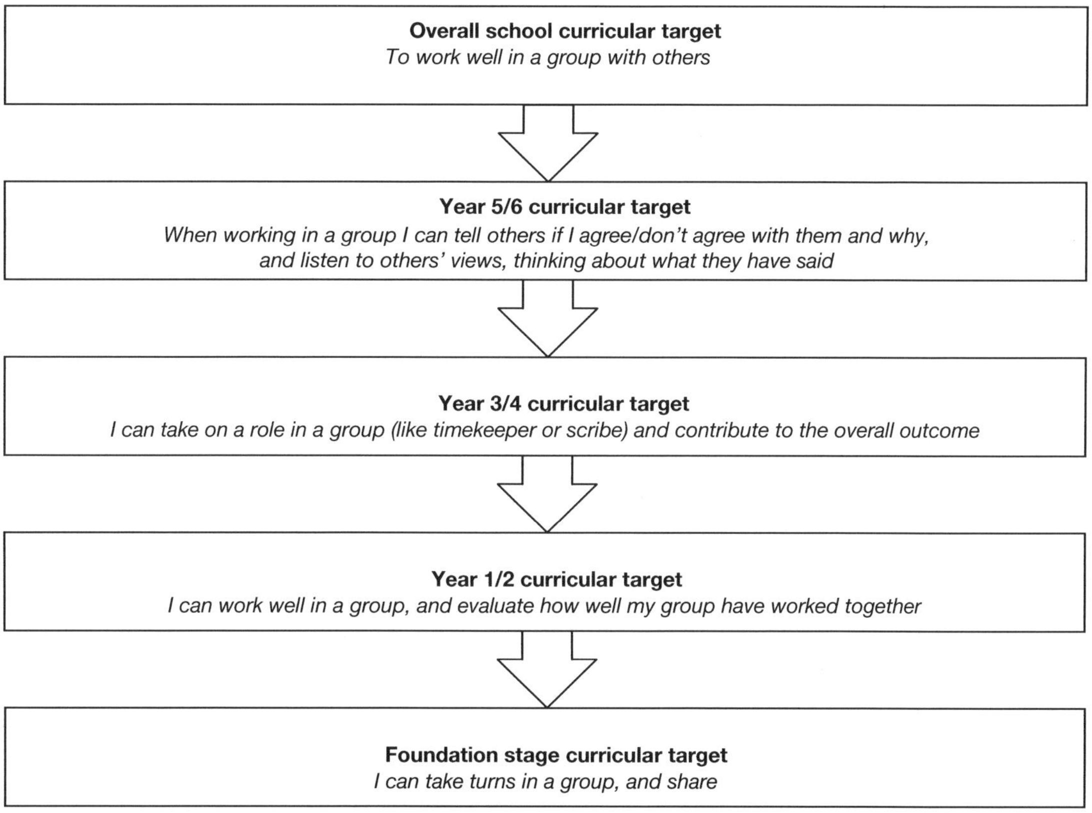

Figure 3.4 Layered curricular target for social and emotional learning

pupil with SEN or a disability. IEP/ISP targets, when arrived at through a shared, group process of prioritising problems (as described in Chapter 1), do help everyone to focus on what really matters. And what really matters is likely to be:

- a problem that the child feels is important and on which they want to work – that is, one that ties in with their main life concerns at the time (like 'learn to do joined-up writing' when the child is really bothered by the difference they have just begun to notice between their written work and that of their peers);
- a problem that underpins others – such as poor concentration, personal organisation or willingness to tackle something new.

Such priorities are often cross-curricular, may relate to outcomes that are wider than just attainment and will not be addressed solely by curricular targets set by subject teachers, or literacy and mathematics targets set by primary teachers.

An example of the need for targets that go beyond attainment is a story told to me by Janet Thompson, former HMI. Janet describes a Year 10 pupil with a visual impairment whom she tracked in school. When Janet observed in class, she saw lots of opportunities for paired and small group work – but her tracked pupil always worked with her TA at these times rather than with other students. The girl said, 'It has to be like that because she understands my disability. I don't go to after-school clubs because my taxi comes at quarter past four. I don't go to lunch time clubs because that's when I do my Braille.' This girl lived in a small rural village and saw few people other than her mother and sister. Her academic attainment was good, but what life chances would she have in the future? For her, some targets around working and socialising with other students would have been helpful.

CASE STUDY

Houldsworth Valley Primary School in Newmarket provides a good example of how to identify meaningful priorities for children. Every child with SEND has a giant Pupil Passport in the form of a Big Book (Figure 3.5) that is kept in class. Children and families have a conversation about the Big Book Passport every half term. In the first half of the autumn term, the conversation will focus on the child's dreams for their future, the parents' dreams for their child and the teacher's dreams for the child. This helps everyone focus on what really matters and develop meaningful goals that will help the child and family reach their dreams. Subsequent reviews gather evidence of progress against these goals and develop new ones where appropriate.

Some schools do have systems for setting and reviewing personal targets, as distinct from simply subject targets. They know that *all* children have particular things they want and need to improve on or achieve that are about themselves as individuals rather than as subject-fodder. In these schools, form tutors or class teachers meet regularly with pupils to discuss their overall learning needs and consider progress not only in subject learning but also in so-called soft or non-cognitive skills such as communication, the ability to work as part of a team, reliability, punctuality and perseverance, knowing how to work independently without close supervision and being resilient in the face of difficulties.

The role of the SENCO may be to ensure that systems in their school do include this element. SENCOs are likely to have considerable expertise in devising such targets and in making them 'SMART'. They might use this expertise to provide pupils, form tutors and class teachers with banks of example targets on which they can draw, covering behaviour, study, organisational, 'learning-to-learn' and life skills. This would be a very good use for the IEP software that many schools have bought, which often has excellent target banks.

If whole-school systems for setting personal targets that transcend subject boundaries are not possible, however, a system for pupils with SEND might be for a member of the inclusion team who knows the student well (a teacher, TA or learning mentor) to join in any meetings students and their parents have with class teachers, form tutors or Heads

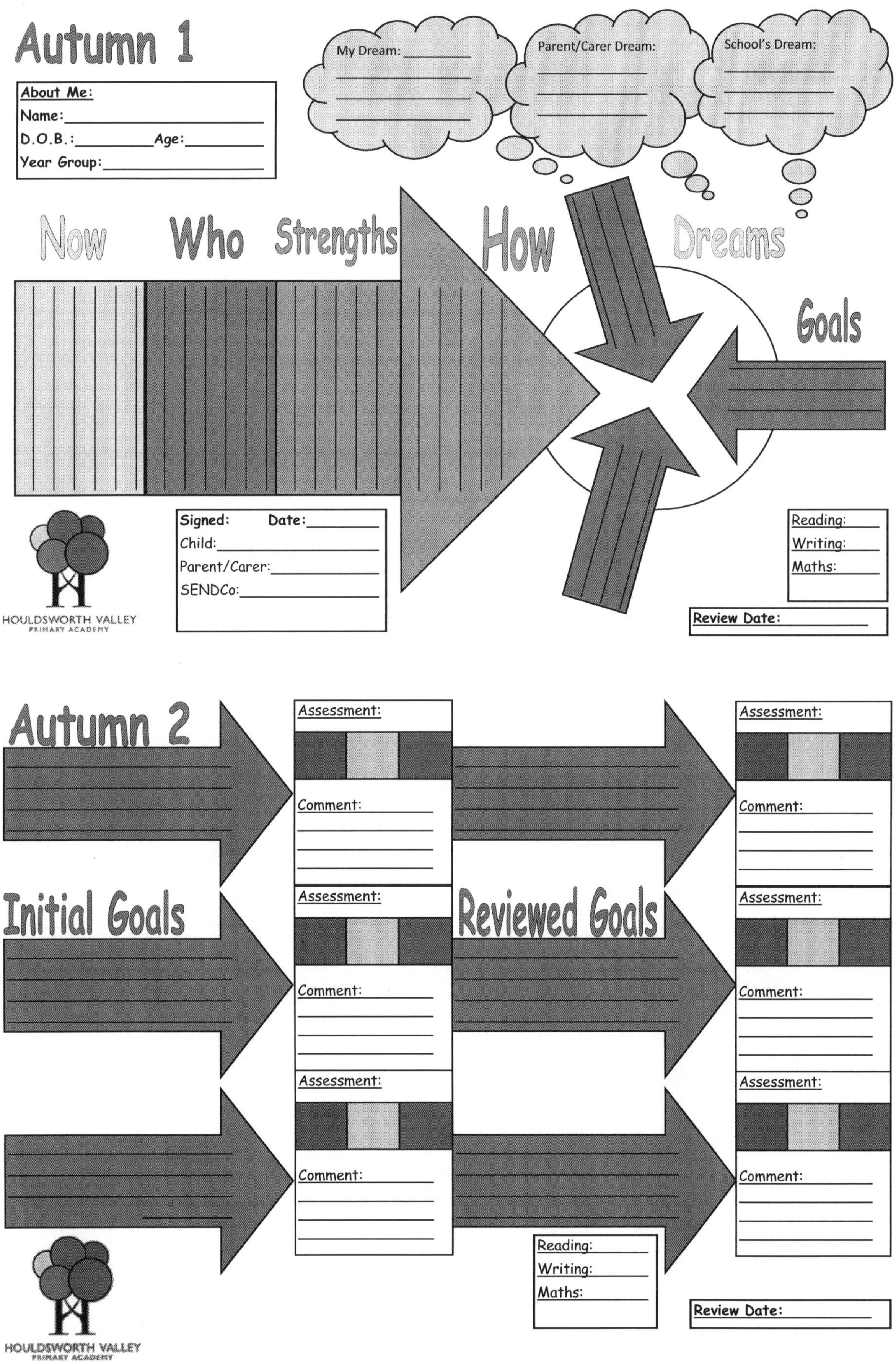

Figure 3.5 'Big Book' Pupil Passport

Source: Used by kind permission of Elizabeth Barneveld, SENCO at Houldsworth Valley Academy

Class xx	
Literacy targets To proofread my work (Morgan) To plan clear sections for my writing (Sayeed, John)	**Speech, language and communication targets** To say if I haven't understood and ask my teacher to say again/explain (Marius)
Behaviour targets To get to class on time (Morgan) To sit a long way away from people who wind me up like Jack (Paul)	Other targets

Table 3.1 Class map of targets

of Year to contribute suggestions for appropriate personal, cross-curricular targets. Another model is where TAs act as key workers for students with SEND and meet with them weekly to jointly set and monitor such targets.

Once set, targets need to be highly visible to children and teachers. That means not being kept in filing cabinets or on laptops but put on post-its on the child's desk, in their books, on the wall or written in their planners. The more visual they are, the better – a photograph of the child doing what the target requires, for example.

Some secondary schools put the targets on the school's intranet, with ideas on how subject teachers can help students achieve them. Others have compiled the targets for pupils into class-by-class composite target maps (Table 3.1).

Systems like these can meet the purposes of effective SEND provision and remove the need for separate individual SEND plans as long as progress against targets is recorded and parents are kept informed.

Tracking progress

Tracking overall curriculum progress

As with target-setting, systems for tracking the progress of *all* pupils on the curricular and numerical targets set with and for them are now expected of all schools.

The most effective tracking systems for pupils with SEND will be embedded within the systems used for the class or group. This ensures that class or subject teachers are monitoring their pupils' progress throughout the year and have ownership and responsibility for taking action where any pupil's progress is causing concern. The SENCO's role will be to develop and refine whole-school tracking systems so that they are fully inclusive and so that all pupils' progress is systematically monitored and reviewed, with the findings acted on.

An example comes from a school in Wiltshire. The school uses a 'Tick/Star/Cross' target-setting system where each student is given a good GCSE grade and an aspirational GCSE grade in each subject from the start of Year 7. These targets are based on all available data on entry. Each year group receives six reports a year. If they are working at their good grade, they achieve a tick; if at their aspirational grade, they receive a star. If they are not achieving either good or aspirational grades, they get a cross. If a student is achieving their aspirational grade three times in a row, then that grade will be upped to maintain the challenge. The students also have their own personal 'flight path' – as a visual representation of their achievement – which they complete after every round of Tick/Star/Cross. The school's Deputy Head noted the advantages of the system for pupils with SEND. Whereas IEPs 'helped to make our SEN students look different, which is certainly not what we wanted', the Tick/Star/Cross system enables the Learning Support team to work effectively:

> Our department has a very high-status role in the whole school process and we work across the whole school with all teaching staff to ensure that our students receive the strategies they need. If it does not work then we change it more quickly than previously, as we have these reports six times a year.

Effective schools will also keep track of pupils' year-on-year progress. If this is not part of whole-school systems, the SENCO can keep such individual records for pupils with SEND, adding information on additional provision that was in place in a given year or term (Table 3.2).

Progress over the course of an intervention

A second element of tracking that is specific to pupils with additional needs is tracking progress over the course of an intervention using 'before' and 'after' measures. A small-group intervention to improve pupils' social, emotional and behavioural skills might, for example, have a before and after assessment using GL Assessment's emotional literacy measures, the Strengths and Difficulties Questionnaire (www.corc.uk.net/outcome-experience-measures/strengths-and-difficulties-questionnaire-sdq/) or the Kidscreen questionnaires (www.kidscreen.org/english). Children in a nurture group would be assessed at the beginning and end of their placement using the Boxall Profile. Children taking part in a literacy intervention might have their reading or spelling age assessed using one of a number of standardised tests. For primary language interventions, the NELI assessment tool, Speech and Language UK's *Progression Tools*

Name:

Attainment[1]																		
			+	*+														
		#+	#	#														
	#+*	*	*															
	Term 1	Term 2	Term 3	Term 1	Term 2	Term 3	Term 1	Term 2	Term 3	Term 1	Term 2	Term 3	Term 1	Term 2	Term 3	Term 1	Term 2	Term 3
	Year 1			Year 2			Year 3			Year 4			Year 5			Year 6		
Provision in place	Social skills 2× week	Sp. and lang. gp. 3 × 20 mins a week Abra Reading intervention 2× week	As for term 2	Place 2 Be plus provision as in Y1 terms 2 and 3	CAMHs referral made													

Table 3.2 Example of a cumulative tracking sheet for a Year 2 child

* Child's reading attainment
# Writing attainment
+ Maths attainment

or, for primary and secondary pupils, the computerised *Language Link* assessments might be used. A helpful proforma for collecting pre- and post-intervention data can be found in the toolkit section of this book.

Reviewing progress

Just as effective SEND systems require that schools track pupil progress made as a result of additional or different provision, so it also requires a regular and frequent review schedule for individuals.

This need not mean a lot of extra work or separate SEND procedures. Many schools manage to combine review requirements for pupils with SEND with what they do for all pupils – normal parent meetings extended from ten to 30 minutes for children with SEND, or Academic Mentoring days at which TAs join pupils, form tutor and perhaps Head of Year to take stock of progress.

Again, these integrated systems have the advantage of keeping ownership of the progress of pupils with SEND where it belongs – with those who are immediately responsible for their subject learning and pastoral care.

Refinements for pupils with SEND will, however, be necessary. Reviews must, for example, look at progress across the curriculum and often behavioural, organisational, study, life and 'learning-to-learn' skills as well as progress in individual subjects. This is particularly important in secondary schools where uneven performance across subjects can often give vital clues about what helps and what hinders a pupil's learning or behaviour.

Review systems for pupils with SEND should also build in a review of the extent to which pupils' classroom curricular and personal targets have been met, as well as overall numerical progress in attainment measures.

They should review not only the pupil's progress but also the effectiveness of the school's actions. Is there evidence from teachers' planning, for example, that staff are taking account of the pupil's individual needs? Have any additional interventions used proved effective on the evidence from before and after measures and evidence from what the pupil, parents/carers and staff all think? Is further intervention necessary, and if so, what types of provision from the school's provision map might be appropriate?

These review questions help hold the school to account for what it is doing to support the pupil. Review meetings also provide an opportunity to hold everyone involved (pupil, parents/carers, staff, outside agencies) to account for any actions they agreed to undertake at the last meeting or review.

Another added dimension to review meetings that involve pupils with SEND is the cast list involved. While reviews for most students may only involve some combination of pupil, parent/carer and class teacher or form tutor, those for pupils with SEND might also involve the SENCO, a TA, perhaps the Head of Year in a secondary school and any outside agencies that are involved.

Finally, there may be additional work to be done with both pupils and parents/carers to secure their confident engagement in review meetings. This is discussed in Chapter 10.

The additional elements in SEND reviews mean that the SENCO may want to build on regular school record-keeping by adding additional headings or prompts. A possible set of agenda prompts, based on the principles of person-centred planning, is included in the toolkit section of this book.

Table 3.3 summarises these 'extra' features that need to be added to parent-teacher meetings, along with adaptations for other whole-school systems for setting targets and tracking progress.

Whole-school systems	SEN adaptations
Target-setting – numerical	Use data to set numerical targets for pupils functioning well below age-related expectations, including those working at pre-key stage standards
Target-setting – curricular	Teach class and subject teachers how to track back to identify curricular targets for pupils functioning well below age-related expectations Provide banks of targets for behaviour, study, organisational, 'learning-to-learn' and life skills
Tracking progress	Monitor the impact of intervention programmes by using 'before' and 'after' data Monitor the progress of pupils with SEN and disabilities towards numerical targets, as a group
Reviewing progress	Ensure that reviews • are cross-curricular; • include a review of the achievement of curricular and personal targets; • are individual, rather than involving a group; • involve others beyond the pupil, tutor or class teacher and parent – for example, SENCO, head of year, TA/key worker, outside agencies; • consider how effective the school's provision has proved to be; • check whether all concerned have completed the actions they undertook to take at the last meeting or review; • are preceded by work to secure the confident participation of pupil and parents/carers.

Table 3.3 Adaptations to whole-school systems

KEY PRINCIPLES

Key take-aways for SENCOs

- IEPs/ISPs were intended to provide individual targets for pupils, against which progress can be monitored and reviewed, but this function can equally be fulfilled through whole-school systems for setting targets for all pupils
- The SENCO's role is to ensure that these systems incorporate meaningful outcomes for children with SEND, and are visible and 'owned' by pupils

Key questions for the wider school leadership team

- Are your school systems for setting targets fully inclusive?
- Do they for example identify appropriate curricular targets for pupils working well below age-related expectations?
- Do they include personal and social as well as academic outcomes?

Note

1 In this column, the school enters the numbers or letter codes it uses to track small-steps progress towards age related expectations, with the code for exceeding Year 6 age-related expectations at the top

4 Adaptations to everyday classroom teaching

There are five things that make a real difference to the achievement of children with SEN or disabilities. They are

- additional provision made by the school, in the form of time-limited, evidence-based intervention programmes to address gaps in children's language, literacy, mathematical and social and emotional learning;
- interventions that extend beyond the school and involve outside agencies, from disabled children's services to early help teams, in providing support to the child in the context of the family and community;
- the meaningful involvement of parents/carers and young people themselves, so as to increase aspiration, motivation and support at home;
- inclusive environments and curricula;
- adaptations to everyday classroom teaching.

This chapter is about the last of these five. It is about whole-school systems that expect all teachers to take account of the needs of pupils with SEND (and for that matter, more able pupils, EAL learners and other vulnerable groups) when they plan their teaching, and monitor whether this expectation is being met.

Successfully embedding thinking about SEND into teachers' planning is essential to beating bureaucracy. Like setting targets and tracking progress for all pupils, it enables schools to use everyday systems that already exist in order to provide for SEND rather than separate paper trails.

IEP/ISPs were intended to be the mechanism for influencing teachers' planning. But as we have seen, there is little evidence that they successfully did so. What really works is supporting class and subject teachers to acquire the knowledge, skills and understanding of inclusive practice to enable them to adapt their teaching to meet the needs of all learners.

Embedding SEN and disability in teachers' planning takes time and effort, however (see Figure 4.1). First, there will need to be professional development for all staff on the basic principles. Second, it may be necessary to introduce new planning formats or amend existing ones. Third, SENCOs need to spend time working alongside class

DOI: 10.4324/9781003313526-4

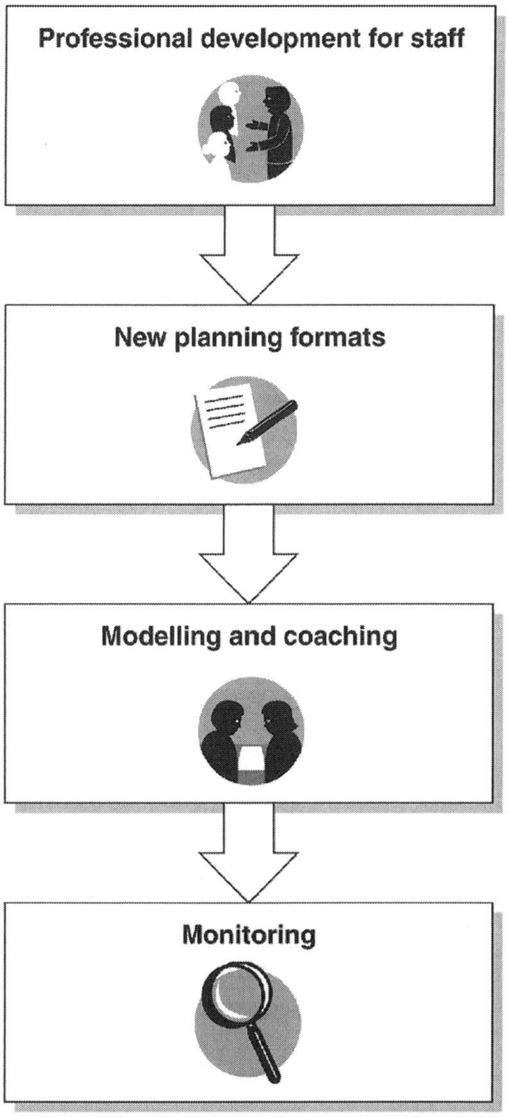

Figure 4.1 A four-part strategy to embed thinking about SEND

and subject teachers to model and coach the process of adapting planning. Fourth, the school will need to consider building the requirement to plan for pupils with additional needs into performance management. They will also need to build in systems for monitoring teachers' planning to identify staff who may need further support or challenge.

Mapping out this four-part strategy can take care of another potential piece of bureaucracy – the requirement to produce an accessibility plan showing how curriculum access will be provided for disabled pupils. The SENCO can simply build the actions that need to be taken (staff training, modelling/coaching, adapting planning formats and performance management) into the School Improvement or

Development Plan. Government guidance has consistently made clear that embedding curriculum access plans into overall school development plans is an acceptable and sensible step.

Professional development for staff

The inclusion section within the National Curriculum sets out key principles essential to planning and teaching:

- Setting suitable challenges
- Responding to pupils' needs
- Overcoming potential barriers for individuals and groups of pupils

These principles form the basis for professional development that SENCOs can provide for staff. They can be translated into practice and represented visually as shown in Figure 4.2.

Learning objectives

SENCOs can explain to staff that when planning for a class, they need first to think about the range of learning objectives that they need to cover. The majority of the class will be working on an objective linked to age-related expectations. A small number of pupils, however, will need to work on objectives that come earlier in the progression set out in the relevant curriculum frameworks or programmes of study. This will apply even in the context of mastery approaches to teaching and learning.

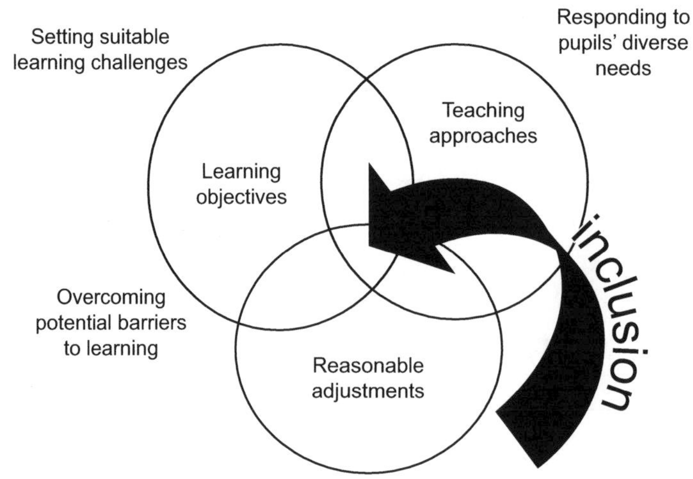

FIGURE 4.2 A model of inclusive teaching

> We use Singapore maths but it is not possible to have everyone working on their year group objectives . . . there's no point in working on fractions when you can't add two numbers.
>
> SENCO, Porters Grange Primary

Teachers often need help in planning for children who are working well below age-related expectations because they are uncertain about learning objectives that lie outside their usual terrain and have not had the opportunity to work alongside an expert in planning how to help pupils achieve them. All too often their planning simply notes that some children will be supported by a TA to achieve the general class learning objective (or at least remain reasonably quiet while everyone else does).

What SENCOs will want to encourage colleagues to do is write into their planning *different* learning objectives for those working very significantly below expected levels, all linked into the same overall class focus.

The principle of identifying different learning objectives for a small number of individuals is one that staff easily grasp. Equally, the teachers will understand that planning differentiated learning objectives will give a focus to the work of additional adults providing support in the classroom. Research (Moyles and Suschitzky, 1997; Blatchford *et al.*, 2012) has shown that TAs tend to focus more on helping children complete tasks successfully (what children are meant to *do*) rather than on what they are meant to *learn*. Carefully chosen learning objectives that are communicated to TAs can stop this from happening.

Even though they see the advantages and support the principle, the idea of incorporating linked but different objectives can still nevertheless sometimes alarm staff. There is no point in pretending that this is easy; better to say that it represents the peak of a teacher's skilled performance, something to work towards and something that even the most skilled teacher will not achieve all of the time. Even so, people will be able to give you examples of how, when they are in the 'exposition' phase of the lesson, they are able to drop in questions at different levels, targeted at different named pupils, or reiterate an explanation of a concept covered in previous years for the benefit of pupils who are still trying to master that particular idea.

They will even more easily be able to give examples of how they design different tasks for the part of the lesson when pupils are working independently or in groups – this is part of every teacher's planning repertoire.

In providing training to colleagues, SENCOs will want to help them consider how they will assess the extent to which pupils have mastered particular concepts or skills. The plenary part of any lesson or unit of work should also be planned so as to use it to assess all children's success – planning should cover not just what will be taught for children working outside age-related expectations or how it will be taught but also how it will be assessed.

Finally, SENCOs may want to help colleagues think about ways of building children's *personal* targets into their planning. Tracked-back learning objectives work well for the majority of children with learning difficulties, most of the time. However, as we saw in Chapter 3, there will be particular things that children with SEN or disabilities need to learn that are a real priority for their overall development but may not always link to the class learning focus. As an example, the absolute priority for a child at a particular time might be to learn to take turns when sharing equipment, or to learn how to use question words when speaking. These are not targets that necessarily relate to learning objectives in a teacher's overall class planning. If a teacher was planning a mathematics lesson on measurement, for example, tracking back through a mathematics framework would not take her to learning objectives about taking turns or asking questions. It could be more important for her to think, in her planning, about how she could use the general context of the lesson to support the child's progress towards these priority personal targets. She might make a note in her planning, for example, to say that she would put the child in a group of three for a practical measuring activity and explain to him beforehand that what she was looking for was to see him take turns with the measuring tape in the playground. If his target was to learn to ask questions using the question word 'What,' she might make a note that in the plenary, she would model the questions 'What did you do?' and 'What did you find out?' and then have the child put the questions to each group in turn.

Building personal learning targets into teachers' everyday planning in ways like this means that children with SEND can do most of their learning with their peers in the classroom rather than be pulled out for separate IEP/ISP-related activities. It is like a child doing their special physiotherapy exercises in the context of a PE lesson, or their own special speech and language therapy activities in the context of mathematics or history.

This will not always be possible; sometimes it is simply more practical, economical and effective to provide the special learning that a child needs outside of the work of the class as a whole. An example might be a child with severe learning difficulties whose priority personal target is to learn how to cross the road safely, find the right bus home or pay the right fare. These would be occasions when separate planning would be appropriate rather than trying to build the learning into the planning of class or subject teachers. Sometimes we do try to stretch 'inclusion' (in the sense of being physically present in every mainstream lesson) too far.

Giangreco and his colleagues (1993) provide us with a vocabulary for thinking about planning for children with SEN, which may be helpful to share with colleagues when providing training.

Giangreco talks about four different options for student participation in general classroom activities.

The first option he calls 'same'. This describes occasions when the student with SEN can pursue the same objectives and the same activities as others in the class. The example he gives is a lesson where a class is practising songs for a concert for parents.

The second option is 'multi-level'. This is where students are all involved in a lesson in the same curriculum area but are pursuing different learning objectives at multiple levels based on their individual needs. This corresponds to the idea of tracking back (or forward) through relevant sequenced objectives in a subject.

The third option Giangreco calls 'curriculum overlapping'. This occurs when a student with SEN is involved in the same lesson as the class but is pursuing objectives from different curricular areas. This would correspond to the example of covering social/emotional or speech and language objectives in a maths lesson about measurement.

Finally, Giangreco describes an option he calls 'alternative'. This refers to times when the regular class work does not offer reasonable opportunities to address the particular priority learning objectives for a student with SEN, and they need to be addressed discretely in a way that is not linked to the work of the class as a whole. It corresponds to the example of work on road safety and independent travel described earlier.

All teachers need to understand the difference between 'same', 'multi-level', 'overlapping' and 'alternative' learning objectives. They can then consider which of these options is most appropriate at any given time for a particular individual or group when planning. SENCOs might want to help them by providing a flow chart of questions, like the one in Figure 4.3.

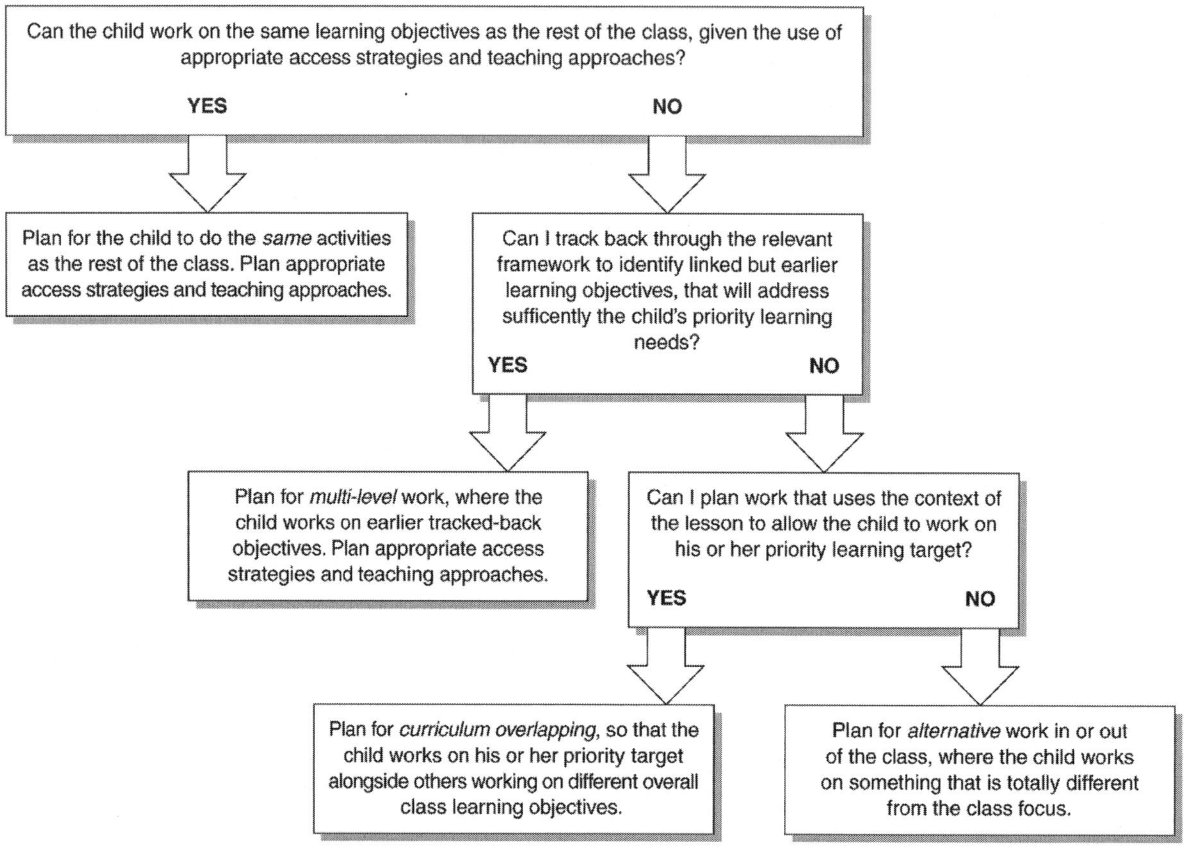

FIGURE 4.3 Questions flow chart

Access strategies/reasonable adjustments

Having explained how everyday lesson planning can note tracked-back learning objectives for children with SEND, or provide the context for priority learning objectives that are not linked to those of the class as a whole, SENCOs can go on to explore occasions when a child with SEN or disabilities *can* work on exactly the same learning objective as the rest of the group or class if appropriate access strategies – or, as equalities legislation frames them, reasonable adjustments – are used to overcome a barrier between the child and the learning.

A good example to give is that of a child with a visual impairment but with no learning difficulties. Staff will readily agree that there is no reason for such a child to work on earlier learning objectives or be placed in a group of 'less able' children. If the barrier created by the visual impairment can be overcome by appropriate access strategies/ reasonable adjustments (by using an enlarged text, for example, or materials in Braille) the child can be expected to achieve the same learning objectives as their peers.

You could then ask staff what they would say about a bright child with behavioural difficulties – one with ADHD, for example. Does this child need work on earlier learning objectives? If he is placed with a group who are working at earlier levels (perhaps because they happen to have a TA with them), what are the implications for his learning? Are there any access strategies the teacher could use to overcome the barriers presented by this child's behaviour to his own learning and the learning of others? Ideas might be increased opportunities to be 'up and doing' rather than sitting, building in breaks when the child can take a message to another class or have a brief period of exercise or providing an individual workstation that is screened at the sides.

> One day, my English teacher taught me about mind-maps and told me to make sure I had paper and pens to hand – now when all those ideas want to burst out, I make my mind-maps. I think the teachers are quite surprised that all that time they thought I was being annoying or naughty, I was just full to the brim with ideas about the lesson. They look at me a little bit differently now; and I hardly shout out at all.
>
> A learner with ADHD, quoted by
> Dr Pooky Knightsmith, 2022

Finally, you could ask staff to think about a child with dyslexia, who can express himself well orally and is quick to pick up new ideas. Do they think they need to plan for different learning objectives for him in science, maths, history, geography and so on? Does his slow reading, his brief and scrappy written work, mean he is not capable of understanding the subject content of a lesson – or does it just mean that he needs reasonable adjustments that provide him with scaffolded or alternative means of recording, such as those described in the toolkit section of this book? Are there subjects where he might need both differentiated learning objectives *and* access strategies? An example would be in English, where the class are working on spelling, and he does need to work on earlier learning objectives but might also need the access strategy of having a buddy read instructions on a spelling worksheet for him.

Questions like these, and the discussion they will prompt, will help colleagues to be aware that many underachieving children can work on the same learning objectives as others in the class as long as the teacher plans access strategies to overcome a barrier between the child and the learning.

The idea of using access strategies extends to the whole area of inclusion, not just to SEND. For EAL learners, the barrier might be difficulty in understanding the teacher's language as she explains a task. The access strategy might be simultaneous use of the child's home language. Or the teacher might plan to 'chunk' her speech into shorter sentences, use pictures or real objects to accompany her instructions and check on comprehension by asking the child to repeat the instruction back – all access strategies that would work equally well for a child in the class with speech and language difficulties. For more able pupils, the barrier might be the difference between the speed of their thoughts and their ability to get these thoughts onto paper. The teacher could overcome the barrier by suggesting the child uses concept mapping, for example, to get their ideas down quickly in a visual format. This strategy would work equally well for a dyslexic pupil in the class.

Access strategies should form part of every teacher's planning. Whenever they design tasks and activities for children, they need to be thinking about what might get in the way of learning and be creative about ways around the barrier. What SENCOs will want them to avoid is using just one, not very creative access strategy – that of allocating a teaching assistant to support the child or group who is likely to have difficulties. This is the most common access strategy used, but it places a heavy burden on the TA, who has to coax a group of children into completing tasks that have not been designed with their particular needs in mind and may not even be addressing appropriate learning objectives. It is also something that Ofsted is now examining closely in inspections – so teachers need to consider carefully whether they are spending less time with pupils with SEND than they are with other pupils, and whether pupils with SEND have opportunities to work independently and to work with peers during lessons.

Teaching approaches

As well as planning access strategies to overcome specific barriers to learning, teachers need to think about the more general teaching approaches that are appropriate to particular types of SEND.

Children with learning difficulties often benefit, for example, from teaching approaches that make abstract concepts real for them by making links to their everyday experiences and to things that are important to them. This is particularly so in mathematics. A good example of this is a child who was learning about subtraction:

> 'Looking at number 2, if I took 2 away how many would I be left with?' his teacher said. 'Two', the child replied. The teacher tried demonstrating with pictures, then bricks, to no avail. Then she remembered that he was interested in money. 'If you have £2 and I take it away, how much will you have left?' she asked. 'Oh I know what you mean', he exclaimed. 'You mean b – er all, don't you!'

These are some further examples of matching teaching approaches to particular needs:

- Children with speech, language and communication needs benefit from visual approaches – pictures or props used to back up a story or an explanation, as will children on the autistic spectrum, along with visual timetables that give a sense of routine and help them understand what will be expected of them and when
- Children whose behaviour presents challenges may benefit from absolute clarity about what is expected of them and opportunities for active and interactive learning that involves them in 'doing' rather than sitting passively
- Children with learning difficulties or those on the autistic spectrum might need tasks that are relatively closed – that is, where the task is structured for them and they do not have to invent their own ways of going about it ('Follow the step-by-step instructions on the card. . . . '). This might contrast with the need of more able children to be set tasks that are more open-ended or extended in time ('Devise your own experiment to explore friction').

Drawing on a variety of teaching styles and approaches (open and closed tasks, short and long tasks, visual supports or kinaesthetic approaches using movement) forms the background to planning for both teacher exposition and modelling and independent or group activities.

Planning a staff meeting or part of an INSET day

The first step, then, for SENCOs who want to influence teachers' planning is to provide training, either at a staff meeting or as part of an INSET day, on the 'three circles' model – getting the learning objectives right, using specific access strategies/reasonable adjustments to overcome barriers to learning and drawing on a variety of teaching styles and approaches.

Teachers might then use discussion questions like those in Figure 4.4, or work with year group or class teams and consider a child with SEND or a child whose behaviour presents barriers to learning. They share an example of short-term planning they have

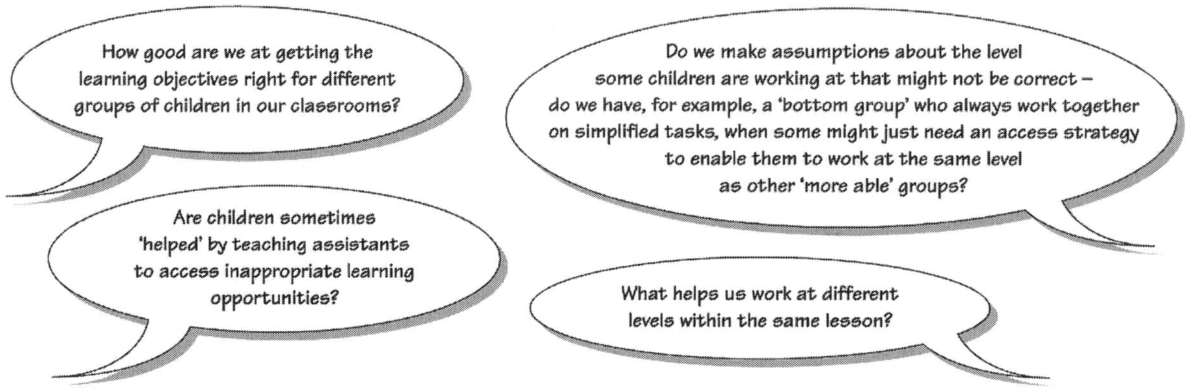

Figure 4.4 Example discussion questions for a staff meeting

brought with them and together identify any teaching styles or approaches that might be particularly effective and any specific barriers that might need to be overcome in order to make sure the child can access the learning, using a checklist of inclusive teaching strategies as a prompt. Groups feed back their best idea for an access strategy or teaching approach.

Training like this should include teaching assistants wherever possible and should tackle the issue of communicating planning to the TA or TAs who are working with a class. In the most effective schools, TAs take an active part in departmental and lesson planning and can often contribute a specialist knowledge about access strategies and teaching approaches that will work for a particular type of SEN or a particular pupil. They cannot be expected to provide effective support unless they know in advance what the pupils are to learn (the learning objectives for the class as a whole and for the pupils they are supporting) and what their role is to be. TAs should be routinely provided with teachers' planners, schemes of work, short- and long-term curriculum plans and class lists with annotated needs.

Planning formats

Having provided staff with a conceptual model to help them think about their planning, the next step might be to consult with them on modifications to the existing planning formats used in school.

Staff might decide that planning formats have a dedicated space (extra boxes, columns or rows) on which they can note particular adaptations they will make for pupils with SEND, more able pupils or other groups such as EAL learners. Table 4.1 shows an example.

<table>
<tr><td colspan="3">Teacher:</td><td>Subject: English</td><td>Date</td></tr>
<tr><td>Class:
9 L</td><td>NOR: 23</td><td>Grouping: mixed ability</td><td colspan="2"></td></tr>
<tr><td colspan="5">Unit of work: Study of Key Stage 3 Shakespeare text</td></tr>
<tr><td colspan="3">Objectives (WALT)
Read and understand key scene from text.
Explore characters and what motivates them.</td><td colspan="2">Outcomes (WILF)
Brief monologues (soliloquies) that give a good picture of what the opinions and feelings of one character are.
Complete reading of key scene from set text; understanding of what has happened and why.</td></tr>
<tr><td colspan="3">Activities
Starter
Paired recap on previous lesson's reading – key actions/characters. Q and A by teacher.
Main
Use interactive whiteboard (IWB) to display a usual wedding and contrast with play. Display still from movie – identify main characters.
Individuals choose one character and write brief monologue exploring the character's thoughts and feelings in the scene.
Paired work – read and comment on each other's monologue.
Complete reading of scene with individuals taking parts, up to Leonardo's losing control.</td><td colspan="2">Adaptations
Pupils to work in their buddy (mixed ability) pairs for starter.
Ask Qs using 'infer', 'speculate' to challenge more able.
Give Ian, Parin, Anthony a copy of the last IWB slide (the still) with starter ideas in boxes for each character – students to choose one and complete in the box.
Dan to work with Robbie – Robbie scribe.
Pupils to work in regular (ability-matched) pairs.</td></tr>
<tr><td colspan="3">Plenary
What will be the effect of the scene on events to come?
Last IWB slide – have students add thought bubbles for all main characters.</td><td colspan="2"></td></tr>
<tr><td colspan="3">Assessment opportunities
Use plenary to check understanding for five target pupils.</td><td colspan="2"></td></tr>
<tr><td colspan="3">Homework
Edit your monologue in the light of others' comments/what actually happened in the scene.</td><td colspan="2">Ian, Parin, Anthony instead to read next two scenes in Comic Book Shakespeare (www.shakespearecomics.com) in preparation for next lesson.</td></tr>
</table>

Table 4.1 Lesson plan

Unit: .... **Date:** .... **Year group:** ....

Key learning objectives: ....

Learning outcome for unit: ....

Planning for inclusion – note here differentiated learning objectives for different individuals and groups, and the teaching approaches and access strategies you will use to overcome barriers to learning.

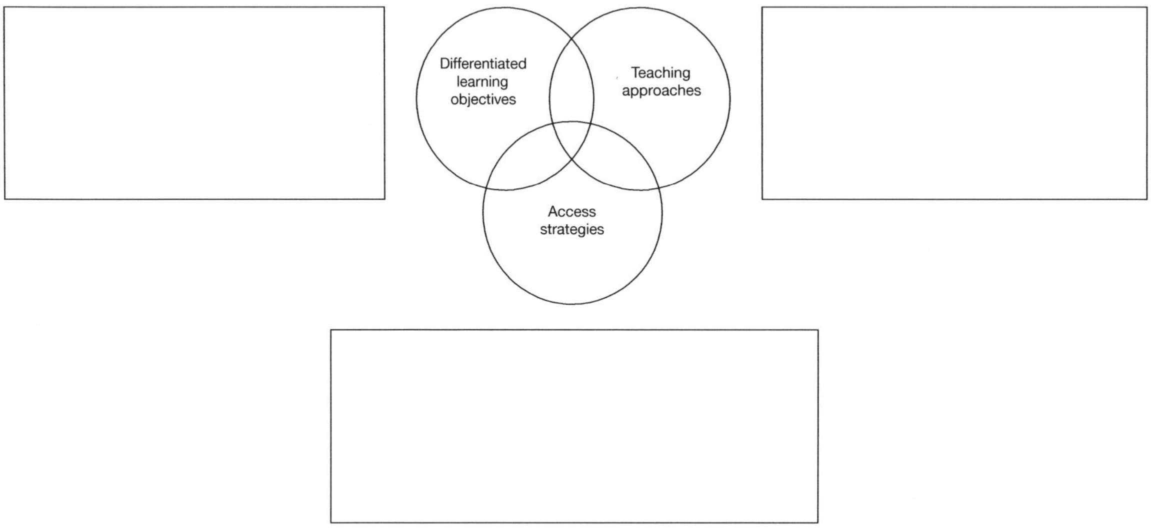

Session	Shared learning and teaching	Independent learning	Plenary	Assessment criteria	Guided learning
1					
2					
3					

FIGURE 4.5 Example planning format

Alternatively, staff might decide to add a blank version of the three overlapping circles to the school's planning format so that they can write in any learning objectives different from those for the class as a whole, any particular teaching approaches they will use to meet the needs of individuals and any access strategies/reasonable adjustments required (Figure 4.5).

Another idea might be for the SENCO to add a standard extra box to the planning format, containing a list of inclusive teaching strategies applicable to a wide range of special or individual needs. When planning for a particular class, the class or subject teacher simply has to reflect on needs present in the group and tick or highlight the strategies they want to use. A possible model for this is provided in the toolkit section of this book.

A final option is simply annotating existing printed plans by hand or electronically, to note the adaptations that will be made to meet the needs of particular groups or individuals. Figure 4.6 gives an example for a unit of work in a class that includes children with speech and language needs, children with difficulties in cognition and learning and several highly able pupils.

Technology has made the process of planning for individuals in the context of the class easier. Such tools allow teachers to do multi-level planning by pulling down into their planning objectives from earlier or later year groups. They allow teachers to cut and paste in questions at different levels of difficulty, which they can use to assess whether individual children have reached learning objectives. Plans that are saved from year to year can readily be amended to include teaching approaches and access strategies appropriate for the particular needs of 'this year's class'. Those teaching approaches and access strategies can be cut and pasted across from subject to subject, saving time and helping to ensure that ideas added to one plan as a result of a discussion with the SENCO or an outside agency will be applied more widely.

When thinking as a staff about how they want to record adaptations on their planning, it is important to avoid people making a rod for their own backs by trying to record every detail of the inclusive teaching approaches they use with a class. Planning is there to guide teaching and assessment, and what goes on it should only be what the teacher needs as a prompt. A teacher who has taught a number of children with autism, for example, is likely to have internalised the sorts of strategies that will be useful and will automatically use visual supports and closed rather than open-ended assessment tasks. The teacher does not need to annotate their planning to that effect. A teacher new to autism, however, might need to record explicitly on her planning a reminder to herself to do these things.

In general, the minimum that might be recorded by all teachers is

- the appropriate tracked-back learning objectives for any children working well below age-related expectations who cannot progress until they have mastered earlier knowledge in the sequenced curriculum;
- the different tasks that groups or individuals will be set, including any different homework;
- what will happen in the plenary to enable children working on different objectives to demonstrate their learning.

Medium-term Plan   Subject: Branching databases (Flexi Tree)   Term: Spring

Key Questions/Activity List	Resources	Teaching and learning intention and how it will be assessed
Show the class a selection of about eight materials, such as marbles, water, oil, salt. Tell the class that you are thinking of one of the objects, and that they must work out which one it is by asking 'yes/no' questions, such as 'Is it a solid?' Discuss which questions work well and point out that questions about small numbers of objects are unhelpful if the answer is no. Encourage them to use questions which divide the set of objects into two. Show the class how to create a tree diagram of branching questions, which can be used to identify each object. Do on IWB. Divide the class into mixed ability groups; give each group a tree diagram challenge. e.g. use a tree diagram to separate the Tudor monarchs. *TP KS MM MLG to do four objects with CT support.* *Plus group of TP/KS/MM/MLG/ JH/RLG* *JH RLG practise yes/no questions about people and sort selves before joining the group.* *ML, NG To relate back to science and use appropriate vocabulary.* *ML, AW – HA in history. Higher order questions What if . . . ?*	Selection of about six materials such as marbles, water, oil, salt. 'Big' and smaller paper trees.	The children will be able to create Y/N questions to categorise information.
Create a branching database in order to create a database to classify different organisms, e.g. Lives on land? *ML, NG include more organisms (with obvious similarities) in order to make the task more challenging. Where would you put a frog? Why? ML . . . ?* *JH, RLG – to have time prior to session with ICT buddy with 1:1 support in setting up a branching database (and after, to consolidate).* *JH, RLG, TP, KS, MM, MLG with CT recap on pics from science earlier in term linked to animal attributes and habitats. Sort 4 on paper tree before transferring onto computer (labels, spellings provided).*	Seven different organisms. Pics from science week. Paper tree. Labels, wordbank.	The children will be able to use their knowledge of branching databases to create a database to classify organisms.

Figure 4.6 Planning annotated for children with SEND and more able

Modelling and coaching

Agreed inclusive planning formats can be helpful in guiding teachers towards appropriate adaptations to learning. As ever, however, it is the *process* used to support teachers' planning that is more important than what ends up being written down. The most productive processes involve a collaborative planning process, like that used in the very interesting Lesson Study approach (www.lessonstudy.co.uk). Here, a group of teachers from different subject areas, which can usefully include the SENCO, plan a cycle of lessons together and observe pupils' response. SENCOs can also work individually with class or subject teachers, listening to the outline of what they want to teach and making suggestions about learning objectives, teaching approaches and access strategies/reasonable adjustments that are appropriate for children in the class who have SEND.

The examples that follow show how this can be done.

PLANNING EXAMPLE

Planning collaboratively with a Year 3 class teacher

A Year 3 teacher was planning work on spoken language, using a unit in which children discuss different scenarios for an ending to a novel they have been reading (*The Battle of Bubble and Squeak* by Philippa Pearce), and decide which is the most plausible. The lesson objective was to use the language of possibility to investigate and reflect on feelings, behaviour or relationships. Children were going to discuss how to talk about things that 'might' happen, using words like 'may', 'might', 'could', 'perhaps', then work in groups to talk about different endings to the story and have a spokesperson to report on their discussion.

The class contained a number of children with speech and language difficulties, so their teacher asked for the SENCO's help in planning adaptations she could make to meet their needs.

The first step was to consider whether the teacher would need to track back to earlier learning objectives for some children. Two of the children were able to express themselves only in simple sentences. The SENCO suggested that an appropriate objective for them would still involve the language of prediction but at a simpler level – learning to understand and use words like 'guess', 'I think', 'I don't know'.

The SENCO and the class teacher then discussed how this learning objective could be brought in to the lesson introduction, in which the teacher was going to explain to the children that we use different language to talk about things which might happen rather than things we are sure about. The teacher wanted then to ask the class questions about what they had done in the morning before they came to school and what they might do after school – using language like 'Are you sure?', 'Is that definite?' to generate vocabulary use that expresses possibility.

The teacher thought she could bring in the learning objectives for the children with language difficulties here. With the help of the SENCO, she decided to use a covered box right at the start of the lesson and ask the children if they knew what was in it, then produce two pictures and ask them to guess which one might be inside the box. This would allow her to use words like 'guess', 'know', 'don't know', 'think'.

The next step was to think about any access strategies that children with SEN might need after the lesson introduction. The SENCO suggested that she might use play people and small models, or a story sack of concrete objects to support her recap of *The Battle of Bubble and Squeak* so far, as the language would present a barrier to the children with communication difficulties, and also to EAL learners in the group.

For the group work part of the lesson, the teacher planned to give each group a different story prediction/ending to work on, and ask them talk about how likely their ending might be, using the clues from the story so far. She wanted the children with communication difficulties to take part, so that they could have access to the role models provided by other children's language, but decided to give them a clear role – that of timekeeper for their group.

In the plenary, she wanted to return both to the overall class learning objective and to the specific objectives she had planned for the children with communication difficulties. The SENCO suggested that she might hold a class vote on which of the different possible endings would be the one in the final chapter of the book. The spokesperson for each group would hold up a card with 'their' ending drawn on it, and children would be asked to go and stand by the ending they thought most likely. First, though, she would ask the children with communication needs to 'guess' which ending would win, encouraging them to repeat and complete the sentence 'I guess that. . . . '. For other children, she would use the language of 'predict', 'might', 'perhaps' and so on.

PLANNING EXAMPLE

Planning collaboratively for a Year 7 history lesson

This class was a mixed ability Year 7 group in which eight pupils had learning difficulties and two had been formally identified as dyslexic. They had been learning in history about Native Americans. The school's SENCO had allocated time to work intensively with members of the history department, modelling for them how planning could be adapted to take account of a range of SEND. He sat down with the teacher working with this Year 7 group and established what the learning objective was for the class – on this occasion to understand how important the buffalo was to the survival of the Native Americans. They agreed that this objective was appropriate for all the children, including those with learning difficulties, as long as appropriate teaching approaches and access strategies were used.

Multi-sensory teaching approaches are important for children with difficulties in cognition and learning, and the teacher had therefore already planned to use a lot of visual support – a PowerPoint presentation on the whiteboard that illustrated key information.

The SENCO suggested that the teacher have a list of key vocabulary on the wall ('nomadic', 'tribe', 'buffalo' and so on) and that she reinforce these in the whiteboard presentation for the benefit of children with reading difficulties.

The lesson was to involve children in writing down what they thought each part of a buffalo (hide, fat, teeth and so on) might be used for. The SENCO suggested supporting those with learning difficulties here by using a buddy system. The teacher would use a seating plan that paired children who found writing difficult with those who wrote fluently (but might not always have good ideas). Children would be asked to talk in these buddy pairs, then have the better writer record their initial ideas to feed back in the class discussion.

Managing to get homework down quickly can be a problem for dyslexic children, and understanding what they have to do in their homework a problem for children with general learning difficulties. The SENCO had been working for some time with staff to get them to spend more time explaining homework and to give it to children in handout form or on the school website rather than expecting them to copy it down quickly from the board at the end of the lesson.

He discussed how this could happen in the history lesson, with the teacher perhaps giving the children a homework sheet in the middle of the lesson and rehearsing with them what they would have to do. This was a good point to suggest, too, that handouts on buff paper using a font like Arial would add to their readability for dyslexic pupils. The SENCO and the teacher looked together at how the homework handout could be scaffolded by providing some pupils with a box of key vocabulary on their sheet or by giving them partly completed sentences to finish.

The SENCO also suggested that in the part of the lesson where pupils had discussed their initial ideas on the use of various parts of the buffalo, watched a further presentation from the teacher and were writing up their learning, some children might use a laptop with the text-to-speech function activated.

The SENCO and the teacher then briefly discussed ways of involving children with learning difficulties in a plenary. The SENCO learned that this teacher regularly used strategies to help less confident children answer questions. In this lesson, for example, he planned to make sure that lower-attaining children had their chance to come up to the whiteboard and drag words into the right places in sentences about the buffalo – but if they struggled, would be ready to offer them the chance to 'phone a friend' or 'ask the audience'.

The advantages of a collaborative planning process like the ones used in these examples are that the process makes strategies for children with SEND live and real for class and subject teachers. The conversation is about the specific content of what the teacher is actually going to work on with a class. The ideas generated are therefore likely to be used and remembered. Training provides the groundwork, but collaborative planning translates ideas into action.

Collaborative planning also leaves something behind. Every minute the SENCO invests in it will have a pay-off far beyond the children involved in the immediate piece of teaching. The joint planning provides the teacher with ideas they can use again and again in the future, even when the SENCO is not supporting them directly.

For children with the more common types of SEND, like general learning difficulties, specific learning difficulties or mild behaviour difficulties, the SENCO may not need to invest very much time before teacher colleagues are able to incorporate appropriate adaptations into their everyday planning. The strategy sheets provided in the toolkit section of this book may be all they need to keep them going.

In cases where children have less common or more complex needs – for example, children with sensory impairment, or those with severe learning difficulties who will function at the earliest stages of the National Curriculum throughout their school career – the involvement of the SENCO or outside agencies will continue to be needed. A primary class teacher working with a child who has little or no sight, for example, should expect to be able to sit down with a specialist teacher of the visually impaired and look in advance at medium-term planning so that the specialist teacher can advise on access strategies and help in the preparation of appropriate resources. Similarly, if a child has severe learning difficulties and is working at levels very significantly below those of the class as a whole, there will be a need to identify in medium-term planning those learning opportunities in which the child can profitably take part, working on either tracked-back learning objectives linked to those of the class as a whole or on separate objectives (curriculum overlapping).

The examples that follow illustrate this process.

PLANNING EXAMPLE

Planning collaboratively for a Year 4 science lesson

This example describes how a teacher planned for a Year 4 class with diverse needs. In science, he was planning work on temperature involving the use of an electronic thermometer/probe. The children were to predict, then measure the temperature of various liquids. Clearly the science learning objectives were not relevant to the needs of Shamina, a child with profound and multiple learning difficulties, whose learning was at a very early developmental level.

The teacher had access to advice from a teacher from a local special school and discussed with her how he might adapt his planning. The specialist teacher used the idea of curriculum overlapping to show how the child with profound learning difficulties could be involved in the class activities but for the primary purpose of pursuing objectives from other curriculum areas – in this case, communication. The objective would be for Shamina to begin to link the words 'hot' and 'cold' with the relevant sensory experience. Appropriate teaching approaches for a child working at this level would need to be based on concrete materials that provide a strong sensory stimulus.

The class teacher suggested that they use two hot water bottles, one filled with hot and one with icy water. A TA would work with Shamina and three other children, encouraging them to first let Shamina feel each of the hot water bottles and hear the words for each of them, then try to engage her in anticipation (an early cognitive forerunner of prediction) by saying 'Ready, it's going to be cold' or 'Ready, it's going to be hot'. The more able children would then predict the temperature in each of the bottles and measure it with a probe. Assessment would involve the TA in using a camera to record Shamina's responses, looking for any sign of anticipation.

PLANNING EXAMPLE

Planning collaboratively across the curriculum

A group of schools in East London working to raise standards through support for vulnerable groups received funding for a curriculum development project. They decided to use the funding to work on inclusive planning with subject faculties in one secondary school.

The project used skilled teachers with prior experience in the relevant faculty, and often with early years and primary teaching experience also. These teachers were asked to 'track' each scheme or unit of work and prepare lesson-by-lesson plans for work appropriate for pupils working below age-related expectations for seven-year-olds when they moved to secondary school at the age of 11. Maths, geography, history, RE and English were covered.

In maths, for example, a Year 8 scheme of work involved the class in working on position (coordinates), straight line graphs and expressing simple functions in words. For one lesson, these objectives were tracked back (using multi-level planning) to the use of everyday words to describe position and direction. Pupils with learning difficulties worked on the key words 'column', 'row', 'left', 'right' and 'position' using a game they played in pairs – each moving counters on a grid and answering the question 'What's your position?' The planning includes questions that the class teacher can use to involve everyone during the plenary, such as 'Can you write instructions using shorthand, for example 2R (move 2 squares to the right)?'

In geography, a potentially challenging lesson on tectonics was made accessible by planning for pupils with learning difficulties to use a simple instruction sheet to construct an 'edible earth' consisting of crust, mantle, outer core and inner core, using three different colours of ice cream, nuts and edible silver spheres. In the plenary, they had to identify each part as they ate their edible earth, sharing it with the class.

In history, a Year 9 scheme of work on women at work in World War I involved the class in studying the impact of the war on the changing roles of women. In planning for differentiation, it was decided that pupils with learning difficulties could access the same learning objectives as the class as long as particular teaching approaches and access strategies were used. These involved adding picture supports to information sheets in the form of black and white photographs of women as bus conductors, nurses, farm workers and so on. Worksheets were simplified and supports provided in the form of sentence starters and picture-word matching activities. The teachers also took the opportunity to develop work on a key life skill for pupils with learning difficulties (writing a CV and job application) in parallel to the main history objectives (curriculum overlapping again). Pupils had to choose a job that supported the war effort and construct a letter of application using cut-up sentence starters and key job vocabulary. Pupils also constructed their own CV using a digital photograph of themselves.

Monitoring

So far we have looked at how a SENCO might provide training for colleagues on how to plan for a range of needs in their class, and how to support this through opportunities for collaborative planning. Ideally, there would also be opportunities from time to time to follow up such planning with review. 'How did the lesson go?' the SENCO might ask. 'How did those with SEND respond? What worked and what didn't? What strategies might you want to use again or apply in other subjects or with other age groups?'

If change is to be embedded, however, it will also need to be monitored and built into existing performance management systems. Teachers might, for a period, all have a target to increase their use of adaptations in their planning. This could form part of the school's curriculum access plan or (better and less bureaucratic) part of a section of the school development or improvement plan concerned with increasing curriculum access.

Monitoring is relatively straightforward. From time to time the SENCO can look at a sample of planning drawn from across the school and provide feedback on issues arising from the monitoring exercise to individual staff and to the senior leadership team and subject leaders. The subject or whole-school issues unearthed will feed into school self-evaluation. Any issues relating to individuals feed into performance management and the provision of extra training and support.

Finally, the school will want to know whether its improved planning is feeding through into teaching. Whoever is monitoring teaching in the school – members of SLT, subject leaders, the SENCO when gathering specific evidence on SEND for the school's self-evaluation – will need to check whether there is a clear read-through from planning to what they see happening in the classroom for children with additional needs.

KEY PRINCIPLES

Key take-aways for SENCOs

- Adaptations to everyday classroom teaching to take account of the diverse needs of pupils increase the range of 'normally available' provision and reduce the need for bureaucratic arrangements for additionality
- SENCOs can help colleagues think about appropriate learning objectives, teaching approaches and access strategies/reasonable adjustments for individuals when planning their lessons
- An important message is that many pupils with SEND can work at the same level as others in the class if access strategies are used to overcome barriers to learning

Key questions for the wider school leadership team

- When monitoring teachers' planning and its translation into classroom teaching and learning, do all senior leaders look at how far the planning incudes access strategies to overcome barriers to learning, varied teaching approaches and appropriate learning objectives for all pupils?
- Do staff tend to rely on a single access strategy – allocating a teaching assistant to coax a group of children into completing tasks that have not been designed with their particular needs in mind and may not even be addressing appropriate learning objectives?
- Are systems in place for your SENCO to support colleagues with their planning in a coaching role?

5 Inclusive environments and curricula

In the last chapter, we looked at how SENCOs can help class and subject teachers make specific adaptations to their planning and teaching so as to meet children's diverse needs. In this chapter we will set those adaptations in the broader context of inclusive provision, remembering that it is this ongoing inclusive **universal** offer that will reduce the need for add-ons to what is normally available to all pupils, and hence the need to identify large numbers of children as having SEN.

There are three aspects to the inclusive offer:

- The classroom and school environment
- The curriculum
- Everyday teaching that effectively scaffolds and supports learning

In this chapter we will look at the first two.

Inclusive environments

> When a flower doesn't bloom, you fix the environment in which it grows, not the flower.
>
> Alexander Den Heijer (2018)

There seem to me to be five key principles to creating inclusive environments:

- Predictability and clarity of expectation
- Attention to sensory overload
- Supporting children to regulate their emotions
- Creating communication-supportive classrooms
- Paying attention to break and lunchtime environments

These are all inspiringly illustrated by the approach taken at Whitefield Primary School.

DOI: 10.4324/9781003313526-5

CASE STUDY

Whitefield Primary School in Liverpool has small open-plan classrooms that run into each other. To overcome the sensory overload problems this creates for children, there is much emphasis on creating consistency across classrooms and predictability from one year group to the next.

Routines and displays are similar in every class. For example, every class has a display board with the school values, concentric circles showing the learning zones (comfort zone, stretch zone, panic zone), the Zones of Regulation and feeling words for each zone.

In the Zones of Regulation approach, children identify whether they are in the blue zone (low, sad, tired), the green zone (calm, alert, focused and ready to learn), the amber zone (worried, excited, frustrated, upset) or the red zone (angry, panicked) and learn strategies to 'up-regulate' if in the blue zone, and 'down-regulate' if amber or red. The Zones approach is used universally from nursery onwards as the school's behaviour policy; children are able to talk about behaviour using the language of the Zones, recognise their own triggers and identify strategies to manage their emotions (in early years, co-regulation – 'I need you to sit with me and cuddle me', in Key Stage 2, 'I need to do my five-finger breathing').

Visual timetables are also used universally, on the wall in every classroom, with cards to put in and take out. Each classroom also has a pod or nest – a safe space to which children who are dysregulated can take themselves.

Children have the same things on their desks in each year group, and there is no clutter, nothing hanging from the ceiling and no displays for displays' sake. Children's artwork instead decorates the corridors outside learning spaces. Bright colours are avoided in classrooms, and there is much use of natural materials such as hessian.

The school have extended playtimes and introduced a range of creative activities based on the Early Years Foundation Stage principles for using the outdoors as a learning space. Classroom staff, including teachers, are all out in the playground, which is seen as part of learning. The school has found that children now come in calmer, so it is less stressful for teachers, and less learning time is wasted in class.

Staff have taught children how to sit at tables for lunch, use a knife and fork, talk to the person next to them and keep to conversational noise levels. Children are served at table by staff rather than queueing up. Marie Beale, Deputy Head and SENCO, notes that 'this is a different approach to many schools, but we find it really supports inclusion and makes for a calming lunch experience.'

In this lesson you will be learning through:

1. Watching a film clip then class discussion	
2. Writing on a questionnaire	
3. Paired work to see who has the same opinions as you	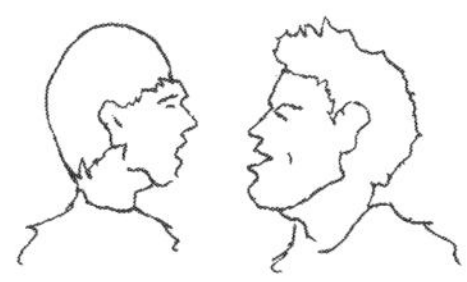
4. Small group work about your favourite conversation topics	

Figure 5.1 Icons for different activities

When creating inclusive environments, **predictability and clarity of expectation** means everything from lesson rubrics for teachers to consistent displays. Other examples would be providing secondary children with a school locker that stays the same every year, or developing an agreed set of icons (Figure 5.1) to be used in all subject areas to indicate what types of learning activities will be used in a lesson – an open book for reading, a TV screen for watching a film, two heads facing each other for paired work and so on. Some schools have a moving marker on all lesson slides to show which part of the lesson has been reached, from starting activities to teacher input, independent work/group work and plenary. Another idea is to colour-code permanent displays in classrooms across the school by subject.

Attention to sensory overload means a decision to be a 'no-shouty' school, providing individual booths and screens for children with autism to work in, or using the top tips from brilliant therapeutic practitioner Shahana Knight (2022). Shahana suggests picking a soothing colour scheme with no more than two colours, decluttering by ensuring, for example, that windowsills are empty and resources kept in storage boxes, using soft lighting (and if you have to use overhead fluorescent lights, checking they are not flickering), adding plants and investing in some flexible seating so that children do not spend all day in uncomfortable hard plastic classroom chairs. Daniel Sobel and Sarah Alston (2021) additionally suggest that we think about providing a variety of furniture in the room so that children can sit at a table and chair that is the right size for them, perhaps by swapping chairs and tables with other teachers.

EXAMPLE

Karen Truelove, SENCO at Cathedral School in Essex, always tries to look at the environment and teaching through the eyes of the child. She describes how staff realised that their classrooms were 'too busy . . . with so many things on working walls that children found it hard to find what they needed.' Now children have on their tables just the limited number of vocabulary words they need for a session. Maths resources like multilink that will be useful in a particular session are also on children's tables, rather than the side of the classroom, so children don't have to think 'I've got to stand up and get them and everyone will know I need help.'

At Priestnall secondary school, some classrooms have sloping ceilings, which provoked anxiety in one autistic student, so his classes were moved to a different room. SENCO Gareth Morewood (Morewood *et al.*, 2011) describes how other students found the open-plan layout in classrooms difficult, so 'for these students, screens and booths inspired by TEACCH workstations, and built by the school's Technology technician, provided a portable solution.'

In planning the environment for children with sensory issues, SENCOS will find useful the sensory audit developed by the Autism Education Trust (https://mentallyhealthyschools.org.uk/resources/sensory-audit-for-schools-and-classrooms/). Can loud noises and bells be avoided, for example, or if not, then can pupils be warned that they are about to happen? What can be done to prevent light reflecting off shiny surfaces? Might carpet squares to sit on be helpful, rather than hard floors?

Supporting children to regulate their emotions will, for primary schools, involve

- displays: visuals of any calming exercise that has been taught (like how to do bubble or square breathing), a check-in board where children can place laminated photos of themselves or sticky-notes onto images or emojis showing different emotions;
- a worry box and a private 'I wish my teacher knew. . . . ' box where children can post messages
- an empathy/conflict resolution area, perhaps with pairs of cut out footprints so children can try standing in someone else's shoes and saying how they might be thinking and feeling;
- a calm-down area of the classroom, which might have intricate colouring-in sheets, lavender-scented cotton balls to sniff, kinetic sand, smooth pebbles to touch, a lava lamp, a rocking chair, soft cushions or a weighted blanket.

Children can also make their own individual calm-down kits in a shoebox, containing things like a small vial of scented oil, smooth material to stroke and a favourite photo.

Some primary schools may choose to have a central calm-down area instead of areas in individual classrooms, or a sensory garden outside; central provision is also the only practical option in secondary schools, where it may be within the SEN department's area.

EXAMPLE

St James' secondary school uses time-out cards for students to show they need to leave the classroom rather than lose control of their behaviour. They are expected to find a member of the pastoral team or SEN team in their respective areas of the school. This adult will help them reflect on the situation, calm down and return to class. All uses of the card are logged and patterns analysed.

At Porters Grange Primary in Southend, there are two rooms for children who need a place to calm themselves and help from adults – one larger room called the Oasis, and a 'Lagoon' room which is smaller and beautifully painted. There is also a large, calm and attractive library where a play and creative arts therapist works with children.

Creating communication-supportive classrooms might involve auditing the environment using the tools suggested in my *Time to Talk* book (Gross, 2018). One aspect of these tools is reflecting on classroom acoustics. Did you know, for example, that the average noise level in classrooms is around 60 decibels, whereas recommended levels are no more than 35 decibels? A number of studies (Shield and Dockrell, 2008) have shown that high levels of background noise have detrimental effects on children's academic performance and also that noise has more of an impact on children with special educational needs than on other children. More recently, studies (Massonnié, 2020) have found that children who struggled with attentional focus, impulsivity and behavioural control were more sensitive to noise than their classmates.

To improve the listening environment, schools can try to reduce reverberation by fitting curtains or blinds, keeping blinds half closed rather than fully open, covering hard surfaces with fabric (for example, as a background to displays), installing special acoustic tiles and panels and door seals. Ways of reducing noise include closing doors, managing the timetable so as not to place noisier activities next door to quiet ones, getting any humming lights, noisy projectors and heating systems serviced regularly and turning equipment like IWB projectors off when not in use. Schools can also consider sticking soft pads (or halves of old tennis balls) on the bottom of chair and table legs, carpeting as many areas as possible, using soft covers on display tables, lining equipment trays with felt and providing a tray of ear defenders for use by any child who needs them.

Another way of managing noise is teaching children to monitor and adjust their own voice levels in class using 'noiseometers' which display different colours according to whether the noise level is low, medium or high.

EXAMPLE

Children at one school designed their own 'quiet meter' with numbers on a sliding scale of one to five to show the level of noise in the classroom. They took turns to be the 'noise monitor' who would quietly get up and change the meter if it was getting noisy. The others quickly noticed this and talked less or talked more quietly.

Finally, **inclusive break and lunchtimes** involves taking a look at the outside area to check for equipment that encourages cooperative and collaborative play, play equipment that encourages children to use all their senses and secluded areas and **cosy places**, which can be enclosed – such as a bubble, cocoon or tunnel. There are excellent ideas for creating inclusive playground designs in an article by Dorothy Lepkowska (2021). Some schools, like Whitefield and Oakwood in the example subsequently, have rethought the whole way playtimes are organised:

EXAMPLE

At Oakwood Primary School in Southampton, staff saw how playground arrangements introduced when children returned to school after COVID lockdowns led to calmer breaktimes. They decided to keep the system in which children eat and play with their year group only, and have consistent allocated lunchtime staff (senior leaders, ELSAs and sports coaches) for each year group 'bubble'.

Before the pandemic, the school offered a break and lunchtime 'Rainbow Room' provision for children with social communication difficulties but have found that the new system works better. Tricia Mahoney, Assistant Head and Inclusion Lead, notes that 'our SEN children are benefitting from quieter, calmer outside environments where the ELSA is able to support with social situations as they arise. A couple of our EHCP children who were unable to participate with groups of peers at lunch times are now able to successfully.'

The inclusive curriculum

Curriculum intent and design have preoccupied schools recently, since Ofsted put them at the heart of their inspection framework. So what makes an inclusive curriculum? Here are some questions SENCOs and other school leaders might want to reflect on:

Does our curriculum

- ? allow all children to experience success?
- ? provide learning that feels relevant to all learners – including clear vocational pathways in Key Stage 4, for example, and learning that relates to pupils' real-life experiences?
- ? teach knowledge in which all learners can see themselves represented – for example, a history curriculum that is not solely based on the history of the UK and its Empire?
- ? start from an understanding of what many learners may find difficult, and plan accordingly?
- ? include a progression in teaching and learning spoken language skills, including but not confined to the vocabulary needed for learning?
- ? teach children about how they think and learn?
- ? teach all children about neurodiversity as part of the curriculum?
- ? include a progression in life skills and social and emotional skills?

Is our curriculum

- ? carefully and cumulatively sequenced, with built-in recap and spiral revisiting of topics and a clearly identified progression in knowledge and skills for all learners?
- ? planned so as to meet social and emotional needs as well as academic learning?
- ? planned so as to build in time for learners to receive extra help when they need it, or pursue particular interest in more depth?

Here are some illustrative examples from schools.

Developing a curriculum that is carefully and cumulatively sequenced, with built-in recap and spiral revisiting of topics

At Woodberry Down Primary in London, the curriculum is carefully sequenced, with knowledge organisers (Figure 5.2) reminding children of previous connected learning and what will come next right through to when they are in secondary school. The knowledge organisers build in recap ('test your knowledge') and important vocabulary – both 'words to know' (topic-specific words that will be explained) and 'words to go' (words that are important for learning beyond the immediate topic, which will be intensively taught to mastery level and regularly reviewed).

<table>
<tr>
<td>Year 6 Summer 1, Geography

Sharing the world</td>
<td>Previous learning
In Year 5 we learned the term globalisation and how trade became global.

In Year 5 we learned about primary, secondary and tertiary stages of production.

Words to know - for this topic
natural resources – materials or substances produced by the environment

commodity – a raw material or product that can be bought or sold

supply chain – the sequence of processes involved in the production and distribution

supply and demand – the more people want something, the more demand there is and the more money that can be charged for it</td>
<td colspan="2">Key vocabulary
Words to go
Fuel – material such as coal, gas, oil that is burned to produce heat or power
Resources- things that can be used to support or help
Natural – present in or produced by nature, fitting in with what normally happens
Unnatural – does not exist in nature, artificial, goes against what normally happens
Produce- as a verb means make, bring into existence. As a noun means food that is grown to be sold
Manufacture – to make
Product – things that are manufactured
Agricultural – to do with farming
Invest – to put money or time into something
Extract – to take out
Distribute – to give out. Distributed – given out, shared</td>
</tr>
<tr>
<td>1 ➔</td>
<td>2 ➔</td>
<td>3 ➔</td>
<td>4 ➔</td>
</tr>
<tr>
<td>There are two types of natural resources – agriculture(crops, food and livestock) and geological (fossil fuels, metals, clay etc.).

Extracting natural resources has led to the destruction of habitats, deforestation, increase in pollutants and decrease in soil quality.</td>
<td>Natural resources are not evenly distributed throughout the world. Countries trade their natural resources to ensure that their needs can be met.

Major natural resources found on the planet are oil, coal, iron, ore, gold, diamonds, copper, coffee, wheat, cotton and natural gas.</td>
<td>Oil is one of the most important natural resources in the world. We consume billions of litres of oil every day.

Oil provides us with energy and fuel to power machinery and in addition it is vital in producing many products such as headphones, candles, computers and deodorants!</td>
<td>World events may affect the price of natural resources. The price of fuel has increased because the price of crude oil, which is used to make petrol and diesel, has risen.</td>
</tr>
</table>

5 →	6 →	7 →	8 →
The term commodity means a raw material or agricultural product that can be bought and sold Natural resources are extremely valuable and there are a complex series of international relationships based on the trading of them.	Africa has a lot of natural resources including arable land, water, oil, natural gas, minerals, forests and wildlife. In recent years China has invested heavily in a number of different African countries and a number of different sectors.	Many natural resources that society has depended on are non-renewable, meaning there is only a finite amount on the planet and supply will eventually run out. Renewable resources include solar energy, wind, falling water, the heat of the earth, (geothermal(and plant materials (biomass).	Approximately 600 million tonnes of material are recycled every year. This generates more than 200 billion dollars a year Using recycled materials directly reduces pressure on natural resources extraction, and less energy is consumed.
9 → Diamonds are a very expensive natural resource and are found under the ground or on the ocean floor. They are then sorted out, polished, manufactured and sold in jewellery. Different countries are involved with different stages of the diamond trade and profits are not fairly distributed.	**Future learning** • In Key Stage 3 you will learn about economic activity in the primary, secondary, tertiary and quaternary sectors.	**Test your knowledge!** • What impact does mining have on the environment? • Why do countries like China invest abroad? • How are natural resources distributed across the world? • Why has the price of petrol recently increased?	

Figure 5.2 Example of a knowledge organiser

Source: Adapted from a model used at Woodberry Down primary school

The CUSP curriculum in the Unity Schools Partnership Multi-Academy Trust (MAT) identifies the critical knowledge in the curriculum, and the desirable. Teachers make sure the teaching in their lessons focuses first on the critical knowledge. Long-term teaching sequences have been planned that are interleaved and include regular retrieval of prior knowledge. The curriculum includes key vocabulary, with vocabulary modules designed to teach vocabulary explicitly (for example 'lava', 'molten',' hardens' in the study of volcanoes). Children have dual-coded Knowledge Notes for each lesson, rich in vocabulary, with high-quality visuals to support the text.

Starting from an understanding of what many learners may find difficult

One example of this might be building in approaches to learning which often benefit children with SEND such opportunities for practical activities. Another is analysing not just the building blocks of learning but also the stumbling blocks and planning a curriculum to tackle them.

St Matthew's Research school, for example, observed that many of its students were struggling with basic understanding of number, As a result, says Assistant Headteacher Hydeh Fayaz, 'we focused our curriculum planning on the representation of number through manipulatives, using 'Ten Frames', 'Rekenreks; and 'Numicon sets' etc.'

Teaching all children about neurodiversity as part of the curriculum

Whitefield Primary has a 'Growth curriculum', part of which is designed to help children learn that we have different brains and not everyone needs the same thing. To help everyone understand autism, for example, the school uses the 1Decision PSHE resources, where there are animated story books and games such as 'Why does purple play differently', covering things like sensitivity to the noise of hand-dryers and preferring to play with a special toy. The films explain how all children need something particular to them; one character needs glasses to see better, another uses a hearing aid, while others need help with classroom routines and how to communicate. Children at Whitefield have developed a good understanding of differences; they are able to say, for example, 'Louise has got a wobbly cushion and Shane's got a fidget toy. . . . I don't need that, but I need help with . . . '

At Henley Bank secondary school, SENCO Rhian worked with a group of children to develop a whole-school assembly called 'Different brains: Respecting differences'. It had a powerful impact, with students coming to Rhian to ask questions about how they could help and what they should do if they saw somebody struggling. Several students also referred themselves for assessment because they recognised in themselves some of the traits described in the assembly.

Another assembly, designed to address growing mental health needs, explained where anxiety comes from, likening it to a parasitic monster that hijacks our brains and distorts our thinking. Rhian used Dan Siegel's hand analogy (https://youtu.be/qFTljLo1bK8) to explain how the different parts of the brain work together and what happens when we 'flip our lid' and find our emotional brain disengaging from the thinking brain. Students worked through breathing and grounding techniques to help them regulate their emotions.

Planning the curriculum so as to meet social and emotional needs as well as academic learning

Inclusive schools will have a sequenced, spiral curriculum that explicitly develops the five social and emotional capabilities described in EEF guidance (van Poortvliet *et al.*, 2019) – self-awareness, self-management, social skills, responsible decision-making and relationship skills. They will include explicit teaching on how to work productively in groups (Gross, 2021). They will also design their curriculum to take account of the particular emotions and vulnerabilities of the children in their community.

At Oakwood Primary, for example, COVID lockdowns led the school to think hard about the curriculum when children returned to school. They provided parents with a statement about the curriculum intent, with a strong focus on children's social, emotional and mental well-being.

To help build a sense of community, there was a whole-school project based on the book *Here We Are* by Oliver Jeffers. Working on this shared project was planned so as to promote a sense of belonging and joint working. The book allowed for children to discuss their time during lockdown, focusing not on what had been 'lost' but what had been gained.

At Whitefield Primary, where children face many potential challenges in their lives, staff know that issues of grooming, drugs, knife crime and alcohol misuse are as important for their learners as English and maths. They have built their 'Growth curriculum' around the Jigsaw PSHE programme, Rights Respecting Schools and Andrew Moffatt's 'No Outsiders' teaching materials. The curriculum includes a progression in learning the language of emotions, using ideas from the book *Language for Behaviour and Emotions* (Branagan *et al.*, 2020). Alongside planned work around the Zones of Regulation, all children are taught aspects of social thinking (www.socialthinking.com), including the idea of rating the size of any problem we face from tiny through small, medium and large, according to how dangerous the problematic event is, how long it will last, the number of people involved and how difficult it is to solve.

Planning the curriculum so as to build in time for learners to receive extra help when they need it, or pursue a particular interest in more depth

Finding time for additional interventions is a perennial problem in a crowded curriculum. Time needs to be built in to address this. One secondary school runs what it calls the 'Getting ahead club', which students attend voluntarily (and enthusiastically) on a Monday after school to work on upcoming learning. Others plan time for same-day masterclasses, where children go over things they may not have grasped and have the opportunity to overlearn key knowledge so that it will be retained.

One school builds in a 30-minute block of time four days a week, when students can take part in various academic intervention programmes or choose electives including peer tutoring and library time. Students choose how they will spend this last half hour of the day, in discussion with parents and teachers. The school faced initial pushback from teachers worried about losing valuable instruction time in an already overloaded curriculum. Gathering and sharing data showing the impact of the programme on attainment convinced them that it was worth it. The school also noticed school-wide improvements in behaviour and a new sense of agency that students felt from knowing they could make choices in their learning.

A final example is Houldsworth Valley Primary school, where there is a 'soft start' to the day, with children coming in at 8:30 for half an hour of activities such as sensory circuits, social group games or, even in Year 6, playing cards. This extra time allows groups of children to work with learning support assistants (LSAs), with the work based around the gaps that their teachers have identified in their learning.

KEY PRINCIPLES

Key take-aways for SENCOs

- Inclusive environments and curricula form a key element of the universal offer that reduces the need for additional 'SEN' provision
- Inclusive environments provide children with predictability and clarity of expectation. They are communication-supportive, avoid sensory overload and provide the means for children to regulate their emotions
- Inclusive curricula offer learning opportunities that are carefully sequenced, with inbuilt recap. They are planned on the basis of common stumbling blocks, not just building blocks
- They teach all children about neurodiversity and focus on social and emotional as well as academic learning

Key questions for the wider school leadership team

- To what extent does the physical environment in your school offer children predictability, avoid sensory overstimulation and provide places where they can go if they need to calm down?
- Does your curriculum allow all children to experience success? Does it include a progression in teaching spoken language skills and social and emotional skills?

6 Inclusive teaching

In the last chapter, we looked at how an inclusive curriculum and environment can be developed so as to increase the provision that is 'normally available' and reduce the need for specific SEND adaptations.

In this chapter we turn to everyday teaching for all that effectively scaffolds and supports learning.

The EEF (Education Endowment Foundation, 2021) have described key features of such high-quality teaching for children with SEND in their 'five-a-day' model: explicit instruction, cognitive and metacognitive strategies, scaffolding, flexible grouping and using technology (which we will explore in Chapter 9). I would add to their list seven more of my own:

- More talk, less writing
- Attending to background knowledge
- Building children's independence and self-efficacy
- Focusing on social and emotional as well as cognitive aspects of learning
- Making learning relevant and engaging
- Making learning social
- Deliberately fostering classroom cohesion and a sense of belonging for all members of the class

Many of these elements are illustrated in the subsequent case study.

CASE STUDY

At Houldsworth Valley Primary Academy in Newmarket, SENCO Elizabeth Barneveld explains how inclusive teaching and high aspirations mean 'We don't put children with SEND in corridors. Lessons have a set structure that provides predictability and teacher modelling: Explain, Example (my turn), Attempt (your turn). Children stick knowledge strips for a lesson in their books, with key information and vocabulary for the lesson. 'Flick back 5' is used for retrieval practice: children stick five recap questions in their books and have to flick back through their previous work to find the answers. This has proved very helpful for children with memory difficulties.

DOI: 10.4324/9781003313526-6

Scaffolding rather than differentiation is used in class. Children with reading difficulties are kept in English lessons, scaffolded by pre-reading. Every child who needs it has time at the end of the day when they are exposed to the text for the next day. Echo reading (where the teacher reads a short segment of text and the student echoes it back) is used to develop expressive, fluent reading.

Writing often involves using Floor Books where the teacher acts as scribe, which is very helpful for children who find transcription difficult. Children have access to laptops, Clicker 8 software and some have daily touch-typing instruction. Talk is central to lessons; children might, for example, draw lolly sticks to form pairs so as rehearse ideas and answers orally. The school uses Voice 21's sentence stems to scaffold discussions, and explicitly teaches vocabulary.

Behaviour is well managed, in a way that takes account of children's social, emotional and mental health needs. The school has a 'reset room' where children take themselves for five minutes if they need to self-regulate. They can sit on a sofa, look at a book and watch a bubble machine. Later in the day, the class teacher will address the behaviour in a restorative conversation.

Explicit instruction

Explicit instruction involves adults modelling tasks, talking through how they are going about them, perhaps live-modelling using a visualiser, developing success criteria and providing children with an example of the finished product – a WAGOLL (What a Good One Looks Like).

EXAMPLE

Success criteria, arrived at with a class by looking at good and poor models of a piece of work, are enormously helpful to children who find learning difficult. One child with SEND, recounts expert Shirley Clarke, put success criteria under the heading 'What helps me learn' on his One Page Profile. Another said, 'It means I can do it'.

On the whole, teachers 'get' the need for modelling and examples. Where SENCOs can often help, however, is in how to give clear instructions to children – by giving instructions in the order in which they should be followed, 'chunking' them and avoiding complex syntax.

EXAMPLE

I recently came across these examples of how **not** to give instructions:

- A poster about how to line up that said 'Leave a space behind the person in front'
- A teacher saying, 'If you want to go out to break you need to listen' (better as 'First listen. Then it will be break')
- A suggestion in a blog post that teachers say, 'By putting your hand up in the air, who can answer question 2?' This one was actually recommended as an illustration of 'front loading', that is, signalling *how* you want pupils to work at the front of instructions, but would not be appropriate for any child with processing difficulties

SENCOs can also help colleagues to

- understand the need to keep information in PowerPoint presentations to the minimum that is actually needed;
- 'chunk' their demonstrations (watch this – then do – come back together – watch this – then do) rather than model everything at once;
- avoid talking at the same time as modelling a practical activity – model first, then talk.

Explicit instruction involves the 'I do, we do, you do' sequence of modelling, then guided practice, then independent practice. It should usefully involve asking children to verbalise after the teacher (for example, repeating 'Five is halfway between 0 and 10').

It involves choosing text with appropriate readability levels, chunking content (dividing it into separate, more manageable components), giving concrete examples and knowing how to ask questions at levels of complexity that are different for different pupils; Marion Blank's well-known levels of questioning are helpful here.

Explicit instruction involves presenting information clearly, with worksheets that use a single consistent font (one designed for general legibility like Ariel, Verdana or Tahoma), a font size of 12 to 14 points and a simple uncluttered layout – like the example in Figure 6.2 rather than Figure 6.1.

Finally, it involves giving children plenty of opportunities for rehearsing new learning, in the practice section of the lesson. Tom Sherrington (2022) suggests what this might look like in a lesson on the parts of a flower:

- Annotating an unlabelled diagram and a photograph from a list of given words

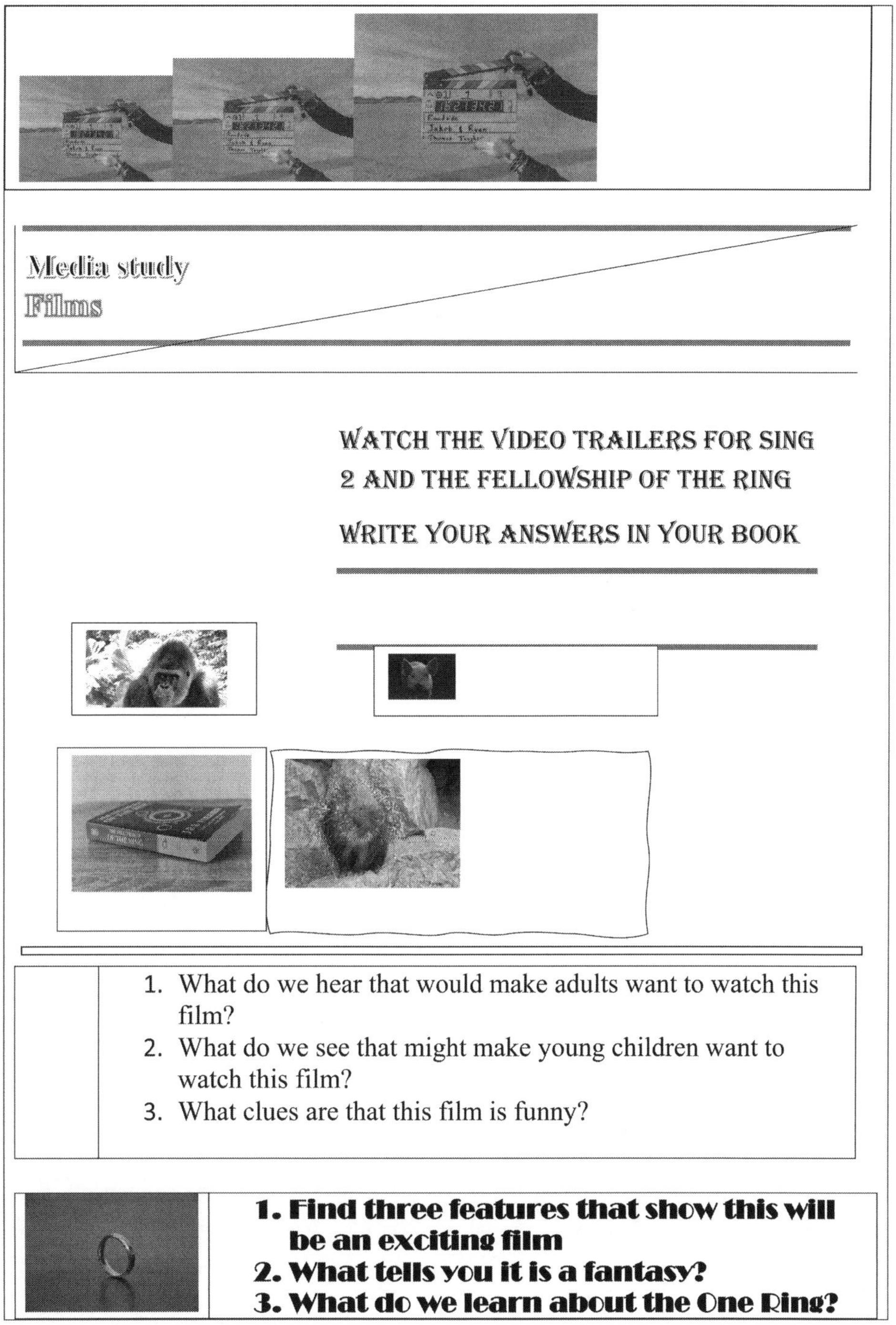

FIGURE 6.1 A cluttered worksheet

- Explaining to a partner, talking through what each part of a flower is called and what it does
- Answering some questions where an expected answer might for example be 'the anthers are parts of a stamen that carry the pollen' – said verbally, not just in writing

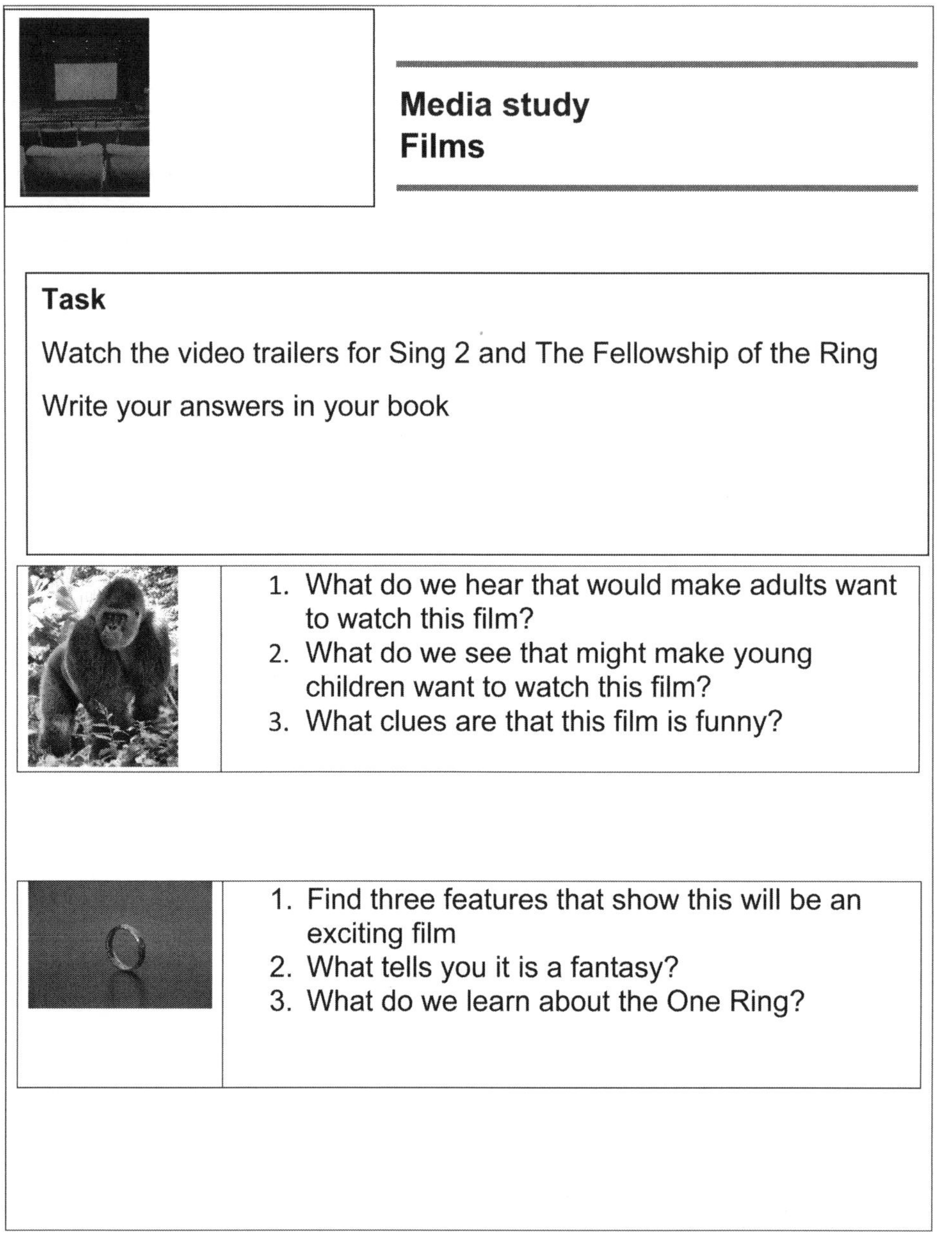

Media study
Films

Task

Watch the video trailers for Sing 2 and The Fellowship of the Ring

Write your answers in your book

1. What do we hear that would make adults want to watch this film?
2. What do we see that might make young children want to watch this film?
3. What clues are that this film is funny?

1. Find three features that show this will be an exciting film
2. What tells you it is a fantasy?
3. What do we learn about the One Ring?

Figure 6.2 The same worksheet decluttered

Cognitive and metacognitive strategies

Metacognition is about helping students understand and be able to articulate how to be a good learner. We know it is central to raising attainment for **all** children, and no less so for struggling learners.

One way to help is for the teacher to model **thinking** using think-alouds rather than just model how to complete a task. Chris Runeckles (2022) illustrated this beautifully (Table 6.1). Modelling making mistakes and correcting them also feels particularly inclusive.

Instead of . . .	Try
The first sentence of our answer always needs to include words from the question.	The first thing I'm thinking is 'How can I make sure I directly answer this question?' I can do that by picking out words from the question to include in my first sentence.
Next I need to include key pieces of precise evidence that will support my point.	Next I'm thinking 'What do I know about this topic that's relevant to the point I've just made?' Here I stop and run through in my head what I know. I choose which pieces of evidence to use. Once I've made a decision, I start writing again.

Table 6.1 Thinking aloud

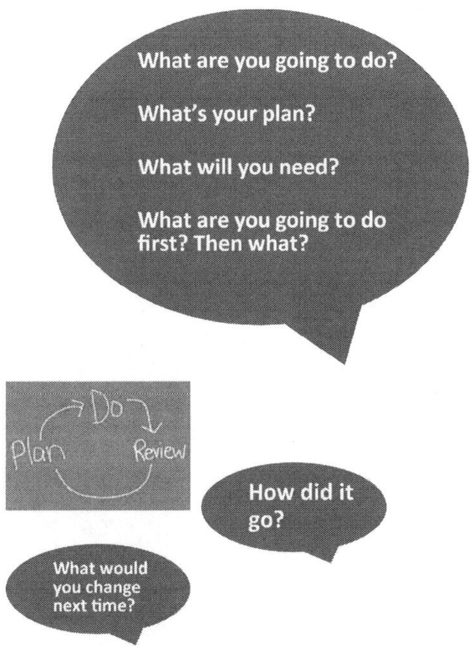

Figure 6.3 Prompts to help children plan, monitor and evaluate their own learning

Pupils also need to be taught to plan, monitor and evaluate their own learning. Figure 6.3 suggests some prompts that teachers and TAs can use to encourage this process, modelling the independent use of a checklist to monitor progress over the course of a task.

Cognitive load is another key concept in the science of metacognition. Inclusive teachers build this into their planning – avoiding overload by not talking while students are reading information from a slide, for example, and by keeping tasks simple (like labelling diagrams or answering factual questions) if a concept they are teaching is complex, while making them more complex (for example, analysing or evaluating information) if the concept is simple or already familiar.

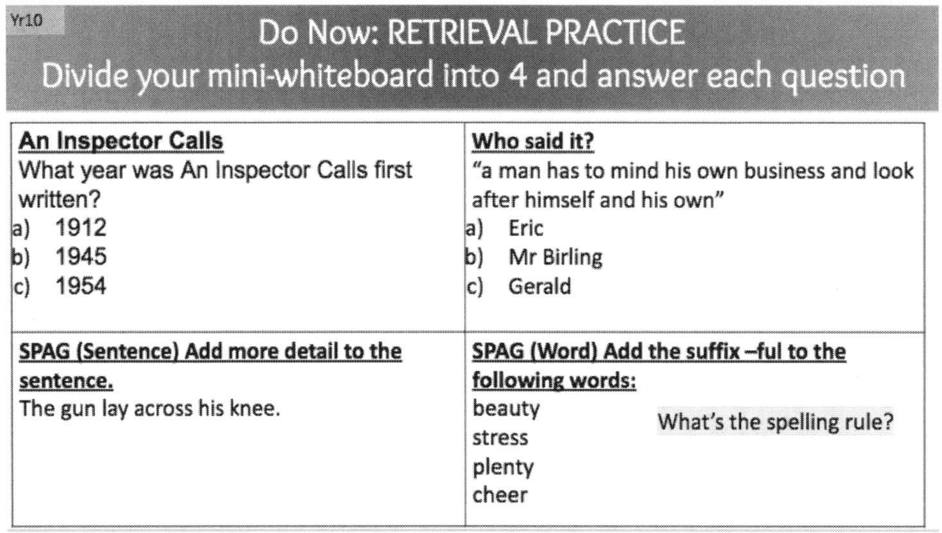
Yr10

Do Now: RETRIEVAL PRACTICE
Divide your mini-whiteboard into 4 and answer each question

An Inspector Calls What year was An Inspector Calls first written? a) 1912 b) 1945 c) 1954	**Who said it?** "a man has to mind his own business and look after himself and his own" a) Eric b) Mr Birling c) Gerald
SPAG (Sentence) Add more detail to the sentence. The gun lay across his knee.	**SPAG (Word) Add the suffix –ful to the following words:** beauty stress plenty cheer What's the spelling rule?

Figure 6.4 Retrieval practice examples at start of lesson

In the cognitive and metacognitive strategies section of their SEND guidance, the EEF includes helping students remember what they have learned. This is useful for all learners – research shows that practising retrieval once doubles long-term retention relative to reading the text once (34% vs 15%) and engaging in repeated retrieval increases retention to 80% (Karpicke and Roediger, 2010). An emphasis on recap and retrieval practice has become a mainstay of the 'mainstream' knowledge curriculum. But for children with learning difficulties, who so often seem to 'know something one day and forget it the next', such practice is especially important.

Inclusive practice for memory will, for example, involve opening lessons with 'Last lesson we learned about. . . . Today we. . . . Next lesson we will . . . ', saving a piece of work that has been modelled on the whiteboard and retrieving it to start the next lesson, using the flick-back strategy we met earlier at Houldsworth Primary, having 'Flash-back Fridays' or starting a lesson with 'Do Now' retrieval practice on mini-whiteboards (Figure 6.4).

But there is more to memory than recap and retrieval. SENCOs can help colleagues realise the power of also using mnemonics, either provided by the teacher (Figure 6.5) or created by the children.

Scaffolding

Times have changed in teaching in the last few years, in ways that can only be good for children with SEND. Planning lesson tasks with three or four levels of differentiation,

- Which is the numerator, which is the denominator? Nice Dog (N before D)
- The mode is the **M**ost **O**ccurring **D**ata **E**ntity.
- All graphs need 'SALT'- **S**cale, **A**xes, **L**abels, **T**itle
- How to spell 'because' – Big Elephants Can't Always Use Small Exits
- How to remember when to use their, there, they're

FIGURE 6.5 Examples of mnemonics

which usually meant those with SEND being placed in a group together to do a simplified version of the learning, has been replaced by the concepts of adaptive teaching and scaffolding – providing, then gradually withdrawing supports that enable all children to access the **same** learning. Tables 6.2, 6.3 and 6.4 and Figure 6.7 illustrate the range of ways in which scaffolding can be applied to classroom tasks – following instructions, reading, writing, response to questions, homework and class or group discussion.

A key aspect of scaffolding is dual coding, or what in the SEND world we know as visual support. This might take the form of animations – for example, using an animation from the brilliant digital resources for teaching science at https://liftlessons.co/science-home?s=03 to explain new vocabulary such as 'compression', or the animations from CENTURY (see this link for an example: www.youtube.com/watch?v=NWhwSn7wmD4).

More often, visual support takes the form of pictures, or symbols – perhaps Widgit symbols or, for older students, the age-appropriate symbols from https://thenounproject.com/. It is important that any visuals are integrated with the text (labels linked by arrows to parts of an image or diagram, for example) rather than separated from it (as in a diagram with a key that corresponds to separate text next to it) so as to avoid cognitive overload.

Following instructions	Ask a child to repeat back an instruction Encourage children to ask for clarification or repetition if they have not understood Provide a task board or checklist for the child to tick off After an explanation, tell children they can start if they are ready, or wait to have the instructions explained again if they would like to Leave instructions on the board or on a laptop in the corner of the room Allocate peer buddies to whom children can go to ask for help Allow students to voice-record instructions Encourage them to write themselves post-it note reminders
Reading	Preview the text and discuss key vocabulary – introduce the class to words they may not know by exemplifying their use in contexts they know or are interested in, inviting them to create a symbol or drawing for the word or completing a Frayer model (Table 6.5) Chunk the text, then read and discuss as you go Use print-to-speech technology
Writing	Provide: • word banks • writing frames – use variations on a class writing frame with more key words/phrases, less complex sentence starters, reduced space for extended writing • ready-made tables or grids • Cornell note sheets (templates for taking notes) • paragraph prompts or structure strips (Table 6.3, Figure 6.7) • graphic organisers Have children record using storyboards, comic strips or infographics (a collection of images, diagrams and minimal text) Paired writing – pair children with good ideas but weak transcription skills with those with good transcription skills but fewer ideas Use speech-to-print technology
Response to questions	Use warm calling (pre-warning of questions) rather than cold-calling – 'Ahmed, please think of the names of the three different types of rock we discussed last lesson. I will get back to you for an answer in a few minutes.' Give choices – is it x or y? Provide clues or sentence starters
Homework	Allow students to voice-record homework instructions Provide worked examples Provide 'Watch again' recorded lessons to be accessed via technology Record supporting guidance

Table 6.2 Scaffolding in the classroom

1. I think that . . . Spell out your point of view clearly Use imperative verbs and hyperbole to create a sense of urgency	Help students to structure any piece of writing with a strip of boxes which students stick down the side of their page, then write next to it. Make each box as long as you would expect the paragraph to be. Put an instruction for this paragraph in the box. This could also include a sentence starter or a feature you'd like them to include, such as a statistic. You can colour-code the boxes with varying degrees of challenge.
2.I think this is because . . . Recount an anecdote that shows why you feel this way	
3.There are other good reasons for my point of view . . . Give at least three different reasons to support your point	
4.It's not just me that feels that . . . Quote an expert	

Table 6.3 Structure strips

Scaffolding class or group discussion
Like any other aspect of learning, purposeful classroom talk requires scaffolding. 'Talk frames or sentence starters are one very helpful approach. SENCOs can introduce colleagues to the progression in language structures developed in Tower Hamlets (https://nrich.maths.org/content/id/14423/Progression%20in%20Language%20Structures%20Tower%20Hamlets%20sentence%20starters.pdf), which has sentence starters for different types of talk, from explanation to prediction and explanation. There is a progression in each from Y1 to Y6, but many students in Key Stage 3 need this kind of scaffolding too
Voice 21, the oracy charity, also has excellent sentence starters for different contributions to a discussion – for example, presenting an idea (I think/We haven't yet talked about/I would like to start by saying), building (Building on x's idea. . . . I agree and would like to add. . . . X's idea made me think . . .) as well as probing, clarifying, challenging and summarising
Inclusive teachers can scaffold contributions to discussion by quieter children by giving everyone a finite number of counters ('talk tokens') which they put in a pot when they speak, which limits the amount that more dominant children say, and enables children to bring in quieter peers by asking for their views
Most importantly, teachers can scaffold the use of academic vocabulary by asking students to reframe answers using words from the board or knowledge organisers. Tom Sherrington (2021) gives a good example:
T: Let's describe the pattern of the graph – Abdi?
Abdi: The line goes up, then goes up less steeply
T: Yes – let's now say what's actually changing and include some key words (gradient, increase, decrease are written on the board)
Abdi: Oh . . . the temperature increases, but then after two minutes, the gradient decreases which means the temperature rises more slowly

Table 6.4 Scaffolding class or group discussion

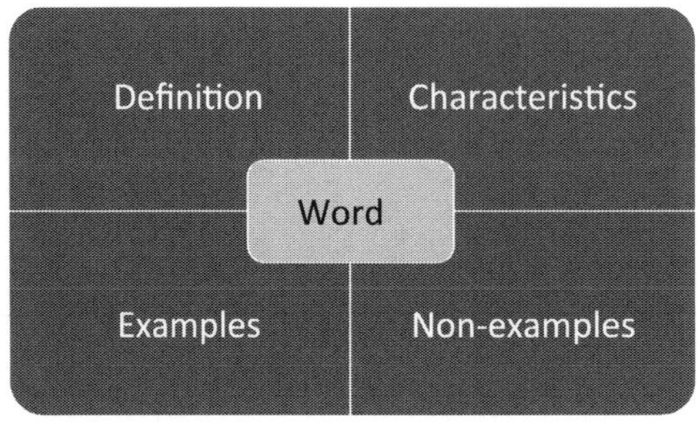

TABLE 6.5 The Frayer model for learning vocabulary

Fishbone	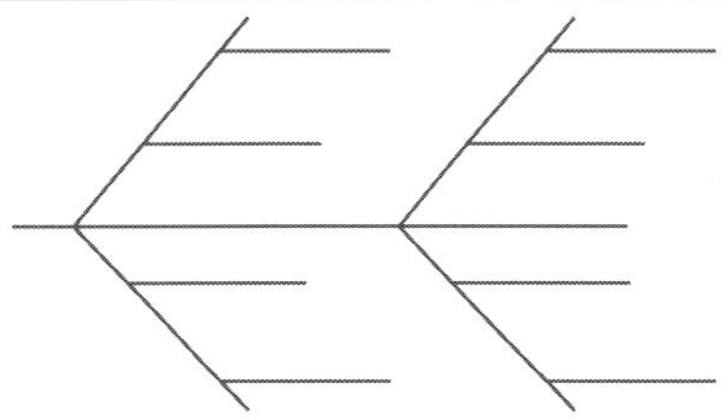	Cause and effect factors for a complex topic. Example: to prepare for a writing assignment, the student starts with the topic (the head of the fish), then lists the big ideas relating to the topic, then the attributes/qualities/functions/effects associated with each of these ideas
Spider	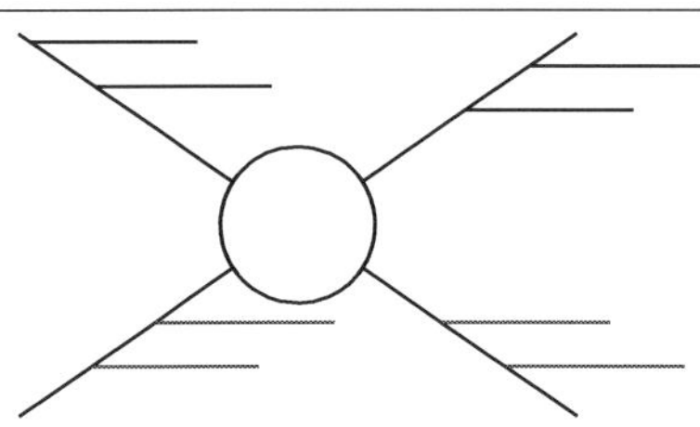	Adding more ideas to a single topic Example : reviewing previous learning, with the topic in the centre, the big ideas branching from it and then recalled information relating to each idea on further branches
Timeline	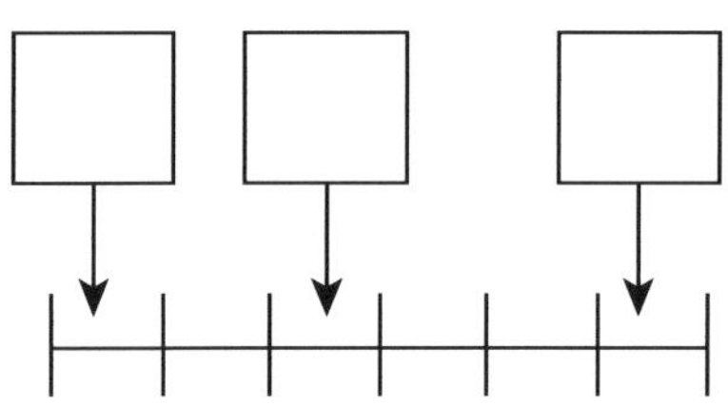	Any sequence of events Example: planning the timings for an event, recording a personal life history or visually representing the changes to the atomic model throughout history
Cycle	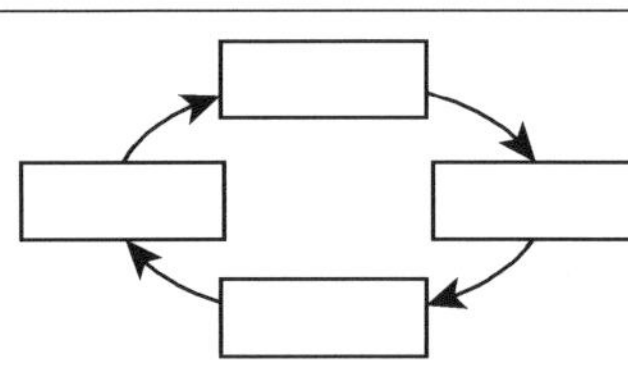	Recurring cycle of events , with no beginning and no end Example: life cycles in nature
Decision tree	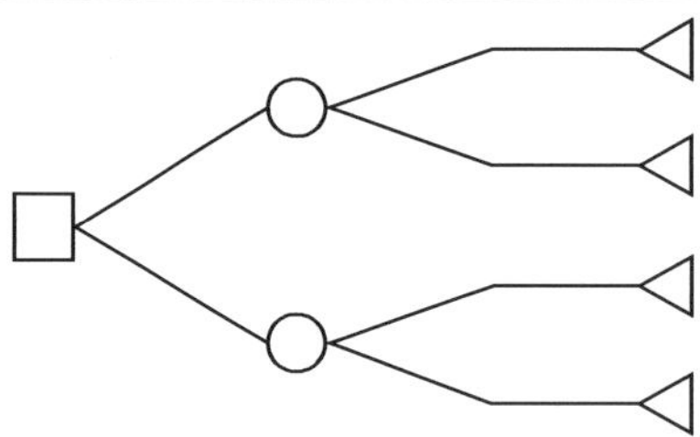	A decision that needs to be made, with possible alternatives, and the pros and cons of each alternative. This chart shows a choice of two decisions, but the number can be increased

FIGURE 6.6 Graphic organisers

Venn diagram	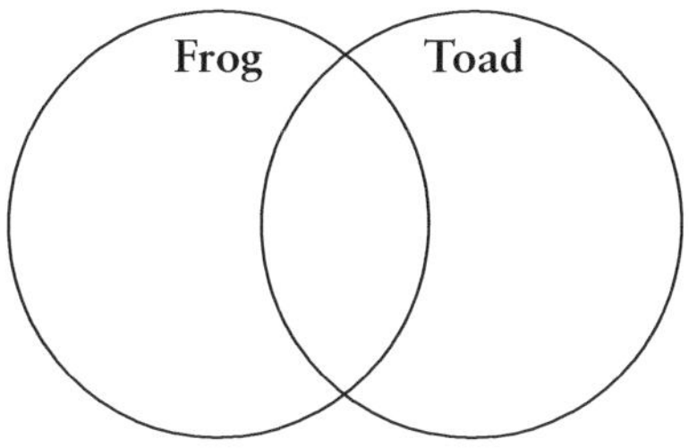	Similarities and differences Example: show the similarities and differences between frogs and toads, or compare two candidates running for office
KWL grid	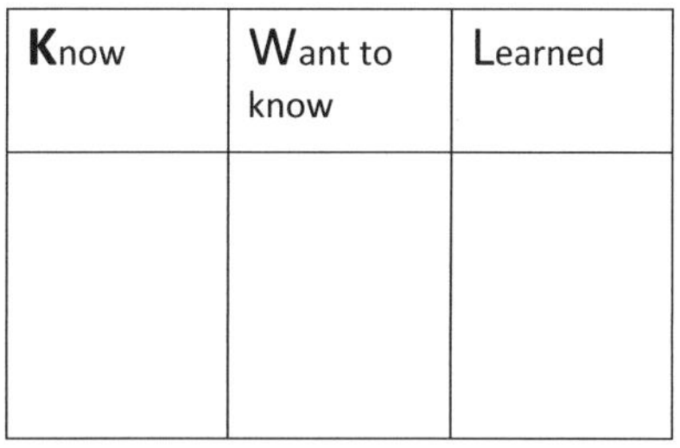	What I know, what I want to know, what I learned Example: Before reading a text children write down everything they know about a given topic, and then generate questions they have. During or after reading, they answer these questions in the last column.
Flow diagram	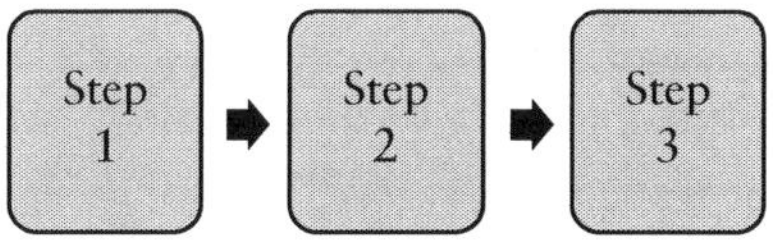	Sequence of events. Example: writing the method for a science experiment
Tree map /flow chart	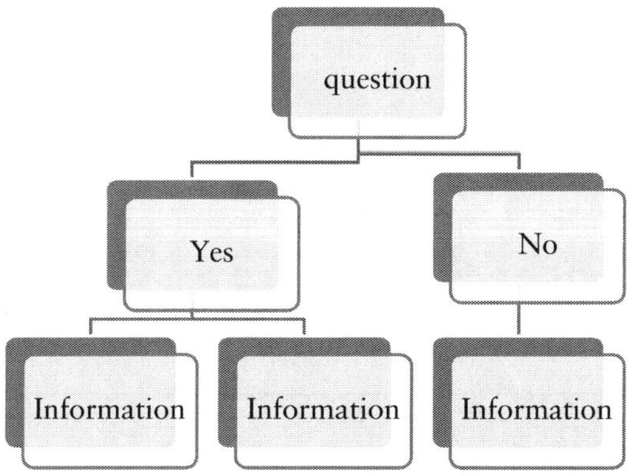	Classification and decision-making Example: when learning about the rock cycle, answering yes or no to the question 'Does the rock dissolve in acid?', and following down for information or further yes/no questions
Persuasion map	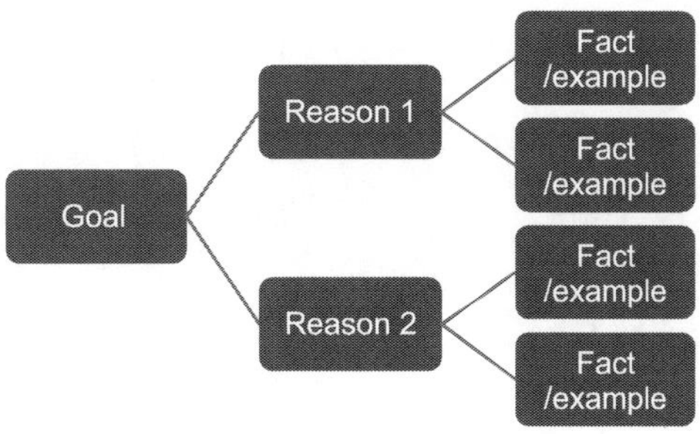	Persuasive talk or writing. Students write their goal in the first box, arguments in support of the goal in the next boxes, and supporting facts and examples in branching boxes

Figure 6.6 (Continued)

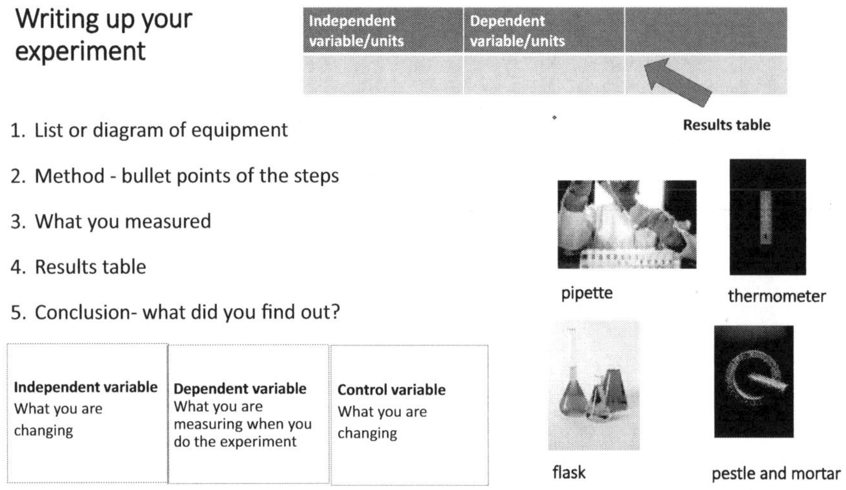

FIGURE 6.7 An example of scaffolding writing
Source: Adapted from a model developed by Rachel Cosgrove (Cosgrove, 2021)

Graphic organisers are an excellent way of presenting information visually. Figure 6.6 illustrates some of the main types, but there are many more. Good sources are

https://creately.com/blog/diagrams/types-of-graphic-organizers/

www.hmhco.com/blog/free-graphic-organizer-templates?s=03

www.edrawmax.com/graphic-organizer/

https://ditchthattextbook.com/15-free-google-drawings-graphic-organizers-and-how-to-make-your-own/?s=03

SENCOs can encourage class and subject teachers to make graphic organisers available in hard copy in their classrooms, or in a shared digital folder, for students to use to record their ideas.

There is good research evidence to show that retention of information is greater when students access it in the form of a graphic organiser, either one provided by the teacher or one they construct themselves, than when they have it only in text form. *Comprehension* of texts, however, only increases when children actively fill in an appropriate graphic organiser themselves (Wang *et al.*, 2021).

In the SEN world, there has always been an emphasis on multi-sensory learning – not just visual support. Unlike dual coding, this gets little attention in current blogs and books on the science of effective teaching, perhaps because of a confusion with the discredited notion of individual learning styles (visual, auditory, kinaesthetic). There remains evidence, however, that adding movement to learning aids recall. Andrä *et al.* (2020), for example, found that children were 73% more likely to recall new vocabulary if they used their hands and bodies to act out a word's meaning, and Damsgaard *et al.* (2022) showed that five-year-olds learned letter-sound correspondences better and recalled them for longer when they were taught whole-body movements for each sound.

As another example, consider how segmenting and blending in early reading instruction can be improved by introducing movement – physically pulling apart or pushing together magnetic letters, stretching a slinky toy, then contracting it. Or how it helps if we ask pupils to draw their own pictures to show what is happening in a maths problem like 'There are seven children on the bus. It stops at a bus stop. Two children get out and one gets in. How many children are on the bus now?'

EXAMPLE

One teacher used a range of modalities when working on the Cold War through the events surrounding the Bay of Pigs and the Cuban missile crisis. She provided an audiotape and a transcript of the then Cuban Ambassador's address to the United Nations, maps charting the invasion, a videotape of Khrushchev, photographs of the Soviet missile installations in Cuba and excerpts from a US Central Intelligence Agency briefing to the US cabinet. Open-ended discussion questions guided students' analyses of the conflicting positions exemplified by these resources. The students then created two scenarios for potentially different outcomes of the crisis and presented them to the class through newscasts that included maps and other visual representations.

'Talk for Writing' is an approach which exemplifies multi-sensory learning, alongside other key principles of inclusive teaching such as repeated rehearsal and gradually withdrawing scaffolds. Children read a text, talk about it, look at a visual of the story and act it out with gestures until they know it really well. At that point they move on to the next stages – innovation (collectively composing new text as a variation on the original) and then to independence (composing their own text individually).

Flexible grouping

The EEF's SEND guidance is clear on the question of setting and streaming; extensive evidence (Francis *et al.*, 2019) shows that lower-attaining pupils do worse in fixed groupings like these.

EXAMPLE

In an episode of *The Simpsons*, Bart is moved to a remedial class. 'Let me get this straight', he says. 'We're behind the rest of our class and we're going to catch up with them by going slower than they are?'

Grouping children by prior attainment **within** their class for specific activities or topics has a better pedigree than setting or streaming. The EEF Toolkit (Education Endowment Foundation, 2022) concludes that such grouping practices, which enable tasks, activities and support to be matched to children's current capabilities, and may involve effective practices such as collaborative learning, on average, benefit all pupils. The evidence suggests, however, that there are fewer benefits for lower attaining pupils than for others, and that within-class attainment grouping may also have an impact on wider outcomes such as confidence, with potentially long-term negative effects on attitudes and engagement.

Laura Teague (quoted in Parr, 2019) highlights another potential negative impact: 'If you struggle in a particular subject and you're working only with students who also struggle, then you lose the opportunity for learn from one another. Similarly, if you are quite able in a subject, it is not always beneficial to work with others who have similar strengths to your own in terms of opportunities to consolidate your knowledge via explaining and teaching your peers.'

What can schools conclude from all this? The evidence suggests that what works best is identifying a group of children who all need help with the same learning content and pulling them together **temporarily** for some focused instruction rather than operating any sort of fixed groups.

More talk, less writing

High-quality inclusive teaching recognizes that writing is a barrier to learning for many students with SEND. 'Do we have to write about it?' is a constant refrain after events from a school trip to getting into an interesting book in home reading.

One way to overcome the barrier is to include more talk-based activities in learning. Such activities benefit all. Language-based approaches, such as Philosophy for Children, Thinking Together, CAME (Cognitive Acceleration in Maths) and CASE (Cognitive Acceleration in Science) are all well-proven, and simply introducing dialogic techniques in classrooms has been found to yield a significant uplift to attainment (Jay *et al.*, 2017).

Tasks we ask students to complete individually can easily be turned into discussions:

> When I teach about the gender pay gap, for example, instead of . . . getting students to read an article or the textbook on the concept, we look at a graph together. We discuss what we can see, and students explain what this means and why it might be.
>
> Together, we are able to explore this new concept through conversation, ensuring that everyone can be a part of it, regardless of their ability.
>
> Megan McKenzie, Director of Key Stage 3 at Ravens Wood School for Boys

There are many creative alternatives to basing lessons on writing. Children can, for example, conduct interviews, make podcasts or prepare and deliver TED talks. I have even seen them act as 'tour guides', showing their parents round a museum of exhibits they have created about a topic they have studied.

Attending to background knowledge

Inclusive teachers don't assume that all pupils have the background skills and knowledge they need before working on a new skill or topic. Rachel Cosgrove, in her brilliant book *Inclusive Teaching in a Nutshell* likens lesson planning to the process of building a house, with laying the foundations coming before adding the bricks of new content. 'If the foundations are shaky, the house will fall down', she notes. This means that teaching needs to start by finding out what pupils already know, without making assumptions that just because they have covered a topic in the past, they are ready for the next steps. It also means thinking about gaps in background knowledge: 'If you are doing a project on rivers in the United Kingdom (UK), do the pupils all know which countries are in the UK and where they are? If you are asking pupils to write a persuasive letter, do they remember the format of general letters?' (Cosgrove, 2021).

A key message from recent research on reading comprehension is the need to prepare children in advance for new vocabulary and make sure they have some background knowledge about the topic of any text they are studying. Exposing pupils to rich content on topics such as history, geography and civics has been found to improve reading skills more effectively than direct teaching of comprehension strategies (Tyner and Kabourek, 2020). The greatest effects on the reading comprehension of six- to 11-year-old children in this study came from the amount of time they spent on what are called 'social studies' in the US rather than the time they spent in English or maths lessons.

The need to broaden pupils' prior experiences, then, means that inclusive teachers think about how class trips, classroom visitors, online searches, videos and the kind of structured subject teaching that builds knowledge cumulatively over time can be used to bolster domain knowledge.

Building children's independence and self-efficacy

An aspect of high-quality inclusive teaching that is little talked about, but very important, is that it will build the child's sense that they can make a difference to their own learning through their own independent efforts. This is called self-efficacy, or agency, or having an internal locus of control. Evidence suggests that this is almost as important for academic success as cognitive ability (Feinstein, 2000; Gutman and Schoon, 2013). Self-esteem, in contrast, though predictive of mental and physical health in adult life, is not a good predictor of academic attainment (Baumeister *et al.*, 2003).

Self-efficacy can often be low in children with SEND because the amount of help they receive leads them to believe they cannot function in classrooms without adult support. We must learn from the story told by HMI Charlie Henry about a classroom where while the teacher was giving instructions, he overheard one boy say to 'his' TA, 'You'd better listen to this, Miss, 'cos you're going to have to tell me in a minute.'

> Sometimes the best way to support a child is to give them safe opportunities to work without support.
>
> Daniel Sobel and Sarah Alston, writing in *The Inclusive Classroom*

A first step in building self-efficacy, then, is to review the deployment of TAs to ensure that children do not become dependent on their support. In Chapter 11 we will look at how SENCOs can work with class and subject teachers on this crucial issue.

EXAMPLE

At Porters Grange Primary in Southend, SENCO Toni Quinn says, 'We don't have Velcro children here.' The school does not allocate LSAs to one-to-one support in class and have done extensive training with teachers so that they understand how to develop children's independence. 'At whatever level a child is working at,' says Toni, 'there must be times in the day when they are working independently, and teachers need to plan smartly so that can happen.'

Children **can** learn to manage on their own if we help them. The teacher might, for example, set up a space in the classroom (the 'Enable Table') where pupils can go to find resources to scaffold their learning – a laptop with a PowerPoint of the lesson loaded up so they can review it, key vocabulary lists, sentence starters and writing frames, a quick read pen that scans words and reads them aloud, spelling resources and maths manipulatives.

Other schools have set up a Help Desk in a corner of the classroom and deployed a pupil to staff the desk and answer questions from those who may need a repetition of instructions, or an explanation, or to be directed to where they can access information they need.

Where TAs are working with an individual or group, they can be trained to use the brilliant scaffolding framework from the EEF's *Making Best Use of Teaching Assistants* guidance (Education Endowment Foundation, 2015), shown in Figure 6.8, which asks

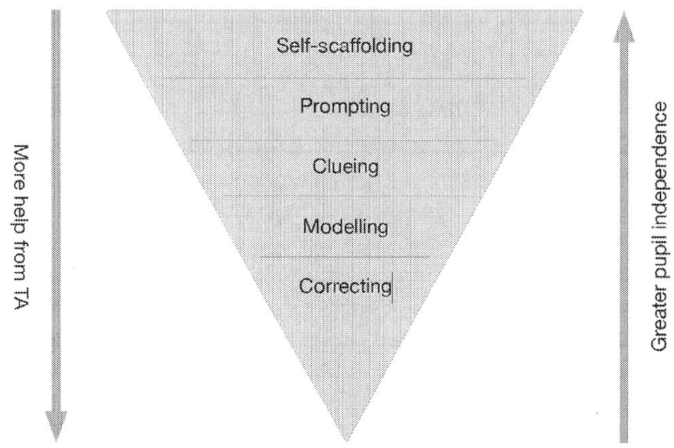

FIGURE 6.8 Scaffolding framework for TAs

Source: Adapted from: Bosanquet, P., Radford, J. and Webster, R. (2016) The teaching assistant's guide to effective interaction: How to maximise your practice, published by Routledge

TAs to identify the degree and type of help a pupil needs, from the rarely appropriate correcting (providing answers, finishing off a pupil's work), through modelling a task that is new to a student, through providing clues for students who do have the strategies or knowledge required to solve a problem but need a hint in order to call them to mind, through prompting to encourage pupils to draw on their own knowledge ('What do you need to do first?'; 'What's your plan?'; 'You can do this!'). The aim is for pupils to ultimately be able to tackle tasks independently by self-scaffolding.

TAs can also be trained to use a 'model and retreat' strategy, in which they first demonstrate the task, then tell the children that they are going to work with another group and will be back later to see how they are getting on. They can make resources to enable children to work independently, such as a task checklist to tick off, with visuals. You will find an example of such a task management board in the toolkit section of this book. Or they can simply jot down the steps in a task on a mini-whiteboard for the child to have on their desk or under their book to refer to.

The way adults – not just TAs but also teachers – provide feedback to children is also central to developing children's sense of agency. I've written extensively about this elsewhere (Gross, 2021) as one of the seven secrets of building self-efficacy, from finding a talent in every child, to giving them responsibilities and opportunities to make change happen.

In giving feedback, a key point is to draw children's attention to strategies they have used to help themselves. I'll never forget the skilled Reading Recovery teachers I watched who would turn back to a specific page in a book a child had just finished and say, 'Show me all the times on this page when you made a mistake and you sorted it out all by yourself. Do you remember how you did that?' Or the secondary teacher who said to a boy who had just done a presentation to the class, 'It looked like everybody was really listening . . . what do you think you did to get everyone's attention?'

We can use this type of feedback for successful behaviour strategies too: 'So yesterday you didn't let yourself get distracted for the first half of the lesson – what was it you did to help you focus?', 'You've done really well to get yourself to school every day lately – 100% attendance up from 80% before. How did you do that?'

If we tell children enough about the strategies that are working for them, they will eventually internalise these messages – like the six-year-old girl who reflected on why her reading had improved (Figure 6.9) using the words that her teacher had used with her over and over again. I know that not only had this child learned to read but she had also learned some important lessons about her own capacity to make change happen, which will stay with her for the rest of her school career.

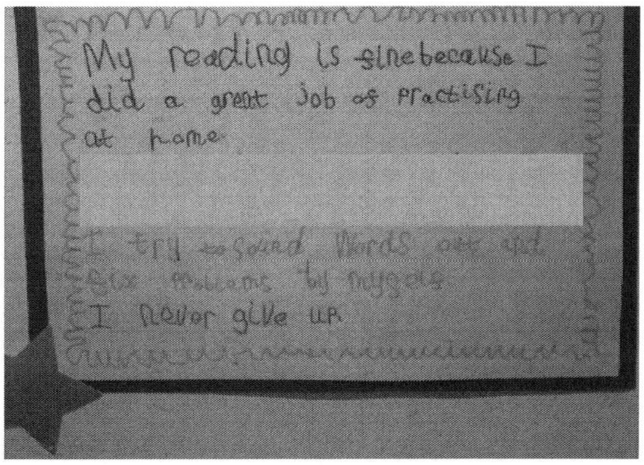

FIGURE 6.9 A six-year-old girl reflecting on why her reading had improved

Valuing mistakes

Another aspect of feedback is how adults respond to mistakes. Inclusive teaching is teaching that conveys that mistakes are an essential and valuable part of learning. I see it in classrooms where the maths working wall has a 'Marvellous Mistake' section, with the teacher choosing a mistake a child has made and showing what everyone can learn from it. I see it in adults who, when children make mistakes, provide feedback on elements that the pupil did get right: 'I can see you used that new formula we learned yesterday.' One teacher's response to a child who got only three out of ten on a test was 'You're a plus three'. Another's might be 'What was it you did that stopped you only getting one or two?'

Inclusive teachers and TAs also avoid comfort words when children get things wrong. Academics (Rattan *et al.*, 2012) have found that when adults use feedback such as 'Don't worry, you'll do better next time' or 'This was a hard test!' this lowers motivation, leads to pupils predicting that they will not improve in future and results in worse outcomes. Instead, when giving critical feedback, we can say, for example, 'This particular piece of work is a little below what I think you are capable of.'

Adults can demonstrate how to cope with struggles when they model a task. In one fascinating piece of research (Schunk *et al.*, 1987), academics randomly assigned low-achieving students aged nine to 13 to receive maths instruction via watching a peer who used either coping modelling, mastery modelling or no modelling of the learning task. In coping modelling, the peer demonstrated the anxieties and struggles that students might experience but gradually improved their performance. In the mastery condition, the models demonstrated faultless performance from the start. Children who were assigned to the coping model had significantly greater growth in self-efficacy and performed better than either the no modelling or mastery modelling groups.

Focusing on social and emotional as well as cognitive aspects of learning

No classroom can be truly inclusive unless teachers understand the need to support social and emotional learning alongside academic learning – for all students, but with particular benefits for children with SEND.

> The brain is made up of a series of complex systems, only one of which (the top part of the brain) is responsible for thinking. These systems are related to and dependent on each other. If a child is emotionally unregulated (upset, distracted, fidgety, or bored) and doesn't have self-regulation skills and strategies, learning is that much more difficult and inefficient.
>
> The best way to make the top part of the brain receptive to learning is to make sure these lower parts of the brain are regulated.
>
> Dr Bruce Perry (2009)

Examples of attending to social and emotional learning would be

- emotion check-ins at the start of the day or after lunch, ranging from emojis to Zones of Regulation to a simple thumbs up/down/sideways in secondary schools;
- explicitly teaching a wide vocabulary of feeling words;
- teaching all children breathing and grounding strategies to regulate their emotions.

There is more to social and emotional learning than emotional awareness and regulation, however. It is important also to develop capabilities like empathy, friendship skills, assertiveness skills, conflict resolution and the ability to motivate oneself and persist through difficulties using PSHE and curriculum subjects like English, history and PE. Again, I've written more about this elsewhere (Gross, 2021; van Poortvliet *et al.*, 2019).

CASE STUDY

At Tetney Primary School, staff recognise that children will not be able to learn if they are feeling anxious, angry or low. Every pupil starts the day with a personal greeting from staff. Then they do a feelings check-in, putting a lolly stick with their name on into a pot. The pots are labelled with characters from Pixar's *Inside Out* – for younger children, just two characters, while Year 4 have four and Year 6 all five.

Built into every day are five short well-being breaks, following the '5 Ways to Well-being' approach originally devised by the New Economics Foundation:

1. Be active: children and staff walk a Golden Mile together
2. Connect: speed dating style chat
3. Keep learning: learning a new quick skill (such as origami or a song)
4. Give: for example, giving out team points to peers meeting the school's values
5. Take notice: a positive reflection to end each day (what has gone well), again linked to the core values

The well-being breaks give staff the opportunity for a private chat with any child who is not feeling good ('Time to Talk'). The teacher can choose a child to talk with during the 'Connect' well-being break or walk alongside them when children are doing the Golden Mile.

Making learning relevant and engaging

Whilst many research-led developments in everyday teaching practice (modelling, retrieval practice and so on) have been very helpful for children with SEND, there have also been some significant downsides to the 'knowledge curriculum'.

Teaching that is based on pouring knowledge into children and getting them to remember it can all too easily fail to engage the learner. Some children – not all those with SEND, but many – also need to have their imaginations captured and their hearts engaged if they are to pay attention and work hard.

So inclusive teaching needs to help learners see the point of what they are doing. They are more likely to engage with endless retrieval quizzes, for example, if their teachers share the science of memory, showing visually how memory traces are boosted by repetition at ever-increasing intervals. They are more likely to engage with any learning if the teacher links it to their real-life experiences:

> A further strategy I deployed was to better understand my students' lived experiences, which is to say that I got to know my students so I could ensure I built new abstract knowledge upon their existing concrete knowledge. By understanding what they already knew and could do, I was able to make connections and teach new information through the lens of what was familiar.
>
> Matt Bromley (2021)

Finally, children are also much more likely to engage if learning is active and, as we have seen, talk-based rather than 'just writing'. There is good research evidence to show that taking an active role in learning rather than passively receiving knowledge helps all children. One study (Thiede *et al.*, 2022), for example, found that children's performance on comprehension tests increased when they were asked not just to listen but to draw organisational sketches showing the relationships between ideas in a science topic. Another (Fernandes *et al.*, 2018) found that drawing pictures of to-be-learned information meant that children recalled it better later on. And as we saw earlier, actions and gestures are also very effective in promoting learning.

EXAMPLE

In one secondary science lesson, children worked in pairs to match pictures of specialist cells with their names and how they are adapted to their function. They then worked in groups from task sheets with diagrams to make models of cells using salt dough, plastic bags, strings and jelly. They took photos of the cells they had made placed next to the name of the cell and drew a diagram of it. Groups had a list of vocabulary describing the structures in the cell, which they had to use when talking to each other during the task. They then had to explain what each part of the model was in the real cell using these words.

Making learning social

Children – especially teenagers – are intensely social beings (with the exception of some children on the autistic spectrum). For the majority of children, any learning activity can become more engaging and motivating if it involves working with others rather than alone.

Inclusive teaching will involve carefully structured pair and group work, using techniques like jigsaw, snowball and barrier games, which I have described in previous books (Gross, 2018, 2021). It will involve explicitly teaching children **how** to work effectively together in groups, building up from pair work with structured tasks to larger groups and more open-ended tasks, using a 'speaking object' pupils hold when they are talking and working with the class to develop agreed 'ground rules' such as "Listen to each other', 'Give everyone a turn', 'Everyone should try to join in' and 'Disagree with the point, not the person'.

Less formally, we can make learning social by letting students bring a peer partner when coming to the board to demonstrate something or give a presentation. We can ask them to explain a concept to a peer or work in pairs to recall taught information – first individually writing down or drawing everything they can remember, then working with a partner to compare notes and create a new shared list before finally using their knowledge organiser, class notes or textbook book to check recalled information for accuracy and add additional information.

EXAMPLE

One teacher made reading a social activity in order to increase children's interest in reading for pleasure. She put children into same-age pairs or threes on the basis of their interests and friendships and suggested a book for them to read in instalments at home. Every day the pair or group would have ten minutes in class to talk about their reading, using guiding questions to steer their conversations, such as:

- How are you liking the book so far?
- What were the best bits you read?
- What feelings is this book evoking for you?
- Which character do you most closely relate to, and why?

Deliberately fostering classroom cohesion and a sense of belonging for all members of the class

It is all too easy for children with SEND to feel different from their classmates, and sometimes isolated. As a first step in promoting belonging, we can deliberately engineer activities which develop bonds in each class or tutor group. Traditional team-building transition activities are very helpful here, and there is no shortage of ideas on the internet. The resources for the SEAL themes 'A Place to Learn' and 'Learning to Be Together'(www.sealcommunity.org), for example, are specifically designed to create bonded and cohesive groups of students.

Some of my favourites, from a variety of sources, are

- having students work in groups to explore how they could create their ideal classroom, making it feel comfortable and distinct to their class, drawing designs and discussing their ideas;
- making a group collage of 'my happy place' – photos or drawings of places where pupils feel happy, safe and comfortable;
- giving each child a paper jigsaw piece which will interlock with others. They decorate their piece with drawings to represent themselves and their interests, then fit their pieces together on a large display.

At the start of the new school year, one Year 6 class teacher introduced her class to West African Adinkra symbols. Each child chose a symbol that they felt represented their qualities, beliefs and interests and printed it on a strip of cloth. Then the cloths were woven together to create a rope representing the whole class. At the end of the year, the rope was unpicked, and the children took their own strip home.

Another good way to build a sense of belonging at the start of the year is to develop a classroom charter, which sets out how people will behave towards each other. Research shows that this will not only build the sense of community but will also lead to greater rule-following.

As the school year goes on, we should continue to give members of a class opportunities to get to know one another better. For example, it is useful to structure paired activities to ensure that everybody has a chance to work with everyone else in the class – randomly assigning children to pairs who work together for a week or so before becoming part of another pair.

Lessons can usefully start with brief cohesion-building activities such as 'Just like me' in which students stand up when the teacher makes a statement that applies to them – 'Everyone who is the youngest in their family', 'Everyone who as a blog or You Tube channel', 'Everyone who has been to more than two schools' and so on.

Alternatively, pupils can be given five minutes paired chat where they respond to a prompt like 'Which one is scarier if you think about it: ocean or space?', 'What was your total screen time yesterday?', 'What's your favourite piece of clothing?', 'What's the best day of the week?'

Finally, to increase pupils' sense of belonging, we can create structures and situations that encourage pupils to show kindness to one another. These can include

- buddying systems, such as pairing Year 11 with Year 7, or Year 6 with Reception pupils;
- friendship stops or buddy benches in the playground, where anyone who temporarily has no one to play with can go and know they will be scooped up by peers and invited to join their game;
- systems of awards for those showing kindness to others, and challenges like the subsequent 'bucket-fillers';
- 'secret friends', in which children draw the name of a peer and have to perform kind actions for them.

Bucket-fillers

At Highfield School in Sunderland, the book *Have You Filled a Bucket Today?* is read in assemblies. The book tells us that we all carry an invisible bucket around with us that fills and empties throughout the day. Your bucket fills up when someone does something to make you feel good. As your bucket fills up, the happier and better you feel in yourself.

'Bucket filling', 'bucket dipping' and 'bucket lids' can act as metaphors for understanding the effects of our actions and words on the well-being of others and ourselves. Dipping is when you dip into someone else's bucket and take stuff out; lids means that if someone tries to take stuff from yours, use your lid and don't dip back.

After hearing the book read to them, every class in school is allocated their own bucket. If a child feels someone has said or done something nice to them, they write it down and put it in the class bucket. The weekly challenge is to see which class is the best bucket-filler.

Making SEND provision universal

There is an old saying that good teaching for pupils with SEND is good teaching for all, and this has become increasingly clear as practices like chunking instructions, modelling, overlearning and visual support for learning, long advocated for SEND, have now become part of the 'mainstream' definition of high-quality teaching.

We can go further than this, however, applying the principle of 'what is good for SEND is good for all' to other practices – like the Zones of Regulation approach originally devised for autistic children but now increasingly adopted in primary schools for whole classes.

As another example, fidget toys are often used for children with ADHD, but research shows that other children can benefit too. One study (Stalvey and Brasell, 2006) looked at the effects of allowing Year 7 students to use stress balls during teacher instruction and independent practice, and found that the frequency of observed 'distraction incidents' decreased during the seven weeks the students used the stress balls compared to the three weeks before they were introduced. Student achievement on writing paragraphs improved also.

Would it not make sense, then, to have a box of fidget toys in class for any child to use when they need to?

Would it not make sense also to routinely turn on subtitles when showing videos rather than having to remember to do this just for a child with a visual impairment?

And what about One Page Profiles? Usually only for those with SEND, some schools now use them for all their pupils – like the example in Figure 6.10, which can be sent home at the start of the school year for pupils to complete with their parents, or in school with an adult if the family are not able to take part.

- My name is ...
- What people like and admire about me ...
- What I'm good at ...
- What I'm interested in ...
- What my teachers need to know so they can help me learn ...

FIGURE 6.10 One Page Profile

CASE STUDY

Chalgrove Primary School in London has extended to all children many of the interventions usually reserved for children with SEND. One example is the use of symbols for different subjects and routines so children can see clearly what is coming next. Classroom resources are also labelled with symbols, and these are displayed on the whiteboard so pupils can get independently what they need for a task. Teachers have symbols on lanyards which they hold up while giving verbal instructions. Victoria Annan, lead for the school's additionally resourced provision for autism, notes that an instruction 'like "It's time for phonics, everyone get your books, pencils and paper out" is a lot easier to process when the resources are shown visually on a card held up while the teacher is speaking.'

Colourful semantics, another visual strategy originally devised for children with communication and interaction needs, is regularly used in whole-class literacy teaching. Teachers colour-code each section of a sentence to show the 'who, what and where' elements on the whiteboard and encourage children to do the same in their books. This, Victoria says, helps 'all pupils who often miss out sentence components, jumble word order, or struggle to speak in full sentences.'

Another example of making provision for SEND the norm for all is the school's use of social stories, which frame an upcoming occasion or situation as short story or comic strip. These are used widely to help all children cope with changes or to explain what will happen during infrequent events like a school trip.

KEY PRINCIPLES

Key take-aways for SENCOs

- Inclusive classroom teaching scaffolds learning for all pupils. It will incorporate explicit instruction, modelling thinking, multi-sensory approaches and strategies to aid recall
- Flexible grouping is more likely to help pupils with SEND than setting, streaming or fixed within-class groups

- Teaching can be made more inclusive by increasing the amount of talk-based learning, attending to background knowledge, explicitly teaching social and emotional skills and building pupils' sense of belonging in their class and school
- Building children's self-efficacy – the belief that they can make a difference to their own lives and learning – is important for all pupils but particularly those with SEND

Key questions for the wider school leadership team

- Do grouping practices (setting, streaming, fixed within-class groups) in your school take account of research evidence on their potential impact on lower attaining pupils?
- Are there strategies used in your school for pupils with SEND that could become universal?

7 Distributing responsibility

So far in this book we have looked at two key ways of reducing bureaucracy and the SENCO workload: reducing over-identification of SEND, and increasing the range of normally available provision through inclusive environments, curricula and classroom teaching. In this chapter we turn to a third: effectively distributing responsibility so that everyone in school plays their part in meeting SEND rather than the weight falling solely on the SENCO's shoulders.

Who can SENCOs share responsibility with?

SENCOs can share responsibility for SEND with senior leaders, middle leaders, class and subject teachers. They can also delegate tasks to teaching assistants and office staff (particularly for administrative tasks like scheduling and arranging meetings). If they have the budget, they can buy in support; SENCO Rhian Williams uses £3,000 to £5,000 of her school's SEND budget to commission a retired colleague to do the paperwork for EHCP submissions. 'She charges £500 for each one and it pays for itself', says Rhian.

Another idea suitable for larger schools is allocating responsibility for all the recording associated with a particular intervention to the person delivering that intervention. One school, for example, pays a teacher to work with children on language and communication interventions; it is this teacher who writes a learning plan for each child, setting out the area of need, the targets and outcomes, which goes to parents and forms part of the school's records should they need to submit to the local authority an account of what the school has provided.

Less often explored, but in my view important, is the potential for pupils themselves to take on some responsibility for getting their needs met – for example, by holding a profile about their needs and what helps them and sharing that with teachers and support staff.

DOI: 10.4324/9781003313526-7

> Having worked in schools where students are often reluctant to be seen as needing additional support, I feel true joy when I am reminded by students that they need their coloured exercise books, asked why they did not receive their extra time in an assessment, or asked to check that their teachers are aware of the information on their student passport.
>
> Rhian Williams, SENCO Henley Bank High School

Responsibility for high-quality inclusive teaching should unequivocally sit with class and subject teachers. When it comes to planning for individuals, in primary schools, the responsibility for co-producing with pupils and parents whatever form of plan/profile/passport the school uses should always sit with class teachers. In secondary schools where form tutors have significant, sustained contact with their tutor group, it could be the form tutor who takes on this role. In schools where Heads of Year have the pastoral role and Pupil Progress leads for each year-group focus on attainment, it might be the Head of Year.

SENCOs whose schools are part of Multi-Academy Trusts should be able to capitalise on the opportunities that provides for joint initiatives, and the extra layer of Trust-wide inclusion leadership capacity that is often available. MATs that include special schools and specially resourced mainstream provision bring an added layer of practical support for SENCOs in developing inclusive practice in their schools.

EXAMPLE

The Unity Schools Partnership is multi-academy trust of 32 primary, middle, special and secondary schools in Suffolk, Essex, Cambridgeshire and East London. Six of its mainstream schools have Hubs (additionally resourced provisions). There are many opportunities for teachers to visit and learn from the specialist provisions. Two full-time MAT leaders have been appointed to support SEND practice across the group. They are able to bring SENCOs together to share knowledge and tips; they provide Trust-wide training and act as a resource for developing tools the SENCOs ask for, such as pyramids of strategies to meet different levels of need, and templates for how to respond to an LA request for a placement for a child whose needs their school cannot meet.

Good practice from schools

Let us now look at some case studies of schools where distributed responsibility is in place or developing.

CASE STUDY

Responsibility sitting with class teachers in a primary school

At Houldsworth Valley Academy, which we met in Chapter 5, the responsibility for SEND sits squarely with class teachers. Before asking for help, they are expected to implement a range of approaches themselves. Elizabeth, the SENCO, describes staff are 'solution seekers – they will first talk to their team, then the SENCO, then the wider Unity Trust to which the school belongs'.

If the strategies staff put in place are not successful, they record on an initial concerns form what they have tried and for how long. Elizabeth will then have a conversation with the class teacher and may look at the child's books and observe in class. She will suggest strategies or a different intervention. There are several rounds of this process; if the child's progress or well-being remains a concern, the school will talk with parents, put the child on the SEN register and do assessments such as the York Assessment for Reading Comprehension (YARC), the Sandwell numeracy test, the Phonological Awareness Assessment Battery (PhAB), the Strengths and Difficulties Questionnaire or the Boxall profile.

Class teachers are responsible for the Big Book Pupil Passports for children on the SEND register. It is they who have the conversation about progress and priorities with the child and family every half term. In the second half of each term, they complete a review sheet, RAG-rating the goals set at the start of term as green (met), amber (partly met) or red (not met). The SENCO records this information on a spreadsheet and is able to monitor the overall school percentage of green, red and amber on the goals.

Every half term the teachers submit their Big Book folder to the SENCO for her comments. She may suggest trying a different strategy or refining a goal. Staff then have one week to make the changes.

Elizabeth is a trained 'instructional coach'. In this type of coaching, the adult being coached will watch a video of excellent practice and discuss it with the coach. The adult scripts and practises an aspect of teaching and then the coach will observe. As well as having this supportive role, Elizabeth is also able to have challenging conversations with staff. 'She is relentless', says her headteacher, 'and she holds people to account.'

Professional development for staff (CPD) plays a central part in enabling class teachers to take responsibility for SEND. Elizabeth notes as particularly helpful the Unity Trust's CUSP reading training, and training in trauma, sensory processing, speech language and communication and Solution Circles. Staff have been freed to sit in on speech and language therapy sessions 'so they know what to do . . . for example if a child can't say a sound'. The school benefits from having specialist unit for up to 18 children with communication and interaction needs, where other staff have observed practice and learned about useful resources such as decodable reading series for older children with gaps in their phonic knowledge.

CASE STUDY

Responsibility shared with subject leaders and teachers and across a multi-academy trust

Ryan Purdy, SENCO at Astrea Academy in Sheffield, set himself the aim of distributing responsibility by developing leaders of SEN across the school. He decided to identify and work with one faculty initially (RE) rather than launch an initiative across the whole school. He met informally with the head of faculty to look at the question 'How do I know that my curriculum and practice are inclusive?' Then the head of faculty led a meeting where self-evaluation helped staff to define their priorities and decide on bespoke CPD to match their needs. As an example, they asked for support on how to make abstract concepts such as reincarnation more concrete. Teachers went away and researched that themselves, with Ryan's role to be a resource and critical friend. They did not, Ryan says, feel 'done to'; they retained ownership of their learning.

Ryan works with other leaders to embed SEND in everyday school improvement processes. He will regularly join heads of faculty and staff with a Teaching and Learning Responsibility payment on learning walks. These are developmental rather than critical, and Ryan will draw attention to good inclusive practice when he sees it on lesson plans or in practice. This has dual benefits – for the subject teachers but also for subject leaders, who develop their own expertise in SEND by working alongside the SENCO.

Ryan's school is part of a wider Trust with 18 primary schools, seven secondaries and one special school for pupils with SEMH needs. Work across the Trust provides another example of how shared approaches can reduce the burden on SENCOs. Historically, provision for pupils with SEND and SEMH was poor, with early identification of need and support inconsistent and underfunded. The Director for Inclusion, working with the Deputy Director for Data Intelligence, led the development of a screening tool for early identification, an audit framework for accessing the quality and scope of SEND/SEMH provision, and a vulnerability dashboard to help develop a picture of Trust-wide need. Before this, some SENCOs had not had the capacity to map numbers and areas of need in their cohorts, or plan training and provision accordingly. The Trust also decided to employ an educational psychologist and three assistant educational psychologists who support SENCOs in accurate early identification. There are in-house Trust training experts who deliver de-escalation and mental health training to staff; the next stage will see development of an in-house trainer in autism and neurodiversity.

CASE STUDY

Responsibility shared with TAs

At Henley Bank secondary, SENCO Rhian Williams has built a strong team of TAs who take responsibility for aspects of SEND. The school has been able to recruit staff with degree-level qualifications and considerable relevant experience, including qualified teachers wanting to change their roles, so that, Rhian says, 'I've been able to delegate responsibility for cognition and learning, communication and interaction and SEMH to the most experienced members of my team.'

Members of the team each support specific curriculum areas, with subject specialisms spanning English, maths, science and humanities. They all attend departmental meetings, understand the assessment criteria for success in the subject and regularly meet with class teachers to discuss the curriculum and assessment foci, as well as the needs of the children in their class. 'I can't know the curriculum for all subjects,' observes Rhian, 'but I can ensure that my team does.'

The TA team also share with Rhian the work involved in meetings with parents of children with SEND. 'I once had 60 children in Year 7 who all needed SEND meetings to be scheduled promptly', Rhian says. 'Members of the team each met with eight sets of parents and guardians, while I met with slightly more, after which we reached agreements and produced student passports outlining the type of provision that would be needed. These student passports were written by my team in collaboration with our young people and their parents and contain important items of information class teachers need to see.'

Sharing responsibility with senior leaders

Despite the adage that 'Every leader is a leader of SEND', many SENCOs feel that their headteachers and other senior leaders believe that all things SEND can be delegated to the SENCO rather than jointly owned.

To secure ownership from the top, SENCOs may need to provide senior leaders with a clear case for making SEND a whole-school priority, using national and school data to show how 'turning the dial' on SEND will help turn the dial on whatever improvement priorities the school is working on, from attainment to closing the disadvantage gap to behaviour, attendance and well-being. A template using national data is provided in the toolkit section of this book.

Ofsted is of course always another card to play, if the SENCO can present evidence that inspectors are likely to be critical of any aspect of the school's SEND work, from what internal data are showing to any hint that the curriculum offer for pupils with SEND lacks ambition or is restricted. SENCOs can also highlight potential parent or pupil feedback to inspectors that might give them cause for concern.

If possible, the SENCO can then suggest the school undertake a whole-school SEND review, either internally or with external help.

The other key motivator for leaders is the risk of litigation. Some SENCOs have used the legal requirements of the Equality Act 2010 to push SEND up the priority list – for example, if there is resistance amongst staff to adapt their lessons, the duty to make 'reasonable adjustments' for pupils with a disability can be invoked. Many senior leaders may not fully understand the Act's definition of disability, and that it includes difficulties such as dyslexia, autism or depression – anything that has a substantial and long-term adverse effect on the individual's ability to carry out normal day-to-day activities.

Sharing responsibility with both senior and middle leaders

In order to distribute responsibility for SEND more widely, SENCOs will want to make it part of the everyday role of middle leaders.

They should try to ensure that staff doing quality assurance – whether through d analysis, work scrutiny or lesson observations – always include a focus on pupil such as SEND. Initially, doing joint quality assurance with subject leads is a goo modelling what to look for so that later the baton can be firmly handed over.

Gary Aubin, Head of SEND for a Multi Academy Trust and EEF SEND Specialist, puts this well:

> Get in on formal processes. Rather than creating your own formal observations that add to the levels of scrutiny in a school, get involved in whatever processes already exist – performance management observations, targeted learning walks, etc. This will also ensure that any feedback you have is integral to these processes, rather than feeling like an add-on.
>
> (Aubin, 2021)

Porters Grange Primary in Southend provides another example. All members of the Senior Leadership Team and subject coordinators have a timetable of learning walks, book scrutiny and sitting in on planning, preparation and assessment time (PPA). In the course of these activities, they are aways looking at whether adaptations to teaching are being made and are relevant to children's needs.

Similar considerations about the role of middle leaders apply to intervention planning, monitoring and evaluation. The English lead should lead on literacy interventions, for example, the maths lead on maths interventions, a well-being lead (if there is one) on social and emotional interventions.

In the most effective schools, there is team approach to provision management, with shared planning to meet the needs of individuals and groups. SENCOs in primary schools, for example, often attend half termly class-by-class pupil progress meetings alongside the headteacher or deputy, the safeguarding lead, subject leads, the EAL lead and so on. At these meetings, shared decisions are made to meet the needs of children whose progress gives cause for concern.

In secondary schools, many SENCOs have had success by developing a 'SEND Champion' in every department to support inclusive pedagogy and curriculum, with the subject Champions coming together, under the leadership of the SENCO, to form a whole-school SEND working group.

Linking up with subject leads is another way of not only sharing responsibility but also increasing the chances that the SENCO's message will be heard. If messaging is seen to come from a teaching and learning source, class and subject teachers are more likely to listen. Similarly, invoking the headteacher will ensure SEND issues get a hearing; in one school, the head sends out a weekly top tip for SEND (supplied by the SENCO) as part of the daily staff briefing emails.

Sharing responsibility with class and subject teachers

Again, despite the 'Every teacher a teacher of SEN' catchphrase, getting colleagues to take responsibility for the children with SEN in their classes is not always easy. There are two possible approaches for SENCOs, which I've characterised as carrot and stick.

The stick is using performance management, which is entirely legitimate and supported by the SEND Code, which says that 'the quality of teaching for pupils with SEN, and the progress made by pupils, should be a core part of the school's performance management arrangements.' An example of using accountability within a framework of positive relationships, where performance management is developmental rather than punitive, is the work of SENCO Toni Quinn, who does regular 'SEN drop-ins' to look at what children are doing in a lesson, how it triangulates with planning, at the work leading up to the lesson and the work that is to follow.

But the carrot approach, which relies on motivating class and subject teachers intrinsically, rather than extrinsically, will often prove more successful than the performance management stick.

Motivating colleagues begins with engaging the heart as well as the head: getting teachers to understand what it feels like to have any sort of difficulty or SEND. To achieve this, it helps to have pupils tell their stories – like the SENCO we met earlier who recorded interviews with incoming Year 6 pupils with SEND about what helped them learn and what got in the way of their learning, and played the resulting videos to the staff. Or a school might set up an inclusion committee of students with SEND, chaired by a school leader for curriculum or teaching and learning, where the students talk about their needs. Their words can then be shared with other staff.

Another school ran training where they invited parents of students with SEND in to provide CPD. SENCO Ginny Bootman organised a carousel so staff could move round to listen to parents of children with different types of need. The parents explained what helped their child and the impact when their needs weren't met. 'It won lots of hearts and minds', says Ginny.

As part of CPD time, subject staff in secondary schools might be freed up to meet 1–1 with students with SEND, using the 'good day/bad day' person-centred tools we will look at in Chapter 10. Pupil tracking – following a pupil around over the course of a school day to look at their experience – can also be very useful.

Another aspect of the carrot approach is providing teachers with easy-to-use ideas to support SEND. Thomas Tillier, Assistant SENCO at Aylesford secondary school, developed 'quick wins' for staff (Table 7.1) – 40 proven strategies he has seen in action or used himself, colour-coded for different areas of need. Tips need to be really practical like Thomas' 'Please make sure that if you enlarge work you don't just enlarge a scan because it blurs and gets pixelated.'

A final element of working with class and subject teachers is being seen as available for support when needed and cultivating an ethos of puzzling out tricky issues collaboratively. At Whitefield Primary, SENCO Marie Beale says,

> I hope all staff feel able to ask for help and, as a SENCO, a large part of my day is talking through how we can support children with complex needs, what routines are and aren't working, what resources would help, and what training we need to access. Staff all know they can come and puzzle out with me . . . they can say "I'm not really sure about x . . ." and I may suggest I come in and observe.

Focusing on professional development (PD)

The most effective way of reducing the SENCO workload is to ensure that class and subject teachers become really skilled in meeting SEND in the classroom themselves so that they identify fewer children as the SENCO's province and only need the SENCO's advice to help them with the trickiest situations. Rhian Williams, SENCO at Henley Bank High School, is making this her priority:

> In the short term, we want to further embed the practice of distributed leadership, since the combined responsibilities of a SENCO can't all be covered within a single position held by someone hidden away in a corner of the school. With new classroom teachers and heads of year having recently joined us, I've been working with them to help them understand what good quality provision looks like.

Quick wins

Task Management Board

1. 'Chunk' instructions rather than saying in one long string
2. Break instructions and verbal information into manageable chunks
3. Jot instructions down on a sticky note, or encourage student to do so
4. Give clear instructions and explain in simple language; new vocabulary, concepts, tasks, questions

Verbal Interaction

1. Check that they fully understand what is expected of them before they settle to work
2. Speak slowly when giving instructions to allow them to process them
3. Include their name when giving instructions to them where possible
4. Meet and greet at the door
5. Explain new words within the context of life experiences
6. Check understanding through asking for instructions or questions to be repeated in their own words

Routines & Environment

1. Carry out classroom routines in the same order to reduce working memory demands
2. They may benefit from being paired with a positive peer (who is a confident speaker and able at problem-solving) in some lessons
3. Develop routines, such as specific procedures for handing in work
4. Don't get them to copy vast chunks off the board – give handouts
5. Pre-warn of upcoming changes

Visuals

1. Support auditory information with visual resources
2. They may benefit from a visual timetable, equipment lists or schedules to help with organisational skills. Encourage them to be actively involved in creating these where possible
3. When writing longer pieces, provide them with a 'WAGOLL' (what a good one looks like/ model text) where possible to allow them to see what is expected
4. Support lesson content and understanding by using pictures, diagrams, modelling and demonstrations as well as providing practical opportunities wherever possible
5. Maybe give them a handout with key words that they can stick into their books (visual for spelling)

Processing

1. Be aware that they may know something one day and forget it the next, may lose or forget equipment they need or may forget what they are supposed to be doing in the course of a lesson
2. Consider reducing the amount of work that is expected to complete in a lesson (if they are struggling to keep up)
3. Consider giving more time to complete tasks
4. Simplify homework and make sure the task is easy to understand for parents at home
5. Ask them to retell what has read/told after every one or two pages. Alternatively, they could be asked a question about what has been read after every one or two pages.

With thanks to Thomas Tiller, Assistant SENCO at Aylesford school

Table 7.1 Quick wins for SEN students

Whitefield Primary has developed highly effective systems for CPD. All new staff have early attachment/trauma training, training on the processes around SEND in the school and training on creating an inclusive learning environment – what the classroom should look like and why. A very experienced Year 4 teacher worked with Early Career Teachers (ECTs) on an apprenticeship model to help them understand what inclusive teaching looks like. First they planned lessons together, then she taught the lesson with the ECT observing, then they discussed the lesson afterwards to unpick techniques like scaffolding and modelling.

Staff personal development meetings are also very important, says SENCO Marie Beale: 'They give us the opportunity to set out the different roles and responsibilities in working with our children with SEND so that it is seen as a team effort.'

One particularly useful approach to PD is to link SEND to what teachers already know or are learning about. Expert SENCO Abigail Hawkins developed PD linking dyslexia to the Rosenshine principles, and adds extra SEND tweaks to PD on topics like memory, modelling or vocabulary. The Greenshaw Learning Trust runs fortnightly Trust-wide 'Developmental drop-ins' for all teachers and support staff, which aim to give staff one small actionable step for high- quality teaching to ensure their classroom practice continues to improve. Again, SEND can easily be linked to ideas about scaffolding or retrieval practice.

PD about SEND needs to be *relevant* to individuals if it is to be absorbed. It needs to be linked, first, to their immediate concerns about students they teach. At Aylesford School, for example, Assistant SENCO Thomas Tillier offers a Monday afternoon SEND surgery. Staff sign up for ten to 15 minutes on a particular student or condition they want to know more about. One session he arranged was on stammering, delivered by an outside expert, when the school had three students with dysfluency.

PD also needs to be relevant to the subjects that staff teach, their role, setting, career stage and ambition. Several SENCOs told me they have used this principle by developing PD for particular subjects based on the EEF's SEND guidance – what 'Five on a plate' looks like for science teachers, for example. Others are making good use of online modules in nasen's Development Pathway, which are tailored to roles and subject specialisms, and nasen's Teacher Handbook, which provides practical strategies for each subject area.

Another example of relevance is setting information firmly in the context of teachers' everyday routines. The brilliant book *The Inclusive Classroom*, by Daniel Sobel and Sarah Alston (Sobel and Alston, 2021), does just this by exploring strategies for each phase of the lesson – entering the classroom and preparing to learn, delivering and receiving instructions and whole-class engagement, individuals working as a class, individuals fitting into a group and the last five minutes of the lesson. As an example, the authors cite 'Callum', who has ADHD. In the entering the classroom/preparing to learn phase of the lesson, he has a clear routine while the class settles (handing out books and equipment) and can see a whole class visual timetable. During whole-class engagement, he uses a whiteboard to jot down his ideas, which stops him shouting out. He has a list of tasks to be completed, each with a sketch. In the last five minutes, an adult checks in with him to help him identify something positive from the lesson so he can start the next one in a calm state.

Getting into existing PD systems and routines used in a Trust or school is also important. Here are some examples I met when writing this book:

- Building SEND into one Trust's school's regular system for having all staff focus on one aspect of teaching for two weeks, such as lesson beginnings
- Short bursts of CPD on SEND; 20 minutes a week works better than one Inset day a year, many SENCOs told me
- Using staff briefings. In one school where there are twice weekly staff briefings, the SENCO uses one per fortnight to talk to staff about a type of SEND, a particular pupil or something she saw going well in a Learning Walk.

Finally, with any shared new SEND learning for staff, it is important to follow up training with opportunities to observe inclusive teaching and be observed, to talk about what they have done and share successes and to 'puzzle things out' with the SENCO if they are not going to plan.

Being clear about the SENCO role

If SENCOs are to share responsibility with others, they need to communicate clearly what their own role includes – and what it does not. Surveys suggest that understanding of the SENCO role by others is currently very low. The most recent SENCO workforce survey (Boddison *et al.*, 2020) found that in secondary schools, only 25% of SENCOs feel their role is understood by senior leaders. Only 17% feel their role is understood by the wider workforce. In primary schools the figures are higher, but still only around half of SENCOs feel their role is understood by senior leaders, and only 30% feel it is understood by other colleagues.

To me this suggests a need for, first, a meeting with the headteacher, armed with a list of possible roles like the one in Table 7.2, to discuss their perceptions of the SENCO's work and try to agree a shared role description that can then be communicated to all staff. It might be useful to arrange the list for the headteacher under the headings 'What I do now' and 'What I could do', or 'What I do now' and 'What SENCOs in highly effective schools do', and go armed with information about the benefits of the SENCO having a wider role than managing individual children's plans, reviews and provision.

Strategic	SEND self-evaluation and improvement planning, SEND policies Analysing data on the progress and participation of children with SEND Working with SEND governor/SEND sub-committee Having a voice within **other** school improvement planning – from teaching and learning to curriculum, attendance, behaviour and mental health Developing, costing, monitoring and evaluating a whole-school provision map of additional interventions for those with SEND or wider vulnerable groups
Curriculum, teaching and learning	Input into curriculum development Joint quality assurance with other leaders – involvement in learning walks to look at the impact of the curriculum and the quality of teaching from a SEND perspective
Supporting class and subject teachers:	Joint planning – contributing to year group/subject planning Surgeries and drop-ins Live-modelling aspects of inclusive teaching Coaching Providing CPD including Early Career Framework and new teacher induction Observing lessons to triangulate planning for a child with what they are actually doing in class
Managing staff	Managing TAs/LSAs
Managing resources	Managing the SEND budget Seeking out/ordering/making teaching resources
Work related to individual children with SEND	Work on individual plans, reviews, reports, meetings Assessment of individuals to better understand their needs
Teaching	Teaching pupils with SEND
Working with parents	Providing information to parent body/groups of parents and working with them to seek their feedback and help them support learning
Working with outside agencies	Liaison with external support services

Table 7.2 SENCO roles

Modelling curriculum development is one example of the benefits of this wider role.

EXAMPLE

Rachel Cosgrove, author and SENCO, noticed that there were issues in science teaching in Key Stage 4 her school. Many pupils with SEND ended up without a grade. Pupils said they did not like science; TAs lacked subject knowledge and felt their role in lessons was just managing behaviour. Lesson observation showed a lot of copying notes from the board, with students with SEND not asking questions or really engaging.

The school decided to create a Foundation Pathway in science for a GCSE cohort that included a large number of pupils on the SEND register and 12 with EHCPs. Rachel, a science teacher herself, developed the curriculum for the Pathway. It included flipped learning – opportunities for students to watch You Tube videos about scientific concepts as homework before working on them in class. Learning was concrete and visual: for example, students created the atomic structure of elements in the periodic table using chalk on tables, smarties and Blu-Tack. Writing was minimised and pupil talk prioritised; for example, students might interview an adult dressed up as a character in science. Wherever possible, teaching linked to real-life experiences, with concrete examples: lessons on the science of food were taught in the Food Technology room so that students could actually handle carbohydrates, fats and proteins.

Initially, Rachel taught the curriculum herself in order to model to other teachers who would later take it on. She and a new specialist science TA created resources to scaffold recording, like the 'Planning an experiment' writing frame we met in Figure 6.7 in the last chapter, which became a permanent resource for other teachers in the faculty.

The new curriculum was a great success. Every pupil in the group attended the lessons well and all received a grade in final exams. The process opened the eyes of the science department to what pupils could achieve; some of the grades children got were higher than those in groups seen as more able.

KEY PRINCIPLES

Key take-aways for SENCOs

- SENCOs in effective schools are able to share responsibility for SEND with other leaders and with class and subject teachers
- Persuading colleagues to take on responsibility needs a 'carrot and stick' approach, based on winning hearts and minds as well as performance management processes
- The best way of reducing the SENCO workload is to upskill teachers in meeting SEND in the classroom, through CPD that is relevant to the children they teach, the subjects they teach and their career stage

Key questions for the wider school leadership team

- What do you see as the role of the SENCO? How do other staff perceive the role?
- What would you say if Ofsted asks who leads on SEND in your school?
- Is SEND a strand that runs through all key school improvement priorities?

8 Planning additional provision

So far, we have looked at a number of key elements of our essential bureaucracy-busting kit that provides the alternative to writing individual plans for every child with SEN or a disability – at whole-school target-setting and tracking systems and at recording adaptations to teaching plans that are already inclusive. In this chapter we tackle another key element, provision maps.

Provision maps were described in *Special Educational Needs and School Improvement* (Gross and White, 2003), and further guidance outlined later in various government publications. Since then, ideas about provision maps have changed, with some people seeing them as almost another form of IEP/ISP, recording all the provision an individual child receives. This chapter will return to the original definition, summarising what a provision map is really meant to look like and the function it fulfils. We will look at what to do to keep the process of developing a provision map as simple as possible, how to build in new developments in quality interventions and how to move from effective provision mapping to effective provision management.

What is a provision map?

A provision map is a way of describing the provision that a school makes for children with additional needs, over and above inclusive class or subject teaching, using additional targeted time from teachers, tutors, teaching assistants or volunteers.

Table 8.1 provides an example of a primary provision map, and Table 8.2 an example of a secondary map.

Provision is best mapped by year group (although in very small schools, it might be mapped by phase) and by types of provision – literacy interventions, mathematics interventions, interventions to boost oral language skills, motor coordination or social, emotional and behavioural skills. Some schools also subdivide provision into universal/ Wave 1, targeted/Wave 2 and specialist/Wave 3 tiers according to the level of need, with universal provision being inclusive classroom teaching, targeted/Wave2 provision being for children who can reach age-expected levels with just a short period of 1–1 or group help from a TA, mentor, tutor or teacher and specialist/Wave 3 interventions being for those with more complex needs that require help delivered by specialists.

DOI: 10.4324/9781003313526-8

PROVISION	YR	Y1	Y2	Y3	Y4	Y5	Y6
Language intervention	NELI		Talk Boost Key Stage 1			Language for thinking group	
Literacy intervention	Phonological awareness group Teacher-led phonics group	Reading Recovery Teacher-led phonics group	Reading Recovery FFT Tutoring with the Lighting Squad	FFT Tutoring with the Lighting Squad	Y6 buddy readers	Paired reading programme	Reciprocal teaching
Maths intervention			Numbers Count IstClass@ number	Numbers Count	Before-school 'Getting Ahead Club' pre-teaching	Pre-and post-teaching Tutoring (Tutor Trust)	Pre- and post-teaching Tutoring (Tutor Trust)
Motor Coordination programme		Weekly breakfast motor skills group plus home programme					
EAL provision	Home language support and additional language work for early-stage learners	Home language support, pre-tutoring and additional language work for early stage learners	Home language support, pre-tutoring and additional language work for early-stage learners	Small group language enrichment for children at later stages of learning EAL	Small group language enrichment and pre-tutoring for children at later stages of learning EAL + additional support for two new arrivals	Small group language enrichment and pre-tutoring for children at later stages of learning EAL	Small group language enrichment and pre-tutoring for children at later stages of learning EAL

Table 8.1 Example of a primary provision map

1:1 counselling/ solution focused work with ELSA			Estimated three pupils per year group				
Small group social and emotional learning with ELSA	Nurture group	SEAL silver sets	SEAL silver sets Circle of Friends for two children	Pyramid Club	SEAL silver sets	SEAL silver sets	Transition group
In-class support	Isaac, Rhys	Abigail	Sadiq	Darren, Alice	James, Oscar, Ben, Leon	Jason	Mohammed, Tyrone
More Able provision					After-school clubs with secondary buddies		
Other	1:1 work with TA on programme devised by speech and language therapist	1:1 TA work with autistic child with on social scripts	1:1 TA sensory programme supervised through outreach from special school	1:1 work with TA on programme devised by speech and language therapist	Social thinking social skills group		

Table 8.1 (Continued)

	Y7	Y8	Y9	Y10	Y11
Language intervention	ELCISS vocabulary and narrative group		Language for Behaviour and Emotions with trained HLTA	Words for Work programme with business mentors	
Maths	Catch Up Numeracy After school 'Getting ahead club' pre-teaching	Tutoring using catch-up funding	Tutoring using catch-up funding	Tutoring using catch-up funding	Tutoring using catch-up funding
Literacy	Lexia Toe by Toe programme 1:1 with teacher Accelerated Reader	Accelerated Reader Paired reading programme organised by Inclusion Coordinator, involving disaffected Year 10 as tutors – approx. 18 pupils involved on a rolling programme		English Tutoring using catch-up funding	English Tutoring using catch-up funding
EAL provision	Grammar for Writing – group of advanced bilingual learners – English teacher	Home language support and additional language work for two children at the early stages of learning EAL	Home language support and additional language work for four children at the early stages of learning EAL	Additional language work and academic tutoring for an estimated three new arrivals	Additional language work and academic tutoring for an estimated three new arrivals
1:1 counselling	CBT-trained school counsellor – estimated 12 pupils per year group				
Focus group work to develop social, emotional and behavioural skills	Nurture group for eight pupils entering Y7 Lunchtime Lego Therapy club	Circle of Friends for three pupils	SEAL friendship skills focus group and two anger management groups run by Learning Support Unit team Lunchtime club		
In-class support for individuals	Kalam, Jamila, Jenny, Cameron, David	John, Rafiq, Attia, Brendan	Stephen, Adam, Parvis, Aki, Jahangir, Sedef	Gareth, Brooke	William B, Patrick, Travis, Sara
Out of school support	Homework/IT club	Homework/IT club	Homework/IT club Outdoor activity programme for targeted pupils	Study support tutorials	Study support tutorials

Table 8.2 Example of a secondary provision map

More able provision	Specialist lunchtime enrichment clubs			Mentoring by university students
Other	1:1 work with TA on programme devised by speech and language therapist Cameron 1:1 TA work with autistic child on social scripts, David Touch typing – two pupils (20 mins, during registration)	1:1 TA work with autistic child on social scripts Anthony, Rafiq, Brendan Social skills group work with this group	1:1 TA sensory programme supervised through outreach from special school Beth	Tailored vocational curriculum group of 12

Table 8.2 (Continued)

It is good practice to include in a provision map all the different types of additional provision a school makes for children – those in need of catch-up provision, those with identified SEND, those who are EAL learners, those who are more able, those with behaviour difficulties and those who are vulnerable for other reasons. This saves the time and effort that might be spent on constructing separate maps for different types of need. It recognises the overlap between needs, in which a child with autism taking part in a social skills group might also require support as an EAL learner. Most importantly, it allows the school to achieve an overview of all the additional needs in each year group and make a coherent plan to meet them.

In so doing, it enables the SENCO to follow the general principle that children with SEN or disabilities are better integrated into systems that personalise learning for all children, rather than separate systems driven by SEND categories and procedures.

The benefits of targeted/Wave 2 provision

A provision map with plenty of evidence-based, carefully targeted Wave 2 provision is the secret of reducing excessive SENCO workload and cutting bureaucracy.

As we saw in earlier chapters, we may in the past have identified too many pupils as having SEN – pupils whose progress has simply been held back by factors associated with social deprivation, a summer term birth date, poor attendance, and even poor teaching. But as the SEN Code of Practice says, 'Slow progress and attainment do not necessarily mean a child has SEN' (DfE and DH, 2014). The Code also notes that 'high quality teaching targeted at their areas of weakness' should be the first response to slow progress, and only if this fails to enable the child to catch up should the teacher and SENCO assess whether the child has SEN.

Targeted/Wave 2 interventions, together with carefully planned universal/Wave 1 inclusive class or subject teaching, constitute this first response. For many children, they will prove effective, so that the child need never move on to requiring specialist/Wave 3 help.

Schools need then only identify those children needing specialist/Wave 3 support as having SEND – as we saw in the case study schools in Chapter 1. This will help differentiate between those children who just need a period of help to catch up with their peers (better universal/Wave 1 classroom teaching and/or targeted/Wave 2 intervention programmes) and those who need a more tailored and long-term approach to address a specific SEN.

This step will make the numbers on the SEND register more manageable and mean that for this smaller number, it will be possible to put in place the true partnership with parents and pupil, and the regular face-to-face meetings, that the Code of Practice requires.

It will also mean that different people within school can share the workload involved in planning, monitoring and evaluating provision for pupils with additional needs. Targeted/Wave 2 provision can be coordinated (as we saw in the last chapter) by primary key stage coordinators/subject leads or the relevant subject leader/head of department in a secondary school.

Steps in developing a provision map

The steps involved in developing a provision map are shown in Figure 8.1.

Auditing the projected need in each year group in the next school year means listing types of provision you could make: literacy, mathematics, language, social and emotional, motor coordination, EAL, attendance, extracurricular, more able provision and an 'other' heading to cover very individual arrangements made for children with less common types of SEND. Then under each, you write the names of children for whom that additional provision would be desirable. It is helpful if on your lists (perhaps using a particular colour) you distinguish those for whom additional provision is essential (your 'MUST' group) – for example, children with an EHCP specifying a particular provision, or children at a very early stage of English language acquisition.

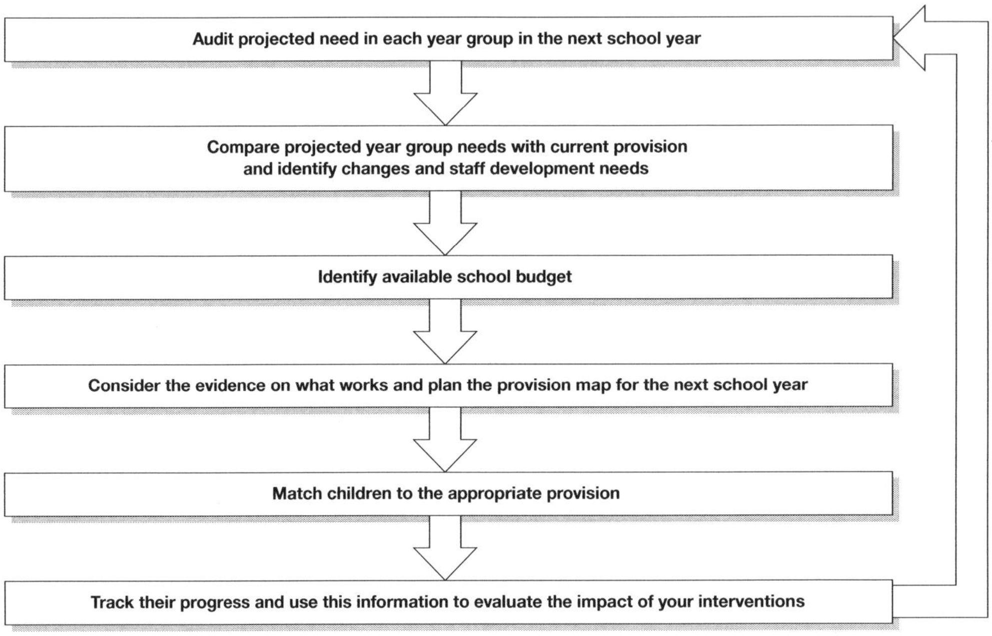

FIGURE 8.1 Steps in developing a provision map

Next, enter in another colour those who have the next highest call on available provision (your 'SHOULD' group). These could be children whose difficulties impact very significantly on their own or others' learning or those who have the potential, with relatively little help, to catch up with their peers and achieve age-related expectations in social and emotional learning, language, literacy or mathematics. Finally, enter the names of children for whom you want to make additional provision, if the budget allows, but for whom the priority is lower (your 'COULD' group).

Comparing projected year group needs with current provision and identifying changes and staff development needs means looking at the audit you have done for each year group for the coming school year and noticing differences between the audit and current needs and provision in that year group. Is there going to be an increase in children in Year 1 who need provision to develop their speech and language skills, for example, that might mean introducing a new intervention and training up staff (in advance) to implement it? Will there still be a group needing a Year 3 literacy support programme, or not? What does the incoming Year 7 look like in terms of need for literacy, maths and social communication support? Does it contain an increased number of children with autism, and if so, what are the implications for provision and staff development? Does next year's Year 9 have a large group of pupils who, according to current tracking, are making poor progress across the board because of lack of engagement with learning, and if so, is there a need for a mentoring programme?

EXAMPLE

One SENCO told me how, in response to an increase in children with SLCN, she invested in ELKLAN CPD for staff rather than fall in with class teachers' 'I need another TA' requests. Another told me how conversations with teachers led her to identify children's memory difficulties as an issue across the school, so she asked the school's EP to provide specific training to staff on long and short-term (working) memory, how they affect learning and how to make sure information enters children's long-term memory and is retained there. And at Henley Bank High, the SENCO audits needs in the incoming Year 7 and plans accordingly – adding TA time for support in PE changing rooms for increased numbers of dyspraxic pupils, doubling speech and language therapy time in response to a high number of autistic pupils, and doubling bought-in counselling time and time from an hourly-paid expert mindfulness practitioner to meet increased mental health needs following the post-COVID return to school.

Identifying the available school budget means pulling together different funding streams, such as a core amount from the school's base budget, delegated SEN funding, the Pupil Premium, catch-up funding and any other local or national funding for priorities such as early intervention or behaviour support. It will be necessary to ring-fence any funding that is allocated through an EHCP which specifies that the child must receive a fixed number of hours of TA support or other specified provision. Otherwise, funding streams should be combined so as to achieve the best possible fit to the priorities identified in the audit. Coherently planned provision that draws together a range of funding sources is more likely to achieve positive outcomes than piecemeal use of pockets of money.

The requirement to account for and report separately on the school's use of the Pupil Premium can be met by

- working out a cost per pupil for each provision accessed by those pupils (cost of staff time and resources divided by the total number of pupils taking part, whether or not eligible for the Premium);
- multiplying this per-pupil cost by the number of pupils in receipt of the Pupil Premium who took part;
- publishing your provision map and adding for each intervention the numbers of children eligible for the Premium who took part, and the cost in staffing and resources for these particular pupils;
- also listing any other Pupil Premium expenditure that links to your pupil profiling – such as CPD costs or financial support for trips or uniform.

The same method can be used for any other ring-fenced funding stream on which you have to provide a discrete report.

The next step in provision mapping, *considering the evidence on what works*, means making choices about what interventions you will put on next year's provision map, drawing on information provided nationally, by your MAT or local authority, from your own research and reading and from your evaluation of interventions used previously in school.

Once the provision map has been drawn up and the new school year has begun, precise tracking information can be used to *match children to the appropriate provision*. This process will be easier, and fairer, if you have established clear entry and exit criteria for each of your provisions.

Finally, 'before' and 'after' measures can be used to *track children's progress* as a result of the intervention, and this information can be used to *evaluate the impact of each provision*. This in turn feeds back into the provision mapping cycle, helping to inform your choice of interventions in the future.

EXAMPLE

At Porters Grange Primary, provision is planned strategically and proactively. LSA time, for example, is allocated to classes by looking systematically at the need in each year group rather than just a fixed historical amount of time per class.

Rich data from teacher assessment and tests is used to evaluate the impact of provisions. Tests such as YARC, PhAB and the British Picture Vocabulary Scales are used termly. Boxall Online profiles are completed and repeated at intervals by class teachers to assess mental health and well-being for those with SEND, children with behaviour programmes, looked after children and children with safeguarding concerns. In Reception, WellComm assessments profile every child's speech, language and communication. Speech and Language UK's Progression Tools are used before and after Talk Boost interventions (Early Talk Boost, Talk Boost Key Stage 1 and Talk Boost Key Stage 2). Termly data drops from the Insight teacher assessment tool also contribute to evaluation of the impact of provision, through judgements of whether each child is emerging/below/working at or exceeding age-related expectations in reading, writing and maths.

SENCO Toni Quinn makes use of all these sources of information to evaluate the impact of different provisions and report to Trustees on what is working – and what is not working. For example, the data showed that the Talk Boost programmes were having a strong impact overall; analysis of impact by pupil groups showed particularly good outcomes for EAL learners.

EXAMPLE

At Henley Bank High, the SENCO has developed a provision map for each of the four SEND areas of need, with a range of provision from pre-teaching of English and maths to 'TLC in the morning' – a breakfast club that opens for all at 8:30 but where children with SEND can stay (for example for equipment checks) while others go to registration with their class. Another provision is 'Positive start', where anxious children who are reluctant to attend school might have a feelings check-in, write a personal ambition for the week or talk to Year 10 mental health ambassadors.

The impact of provisions is evaluated using measures such as changes in standardised scores on reading tests, changes in predicted GCSE grades, improvements in attendance, changes on the PASS scales and (for the school's recently introduced mindfulness provision) reduction in incidents of needing to be co-regulated. Even the impact of in-class support is looked at by assessing improvements in confidence (putting hand up, answering low-stakes quizzes). Rhian is also planning to collect data on whether pupils are progressing up the EEF scaffolding triangle discussed in Chapter 6, as a result of skilled TA support in their lessons.

What are provision maps for?

A provision map is fundamentally a management tool, based on auditing the needs of year groups, deciding as a result what provision is needed in which year groups and using this to determine budgetary and staffing arrangements. Its main value is 'the strategic view that it gives, and the opportunities that it then affords to carry out some intelligent, and evidence-based planning for predicted needs, rather than simply reacting on an individual basis' (Cochrane, 2006).

EXAMPLE

When schools reopened after Covid-19 lockdowns, leaders in the Astrea Academy Trust undertook an analysis of need for primary pupils. Historical data showed that the proportion of pupils achieving a good level of development in the Early Years Foundation Stage Profile was 5–7% below the national average. Results on the phonics check and end of Key Stage reading assessments were around 10% below the national average.

These attainment issues were exacerbated by the fact that more than a quarter of primary pupils with identified SEN had speech, language and communication needs. Another factor was the disruption to children's education caused by Covid-19.

In order to address the challenges identified, leaders decided to invest in

- supporting early language acquisition and addressing developmental language disorders to ensure access to the full curriculum, whilst closing academic gaps;
- using evidence-based targeted interventions for reading in Years 1–3;
- providing additional staff to each Trust school, with the flexibility to respond quickly to barriers to learning, ensuring that children were not disrupted further post-lockdown.

Adapted from *The inclusive and nurturing schools toolkit* (RSA, 2022)

Developing a provision map helps schools manage different funding streams coherently to target particular patterns of need in different year groups. Priorities are established and made transparent so that staff can see, for example, why the TA who was formerly attached to their class full-time now needs to work differently, running time-limited interventions in a number of year groups. Provision maps help schools to avoid situations where in one class there might be a teacher and three TAs, each attached to support individual children, while next door in a parallel class the teacher is struggling alone with no additional support. They also help schools to check the overall pattern of their provision and make sure children do not become demoralised by repeating very similar interventions year after year.

Another advantage of provision maps is the basis they provide for systematic evaluation of the impact of interventions. Combined with data on pupil outcomes, the map gives substance to the school's SEND self-evaluation and will be helpful to Ofsted inspectors.

For parents, a provision map provides very useful information about what they can expect the school to provide for their child, putting flesh on the bones of the school's contribution to the local offer required under the 2014 SEN reforms.

From the standpoint of this book, an even more important advantage of provision maps is that SENCOs and class teachers can avoid the need to write particular provisions down over and over again on a series of IEP/ISPs. Provision for individual children can be recorded by simply highlighting on a copy of the school's provision map the provision a particular child is receiving, dating the map and storing it with the child's records. This personalised map will provide good information for parents/carers and increase parental confidence that their child's needs are being comprehensively met.

Provision maps as a management tool are mainly a way of planning strategically for children with high-incidence (more common) types of additional need, and for planning the provision over which the school has control – that which it makes from its own budget, including any delegated SEN funding. For the majority of children, therefore, it will be sufficient just to highlight a standard, whole-school provision map when recording the provision made for that child.

Provision maps are also mainly about planning targeted intervention – time-limited group or one-to-one programmes used in class or on a withdrawal basis, rather than planning for general in-class support. This is because the evidence for the efficacy of such generalised support for children with the more common types of SEN is weak (Giangreco *et al.*, 1997; Gerber *et al.*, 2001; Howes, 2003), with large-scale research at the Institute of Education in London (Blatchford *et al.*, 2012) finding that for pupils with similar prior attainment, social class and SEN status, there was a negative relationship between the amount of TA support received and academic progress – in other words, the more TA support a child receives, the less progress they make on average. Schools are, in general, better advised to spend their money elsewhere.

Some children, however, such as those with physical impairments, medical conditions or major social, emotional and mental health needs, do require in-class support. So as to have all the information about the child in one place, these very individual arrangements can be recorded in the 'other' row on the provision map. The same row can be used to record the support provided by external agencies.

Keeping it simple

There is something about SEND that seems to make us manufacture complexity where none needs exist. With provision maps, what started as a simple planning tool for school managers has degenerated in many local areas into yet another bureaucratic burden. These are some examples:

- Provision maps that include universal/Wave 1 class or subject teaching, and try to list every single adaptation that teachers make to meet particular types of SEND
- Provision maps written individually for every child, aimed at showing exactly what is being done to meet their needs, and often running alongside IEP/ISPs
- Provision maps that must be submitted annually to the local authority, with each provision costed so as to 'prove' that the school has spent every penny of its delegated SEND budget

Let us consider each of these common mistakes in turn.

It can be useful as a one-off professional development exercise for a staff group to collate a list of teaching approaches and access strategies that they already use to support children with particular needs – dyslexia, for example, or autism or language difficulties. Such an exercise enables teachers to reflect on what they are already doing well, to learn from others' practice, and produce one collated ideas list of which they will have ownership, and therefore be more inclined to use. It will energise everyone because it follows the best principles of managing any sort of development or change – identifying what people are already doing that works, so as to do more of it in the future, more often and more systematically.

But why go to all the trouble of writing all these strategies on a provision map that is produced annually and will become so long and complex that it loses its usefulness? Instead, the SENCO might want to develop the school's own bank of IT-based strategy sheets for each main type of SEN or disability, drawing on the ideas from the toolkit section of this book as well as those generated by staff. Once on the school's networked system, staff can quickly look up the strategy sheets when they want help in knowing how to plan differentiated learning and teaching for a child in their class.

Next, it is important to avoid turning provision maps back into another form of IEP/ISP by writing one for each individual child. This misses the point of provision mapping altogether. The questions a provision map seeks to answer are these:

- How many children have we in each year group who need additional interventions for language, literacy, mathematics, social and emotional learning and so on?
- Where do the greatest priorities for additional provision lie?
- How can we best deploy additional adult and peer support so as to meet these priorities?
- What particular interventions will we choose to use on the basis of their impact?
- Looking at our tracking data from last term/year, which provisions have had the desired impact, and which we ought to review?

These are very different questions from the more familiar 'What does this individual child need in the way of extra support?', which might lead a SENCO to begin by constructing a provision map for each child. That was the question to which we were led by an IEP-driven system. And an IEP-driven system led us to patterns of provision based mostly on attaching TAs as if by Velcro to individual children, to provide generalised in-class support or teaching geared around three or four IEP/ISP targets.

As we saw in Chapter 1, such a system failed to serve our children well, and failed to serve the SENCOs and teachers who drowned in paper while struggling valiantly to make it work. It is essential that provision maps do not replicate the weaknesses of the past. We need to construct them on a whole-school basis, to plan the provision in year groups, not for Saleem or Sam or Sarah. We can print and date a copy, highlighting on it the provision that Saleem receives, so as to have an ongoing child-level record on file. We can as we have seen add to it, in the 'other' column, the very individual arrangements, like help with toileting, and a physiotherapy programme that Sam might need. We can add to it the multi-agency support – speech and language therapy, advice from a specialist VI teacher, advice from a teacher in a local special school – that Sarah might access. We can, as we will see later in this chapter in the section on evaluation, add provision columns to the pupil-level attainment, behaviour an attendance data, on the school's Management Information System (MIS) and, from this, print out individual provision records. We can, as we will see in the next chapter, use technology like Tes Provision Map (formerly known as EduKey) for the same purpose. But we must start our provision planning with a proactive, strategic, whole-school focus rather than ad hoc child-by-child arrangements.

Finally, what about costing provision maps? It is not uncommon now for local authorities to require schools to produce costed maps in order to make sure that they are using all their delegated SEND funding for its specified purpose.

There is not a single headteacher, however, who cannot, by canny accounting, demonstrate that their school is spending not only what the local authority have provided to meet SEND in the school's budget share but far more besides. Almost any arrangement, such as running smaller class groups or sets, providing each class with its own TA, having extra adults around to keep order at lunchtimes, having extra pastoral staff to enable a school in a difficult area to run smoothly or buying extra laptops can be allocated to a school's notional SEN budget and its provision map if the school so chooses. The definition of what constitutes SEND provision is so wide as to be meaningless. And in a sense, accounting for spending is an irrelevance: what matters is the impact that the school's spending choices have on pupils. If the school chooses to spend its SEND budget on refurbishing the staffroom, and can demonstrate that the attainment and well-being of pupils with SEN or disabilities improves, then the local authority has a poor case for challenge.

Unless your school has developed a sophisticated IT system that holds data on average hourly staffing costs and does the necessary calculation, costing a provision map is a lot of work – though the IT-based systems we will look at in the next chapter are making it easier, and nasen has a useful free template that includes drop-down lists of interventions and will calculate costs if you add relevant background information. The costing work should not be undertaken to fulfil someone else's purposes if those purposes can be met in other more sensible ways. This is the case for local authorities' current duty to hold schools to account for the progress of pupils with SEN or disabilities. Providing data on pupil *outcomes* is a more sensible way of meeting that purpose.

It may be useful to highlight or print a provision map for an individual child and cost it if you have to give evidence at a tribunal or need to convince a parent that you are fully allocating funding provided through an EHCP. Otherwise, the only reason for costing a whole-school provision map is if doing so will meet your *own* school purpose, to raise standards and promote pupils' well-being. Here, there may be a case for costing different provisions so that you can do a cost-benefit analysis – that is, compare the costs and impact of different provisions to see which gives best value for money (the highest impact at the lowest cost). An anger-management group run by a learning mentor, for example, might prove to have an impact as great as that of one-to-one counselling from a clinical psychologist for the four individuals involved, but provide better value for money because the unit costs of a learning mentor are very much lower than those of a clinical psychologist, and because the pupils work as a group rather than one-to-one.

Even here, however, schools may want to be cautious. In the example earlier, they would need to be sure that the pupils were comparable – that those working with the learning mentor in this case had needs just as great as those working with the clinical psychologist. One also needs to be aware that analysis that considers only *immediate* benefits and immediate costs can sometimes lead to unhelpful conclusions. Consider, for example, the Head Start programme in the US, which provided intensive pre-school intervention for disadvantaged children. Immediate analysis showed costs to be high and the differential benefits (when compared with outcomes for similar children not involved in the programme) to be limited. It was only when the Head Start children were followed up to adulthood and found to be much less likely to have dropped out of school or to have been involved in crime that the benefits became clear. This long-term cost-benefit analysis showed that for every dollar spent on the programme, over seven dollars was saved by society.

A study carried out in this country (Every Child a Chance Trust, 2009) makes a similar point. Here, researchers compared the costs of providing the intensive, one-to-one teacher-led Reading Recovery programme to six-year-olds with literacy difficulties with the costs incurred by schools and society if the children's difficulties remained unaddressed. The one-off cost of providing Reading Recovery was £2,610 per child (at 2009 prices) – much more expensive than an intervention delivered by a TA or delivered in a group. Yet the same six-year-old receiving less expensive but also less effective provision would cost their junior school £2,390 in special needs support over the course of Key Stage 2, and the secondary school £3,850 over the course of Key Stages 3 and 4 – over £6,000 in total. With the longer-term costs of crime, ill-health and reduced employment opportunities also taken into account, the researchers estimated a return on investment of between £11 and £19 for every pound spent on Reading Recovery.

Special educational needs that are not effectively addressed carry life-long consequences for individuals and for society. Cost-benefit analyses can be misleading if the benefits assessed are only short-term and if the cost-benefit analysis focuses only on the costs and benefits for the institution rather than on the wider issues of every child's right to the best possible future.

Developments in provision mapping

Extending your provision

One notable development in provision mapping in recent years has been the extension of the range of provision that is planned for. Early provision maps were often dominated by provision for pupils with literacy difficulties, with perhaps a nod to numeracy and speech and language provision. Now a primary provision map might include four or five different literacy interventions, one or more maths interventions, an oral language scheme, a social use of language programme and the use of social stories for children on the autistic spectrum, perhaps a motor coordination skills programme and a range of provision for children who need extra help to develop social, emotional and behavioural skills. In a secondary school, there might be a small Year 7 nurture group for vulnerable pupils, a range of one-to-one mentoring programmes, study support, a language programme, skilled counselling or cognitive behaviour therapy and social skills groups, as well as the usual literacy and mathematics catch-up interventions.

An important growth area is provision for pupils with social, emotional and mental health difficulties. The development some years ago of a 'universal' curriculum framework to teach all children social and emotional skills (the SEAL primary and secondary resources) helped about us to think about applying a tiered or 'Waves' model, originally devised for literacy and numeracy, to social and emotional learning (Figure 8.2). Schools were encouraged to identify pupils who with just a little help could catch up with their peers in this area of learning, as a result of taking part in a structured group work programme. Materials were developed (DfES, 2005b, DCSF, 2007) to help them plan, deliver and evaluate such groups; these are all now available at www.sealcommunity.org. These targeted/Wave 2 developments throw into sharp focus the needs of pupils who require intervention that is much more intensive and personalised – a specialist/Wave 3 intervention delivered by a highly skilled professional, often in a multi-agency context where there is work not only with the pupil but with the family and in the community. Provision for children with attendance problems is beginning to figure on provision maps too – like the school that has organised a 'walking bus' to pick up the 20 children who used to be late or attend irregularly.

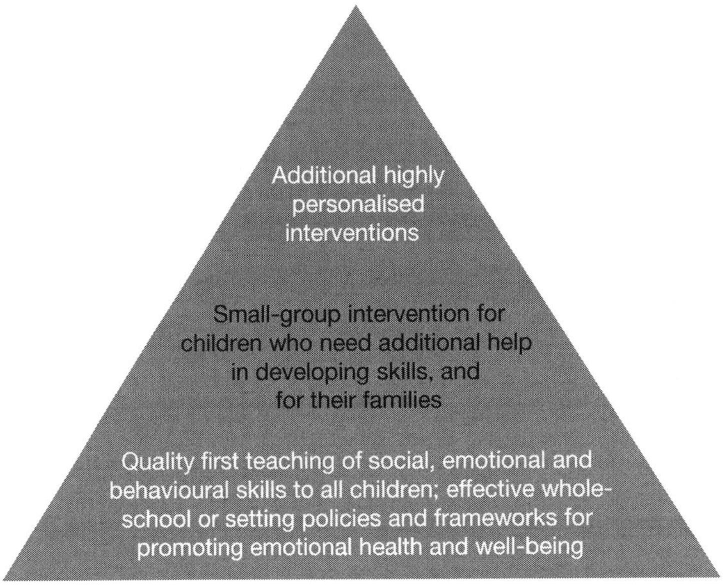

Figure 8.2 Waves model: social, emotional and mental health and well-being

Another area of need that has shown a huge increase in recent years is autism. At Porters Grange, for example, after the COVID lockdowns, there were five non-verbal autistic children on the SEND register, so SENCO Toni Quinn needed to add to the school's planned provision a dedicated room where children worked very successfully on a sensory, communication and early phonological awareness curriculum that would enable them to access the EYFS.

Provision maps for groups of schools

Another aspect of provision mapping is the idea of groups of schools, perhaps within a MAT or Federation, coming together to pool funding, map needs and plan shared provision. A secondary school and its feeder primaries, for example, might share a highly trained speech and language assistant who works across the schools, a parent support adviser, a primary mental health worker and a Reading Recovery teacher.

EXAMPLE

Headteachers of secondary schools and their link primary schools in County Durham met half-termly to discuss SEND priorities and how best to spend funding delegated by the local authority. Provision funded this way and shared by a cluster included a speech and language assistant, a parent support worker and the Lexia literacy intervention programme.

Leadership that promotes the achievement of students with special educational needs and disabilities, Chapman *et al.*, 2011

Defining effective provision

Another development in provision mapping is the greater sense we now have of which provisions have the greatest impact on children's progress.

Research evidence for the impact of different provisions is regularly published by the EEF, Early Intervention Foundation, and other agencies. Sources like the Dyslexia/SpLD Trust's *Interventions for Literacy* website, The Early Intervention Foundation's Guidebook (*programmes for children with recognised or possible special education need spotlight*) and Speech and Language UK's *What Works* database of language interventions provide searchable summaries. Information from all these sources, and from a recent literature review (Pegram *et al.*, 2022), has been incorporated in Table 8.3. The table lists the interventions that schools can use with some certainty that they will have the desired effect.

	Primary	**Secondary**
Language	Language for thinking (http://thinkingtalking.co.uk/language-for-thinking/) Language Link (www.speechlink.info/primary-schools.php) Nuffield Early Language Intervention Programme (NELI) (www.teachneli.org/) Nursery Narrative, Key Stage 1 Narrative, Key Stage 2 Narrative (Black Sheep Press) Speak Out and Speech Bubble (www.londonbubble.org.uk) Talk Boost (https://speechandlanguage.org.uk/talk-boost/)	ELCISS (Speechmark)
Reading	Abracadabra (https://educationendowmentfoundation.org.uk/projects-and-evaluation/projects/abracadabra-abra) Accelerated Reader (www.renlearn.co.uk/accelerated-reader/) Headsprout (www.learninga-z.com/and https://educationendowmentfoundation.org.uk/projects-and-evaluation/projects/headsprout-early-reading) FFT Tutoring with the Lightning Squad (https://fft.org.uk/tutoring/and www.successforall.org/wp-content/uploads/2020/08/Ross-Laurenzano-Madden-2017.pdf) Lexia (www.lexialearning.com/)	Accelerated reader (www.renlearn.co.uk/accelerated-reader/) Catch Up Literacy (www.catchup.org/interventions/literacy.php) Peer tutoring (https://educationendowmentfoundation.org.uk/education-evidence/teaching-learning-toolkit/peer-tutoring and www.moray.gov.uk/moray_standard/page_62204.html) REACH (https://educationendowmentfoundation.org.uk/projects-and-evaluation/projects/reach)

Table 8.3 Interventions with evidence of impact from randomised controlled trials/quasi-experimental studies with well-matched control group

	Primary	Secondary
	Peer tutoring (https://educationendowmentfoundation.org.uk/education-evidence/teaching-learning-toolkit/peer-tutoring and www.moray.gov.uk/moray_standard/page_62204.html) Reading Educational Assistance Dogs (https://therapyanimals.org/read/) Reading and Language Intervention for Children with Down Syndrome (www.dseinternational.org/en-us/) Reading Recovery (www.ucl.ac.uk/reading-recovery-europe/reading-recovery) Reciprocal Reading (https://fft.org.uk/fft-literacy/reciprocal-reading/) Success for All Phonics https://fft.org.uk/phonics Toe by Toe (https://toe-by-toe.co.uk/)	Read Write Inc Fresh Start (https://global.oup.com/education/content/primary/series/rwi/fresh-start/?region=uk) Switch On (https://educationendowmentfoundation.org.uk/education-evidence/teaching-learning-toolkit and www.targetliteracy.co.uk/interventions/switch_on/) Toe by Toe (https://toe-by-toe.co.uk/)
Writing	Reading Recovery (www.ucl.ac.uk/reading-recoveryeurope/reading-recovery) Using Self-Regulation to Improve Writing (https://educationendowmentfoundation.org.uk/education-evidence/teaching-learning-toolkit) Write Away Together (see www.theschoolpsychologyservice.com)	Grammar for Writing (https://education.exeter.ac.uk/research/centres/writing/grammar-teacher-resources/grammaraschoice/thegrammarforwritingpedagogy/) Using Self-Regulation to Improve Writing (https://educationendowmentfoundation.org.uk/education-evidence/teaching-learning-toolkit)
Mathematics	Accelerated Maths (www.renlearn.co.uk/accelerated-maths/) Catch Up Numeracy (www.catchup.org) Improving working memory plus arithmetic (https://educationendowmentfoundation.org.uk/projects-and-evaluation/projects/improving-working-memory) 1stclass@number (https://everychildcounts.edgehill.ac.uk/) Numbers Count (https://everychild counts.edgehill.ac.uk) Peer tutoring (https://educationendowmentfoundation.org.uk/education-evidence/teaching-learning-toolkit/peer-tutoring and Topping and Bamford (1998), *The Paired Maths Handbook)* SAFMEDs precision teaching (http://cierei.bangor.ac.uk/projects/safmeds.php.en) The Tutor Trust (www.thetutortrust.org/who-we-are)	Catch Up Numeracy (www.catchup.org/interventions/numeracy.php) Peer tutoring (https://educationendowmentfoundation.org.uk/education-evidence/teaching-learning-toolkit/peer-tutoring and Topping and Bamford (1998), *The Paired Maths Handbook)*

Table 8.3 (Continued)

	Primary	Secondary
Parenting programmes for children with social, emotional and mental health difficulties	Empowering Parents, Empowering Communities (www.cpcs.org.uk) FAST (Families and Schools Together) (www.savethechildren.org.uk/) Families Connect (www.savethechildren.org.uk/) Incredible Years (https://incredibleyears.com/) Triple P (www.triplep-parenting.net)	Level Group Teen Triple P (www.triplep-parenting.net) Parents Plus Adolescent programme (www.parentsplus.ie/) Strengthening Families (www.extension.iastate.edu/sfp10-14)
Social and emotional learning	Friends for Life (delivered by mental health professionals) (https://friendsresilience.org/friendsforlife) Incredible Years Dinosaur School (https://incredibleyears.com/) Lego based therapy – (www.legotherapy.com/) Mindfulness – Paws.b (www.mindfulnessinschools.org) Seasons for growth (https://seasonsforgrowth.co.uk/locations/wales/https://carolgraysocialstories.com/social-stories/what-is-it/) Social Stories (https://carolgraysocialstories.com/social-stories/what-is-it/) SEAL group work (www.seal community.org) Story Links (www.storylinks training.co.uk and www.young minds.org.uk) Therapeutic Story Writing Groups (www.therapeuticstorywriting.com and www.youngminds.org.uk)	.b mindfulness (www.mindfulnessinschools.org) Blues Programme ttps://www.actionforchildren.org.uk/our-www.legotherapy.com/work-and-impact/children-and-families/good-mental-health/blues-programme/ FRIENDS for Youth (www.friendsresilience.org/myfriendsyouth) School-based humanistic (counselling (www.thelancet.com/journals/lanchi/article/PIIS2352-4642(20)30363-1/fulltext) and www.relate.org.uk)
ADHD	Attention-training computer games Contact specialist advisory services for advice on these interventions: For moderate difficulties, relaxation training, group-based parenting programmes and small-group or individual cognitive-behavioural/social skills programmes as for social, emotional and mental health difficulties For severe difficulties or in cases of lack of response to parenting/small group programmes, drug treatment in addition	Attention training computer games Contact specialist advisory services for advice on these interventions: For moderate difficulties, relaxation training, group-based parenting programmes and small-group or individual cognitive-behavioural/social skills programmes as for social, emotional and mental health difficulties For severe difficulties or in cases of lack of response to parenting/small group programmes, drug treatment in addition

Table 8.3 (Continued)

	Primary	Secondary
Autism	Contact specialist advisory services/speech and language therapists for advice on these interventions: Augmentative and Alternative Communication Cognitive-based social skills training Circle of friends and other forms of peer-mediated support COMPASS Intensive Behavioural Interventions Intensive adult – child interaction LEAP Music therapy Picture Exchange Communication Systems (PECS) Pivotal response training Sensory integration Structured small group play activities e.g. Lego therapy Social stories, Comic strip conversations Social Communication Inference Programme (SCIP) TEACCH Therapeutic touch (massage)	Contact specialist advisory services/ speech and language therapists for advice on these interventions: Augmentative and Alternative Communication Cognitive-based social skills training Circle of friends and other forms of peer-mediated support COMPASS LEAP Music therapy Picture Exchange Communication Systems (PECS) Sensory integration Social stories, Comic strip conversations TEACCH Therapeutic touch (massage) UCLA PEERS social skills programme for adolescents and young adults
Developmental coordination disorder	Mentis-XL – child development programme for three- to five-year-olds (www.mentisxl.org) Wii Fit video games (age seven to eleven) Contact occupational therapists for advice on this intervention: CO-OP (Cognitive Orientation to Daily Occupational Performance)	Contact occupational therapists for advice on this intervention: CO-OP (Cognitive Orientation to Daily Occupational Performance)

Table 8.3 (Continued)

Moving from provision mapping to provision management

Constructing a provision map is one thing. Making sure that the provision it describes proves effective is another. Like ISPs/IEPs, provision maps run the risk of sitting on someone's laptop, to be pulled up at the times when Ofsted come, but not in between.

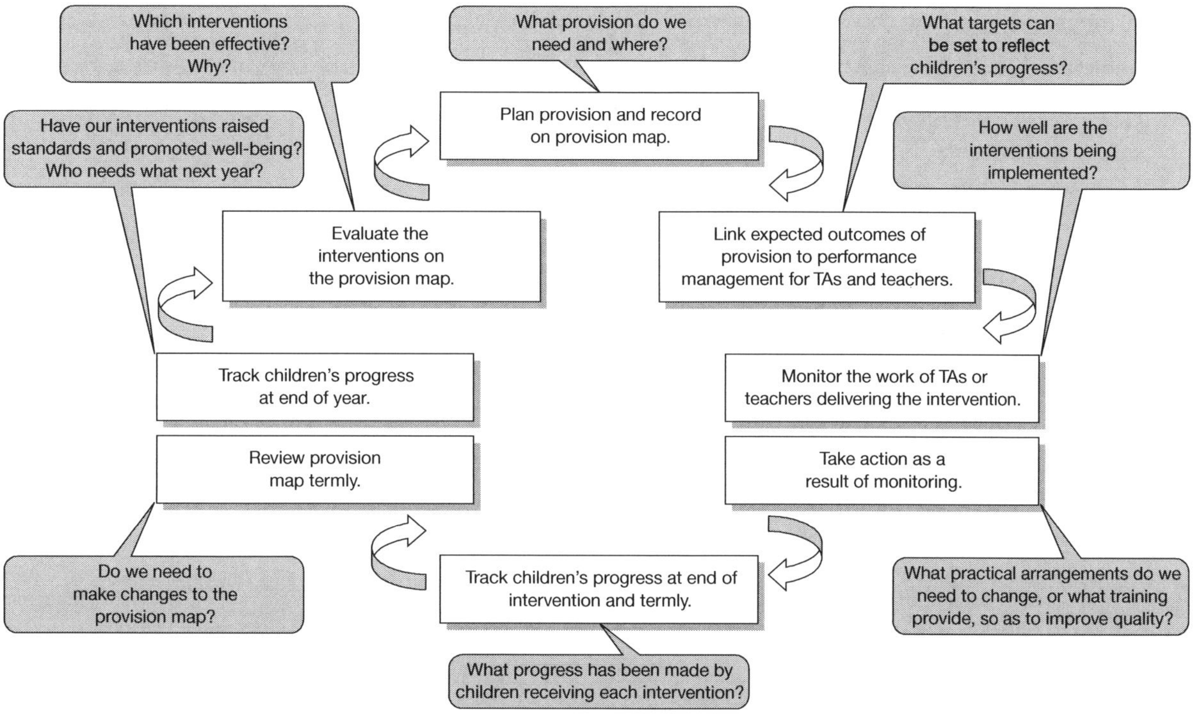

FIGURE 8.3 Provision management cycle

Key to making provision maps effective are the processes that link the map to tracking information. Tracking, too, can become meaningless paperwork – 'fantastic folders of pupil tracking, kept in the deputy head's office but nothing done about them,' as one school put it. Linking your provision map to electronic data on attainment and wider outcomes means that the map can be regularly adjusted to meet changing needs.

Also key are the systems that are in place to monitor the quality of the provision and to evaluate its effectiveness. The steps involved are shown in Figure 8.3.

Linking provision to performance management is a relatively new area. Although we are used to linking the progress of a class or classes to teachers' performance management, and monitoring the quality of classroom and subject teaching, many schools are only just beginning to identify clearly the outcomes they expect for groups of children taking part in intervention programmes and link these to performance management targets for the adults involved. Usually, this will be a teaching assistant who is delivering the intervention – but it is also important to make similar performance management arrangements for the class teacher or subject teacher managing the provision. This is because with an intervention, it is essential that the class or subject teacher retains overall ownership, with the TA working under his or her direction and very good links made between the work the children do in the intervention programme and the work they do in class. As the 2014 SEN Code of Practice says:

> The class or subject teacher should remain responsible for working with the child on a daily basis. Where the interventions involve group or one-to-one teaching away from the main class or subject teacher, they should still retain responsibility for the pupil. They should work closely with any teaching assistants or specialist staff involved to plan and assess the impact of support and interventions and how they can be linked to classroom teaching.
>
> (DfE and DH, 2014)

It is important, too, that adults delivering intervention programmes are observed from time to time. Such monitoring has several purposes. It enables a SENCO or other manager to check that the intervention is being delivered in the way intended by those who originally constructed and evaluated the programme. We know from research that such 'fidelity to the programme' is both highly important, in terms of programme impact, and relatively rare. Training has an immediate impact on the way we teach, but most of us are programmed to return to our default settings (the way we behaved before we had the training) over time – unless we have top-up training, observation and feedback.

Observation of interventions will also inform the professional development that should underpin any performance management cycle, and enable any practical problems to be spotted and resolved. The TA or teacher may be working in a noisy place, for example, or have children arriving in dribs and drabs to their session, without the materials they need, or opportunities for liaison between the TAs and class teacher may be limited. Picking these practical issues up early will make the adult delivering the programme feel valued and enable them to make the most of the precious time they have with the children with whom they work.

The toolkit section of this book provides an exemplar framework for monitoring the quality of interventions, which allows for professional development needs to be identified and practical problems resolved.

Evaluating impact

Also in the toolkit section are examples of proformas for use when setting up an intervention programme. They support the management cycle of planning, developing, monitoring and evaluating provisions in Figure 8.3: they describe the entry criteria for the intervention, the expected outcome (exit criteria), how and when delivery will be monitored and the evaluation method that will be used. Essentially, they enable SENCOs to manage the school provision for children with additional needs once they have mapped the provision that is needed.

It is always useful to set out the expected impact of the interventions on your provision map so that you can report, at the end of the school year, on whether the expected impact was achieved. Table 8.4 provides an example of how to go about this.

To fully evaluate the impact of provisions, it is necessary to have a way of framing outcomes numerically and in a standard way so that you can calculate an average impact for all the students taking part and compare one intervention with another. One idea is to record the expected impact of an intervention in terms of attainment points score gains or behaviour change (as in Table 8.4), then for each child enter a

Intervention	**Expected impact**	**Actual impact**
Reading Recovery 1:1 help for children in Y1	At least four out of every five children taking part catch up completely in their reading, reaching the levels expected at their age	✓
1stclass@number small group maths help for children in Y2 and Y3	Children taking part make, on average, at least eight months' progress on Sandwell numeracy test after two months' help	✓

Table 8.4 Primary example

Intervention	**Expected impact**	
Nurture group provision in Y7	At least 75% of pupils involved avoid fixed term exclusion during Y7 At least 30% of pupils return to no problem range on SDQ by end Y7 60% achieve nationally expected standard in English and maths	✓ 80% avoided fixed term exclusion 40% returned to no problem range on SDQ 62% achieved nationally expected standard in English and maths
ReadWrite Inc Fresh Start/ Abracadabra/Toe by Toe, etc . . . in Y7 to Y9	e.g. Average reading age gain of at least 12 months after three months	✓

Table 8.4 Secondary example

green judgement (if the child exceeded the expected outcomes), an amber judgement (if the child met the expected outcome) or a red judgement (if the child did not meet the outcome). For any intervention or intervention provider, the percentage of children involved who met or exceeded the expected outcome (amber and green) can then be calculated. The same calculation can be made for pupils eligible for free school meals and receiving the Pupil Premium, for children with different types of SEND, for EAL learners and so on.

Another, simpler method is simply to record for each child a Yes or No according to whether the intervention enabled them to get back to the expected level for their age – in essence, to 'catch up'. Standardised assessments or teacher judgements can be used to decide whether or not a child is now at the expected level in literacy or maths. Tools like the SDQ, used before and after a social and emotional intervention, will show whether a child is no longer scoring at the level of clinical difficulties; some intervention programmes, like Speech and Language UK's 'Talk Boost,' have built-in assessment tools (the Progression Tools) which allow objective judgements to be made about whether a child is now at age-expected levels – in this case, in language.

Abigail Hawkins of SENDCo Solutions has developed an elegant way of quantifying impact, which is used in the Tes Provision Map (previously known as Edukey) provision mapping software. A scoring system is used, called a GAS (Goal Attainment Setting) scale, with these progress measures:

–2 points Significantly less than expected

–1 point Less than expected

0 points As expected

+1 point More than expected

+2 points Significantly more than expected

The system allows SENCOs to determine what constitutes expected and less than expected progress for each intervention. Marie Beale at Whitefield Primary has begun this process, and Table 8.5 provides examples for some of the interventions on the school's provision map. Each intervention has its own carefully chosen evaluation criteria – looking at the extent of any reduction in playground incidents, for example, for SEMH interventions. All this impact data is used to evaluate the effectiveness of different provisions and whether the school should continue to use them or cease.

Table 8.5 Defining progress at Whitefield Primary School

Cognition and learning

Reading Recovery Programme: An intensive Reading Recovery programme to accelerate reading attainment. Pupils will be taught strategies through a daily lesson with a specialist teacher over 12–20 weeks.

–2	Child will not have made much progress through the banding
–1	Child will have moved up one book band over the term
0	Child will have moved up two book bands each term
+1	Child will have moved up two book bands each term and have made at least two steps of progress on Target Tracker (TT)
+2	Child will have moved up two book bands each term and have made more than two steps of progress on TT

Daily handwriting practice with fine motor activities

Targets must be specific – include the specific letters that children are working on.

–2	No progress is seen in child's handwriting
–1	Child is working towards the set target
0	Child has achieved target set at the start of the intervention
+1	Improved handwriting in some pieces of work
+2	Improved handwriting in any writing task

Reading Plus: online programme to develop reading efficiency

–2	No significant progress shown (not accessing for planned mins per week (45/90/145)
–1	Child is working towards the set milestones within the programme
0	Child has achieved target set at the start of the intervention
+1	Child has made two levels progress
+2	Child had made three plus levels progress

Toe-by-toe: A highly structured multi-sensory reading approach

–2	Child's reading age did not increase
–1	Child's reading age increased by 3–5.11 months over a term
0	Child's reading age will increase by six months over a term
+1	Child's reading age will increase by over six months, progress observed in daily reading, and child made two steps of progress on TT
+2	Child made more than two steps of progress on TT

TABLE 8.5 (Continued)

Communication and language

WellComm programme: assessment and focused teaching and intervention activities to meet individual speech and language needs.

−2	Child did not engage in the WellComm sessions, and different intervention should be sought
−1	Child is working towards target age band, score increased
0	Child has increased by one age band
+1	Child has increased by two age bands
+2	Child has increased by two or more age bands

Lego Therapy: social skills programme for children and young people with social communication difficulties

Complete pre-assessment and session assessment form

−2	No progress in social communication is observed within the group or outside the group
−1	Child is making some progress towards a score of 288 and needs to continue with the group
0	Child receives a score of more than 288 on the assessment form (360 possible total) after six weeks
+1	Progress in social communication is observed in class
+2	Significant progress made and intervention no longer required

Social and emotional health

Seedlings/play therapy/seedlings domestic abuse support/bereavement support/drawing and talking/think yourself great

−2	Child did not engage with the sessions and alternative intervention should be sought
−1	Child is working towards objectives
0	Child has met therapeutic objectives
+1	Child has met therapeutic objectives and teachers/parents observe positive outcomes
+2	Child has met therapeutic objectives and no longer requires support

Physical and sensory

Sensory breaks

−2	No significant progress is observed
−1	Child is able to engage in learning for an increase between 25–49% from their baseline
0	Child is able to engage in learning for an increase of 50% from their baseline, for example, at the start of term they could sit and attend to task for five mins, they are now able to sit for (roughly) 7.5 mins
+1	Child is able to engage in learning for an increase of up to 70% from their baseline
+2	Child is able to engage in learning for an increase of more than 71% from their baseline

Management Information Systems (MIS) provide a rich source of data for use in evaluating impacts. The pupil-level data function will hold and import data about each of the school's pupils – name, gender, date of birth, SEND status, Free School Meals status, ethnic origin. It may hold data drops on attainment, based on teacher assessment, using systems like Insight Tracking, or based on tests (PiXL assessments used termly, for example, or GL assessment tools used to 'bookend' attainment at the start and end of the year). It is likely to include attendance data and some form of behaviour data in the form of codes for various disciplinary measures. To the basic information, a school can add further columns, one for each of the provisions on the school's provision map.

You can then use the filtering function to look at only those pupils who have received a particular intervention, such as anger management groups, for example, and pull out their exclusion data, attendance data, destination after completing 16–18 study, end of key stage test results and results of any additional assessments (such as optional tests or reading ages) that have been entered onto the system. You can refine your evaluation by, for example, pulling out only boys who have had a particular provision, or only girls, or only those in a certain year groups, or with a particular type of SEND. You can even, in some systems, look at intervention outcomes by the member of staff delivering the programme.

The sophisticated uses of data that IT now allows provide a powerful tool for evaluating a provision map and promise much for the future in terms of reducing the workload involved in proper evaluation. It is to these that we turn in the next chapter.

KEY PRINCIPLES

Key take-aways for SENCOs

- A provision map is a way of describing the provision that a school makes for children with additional needs, over and above inclusive class or subject teaching, using additional targeted time from teachers, tutors, teaching assistants or volunteers. A provision map is fundamentally a strategic management tool.
- A provision map with plenty of evidence-based, carefully targeted Wave 2 provision is the secret of reducing excessive SENCO workload and cutting bureaucracy
- Provision maps form the basis for a cycle of provision management that involves monitoring quality and evaluating impact

Key questions for the wider school leadership team

- Does your school have a strategically planned provision map for each year group, which brings together different funding streams?
- Is it based on a forecast of projected need in each year group?
- Is the impact of each provision evaluated using quantitative measures?

9 Using technology

This will be a short chapter since most of what SENCOs need to know about using technology needs to be found online, rather than in the pages of a book, but it is nevertheless an all-important one. The use of technology has transformed the SEND landscape, helping us beat bureaucracy by

- enabling children to access the curriculum through assistive technology, so that there is less need for the adaptations to teaching that have historically been recorded in individual education or support plans;
- exploiting the potential of digital learning to provide scaffolding for those who need it, similarly increasing the range of 'normally available' provision;
- enabling SENCOs to communicate easily and effectively with staff and parents;
- enabling SENCOs and other leaders to use time-effective IT systems to plan provision across the school, record uptake and outcomes, evaluate impact and pull off records of provision for individuals when needed.

Let us look at examples of each of these in turn.

Assistive technology

I have long been of the view that one of the very best investments of SEND funding is to appoint or buy time from an IT expert who can identify available assistive technology, advise on matching it to the needs of individuals, coach staff and pupils in its use and troubleshoot the inevitable glitches that still beset all forms of tech.

In the absence of such an expert, the SENCO needs to make 'keeping up with assistive technology' a core part of their CPD, starting with a good awareness of all the free cloud-based tools that are built into everyday software. Whilst many SENCOs are familiar with and use SEN-focused software such as Clicker 8, and teaching programmes like Nessy (for dyslexia), they are often less familiar with accessibility options in Google, Microsoft Office and Immersive Reader, iWork, Adobe Acrobat and so on.

These basic systems now have the facility to enlarge text, change the background colour and check spelling and grammar. All have the facility for print to be read aloud, and using a Bluetooth headset or an earbud in one ear makes text-to-speech possible in a busy classroom if this facility is enabled (for example, on an iPad or Chrome book).

DOI: 10.4324/9781003313526-9

Using speech-to-print options is possible at home but more difficult in class, though directional microphones can help. Combining speech-to-text with text-to speech can transform children's written work if they first 'write' by dictation, then play back what they have written so as to proofread it and see if it makes sense.

Text-to-speech functions allow children with reading difficulties to access texts with readability levels above their reading age – essential for their learning. They can look for the 'BrowseAloud' logo to find websites that have this facility enabled, or download the Read&Write Google Chrome extension to translate all web text into spoken words.

Free browser extensions are another way of increasing access to the curriculum. Google Dictionary allows children to look up the meaning of any word they don't understand, while BeeLine Reader helps them cope with online reading materials that are text-heavy and dense; it automatically adds colour to the digital text, improves readability and keeps students' focus.

Microsoft One Note is a good digital note-taking tool. Students with auditory processing issues or limited fine motor skills, who may not be able to take notes quickly, can ask their teachers for permission to record the lessons and have the recordings sync with their written notes, keeping all their class notes in one place. Children with processing difficulties can also record important assignment instructions and lectures for playback with voice notes using Siri from Apple or Read&Write, a free Google Chrome extension from TextHelp. They might also want to explore note-taking apps like Notability or Evernote, which allow them to take pictures of what is on the board to review and study later, rather than having to copy them down.

When using Adobe Acrobat, students can use its optical character recognition (OCR) to first convert the files into searchable text documents and then use the text-to-speech feature Read Out Loud to have the computer read the documents to them. If they come across any word they don't know, they can highlight it and have the application look up its meaning online.

With so much available as pre-installed or free online applications, an absolutely key role for the school is to teach children how to use all that is available, on all their devices. They need to start this learning in primary school and become fully accustomed to using assistive technology in class and for homework so that by the time they come to take exams, it is established as their normal way of working.

Access to laptops or notebooks is often an issue, of course, although this is another area where what used to be SEND-specific provision for individuals has now become a more universal offer for all pupils. If provision is nevertheless poor, then allowing a pupil to use their own mobile phone offers a solution. If their school has a no-phone rule, the SENCOs might wish to challenge this, citing equalities legislation. For many learners with SEND, the mobile phone is as essential to accessing the curriculum as a lift is to a child who uses a wheelchair.

Universal touch-typing lessons seem to lag behind the provision of 'kit', but some schools build these into the curriculum and are moving away from the 'pen licence' to the more imaginative keyboard certificate.

It is not just children who need to understand the full range of accessibility options available to them on their phones and tablets. Giving class and subject teachers simple tips can make all the difference. Do they know, for example, how to boost accessibility in Google Slides by switching on automatic captioning, which displays the speaker's words alongside each slide? After entering presentation mode, they can hover their cursor in the bottom left corner of the screen to bring up the menu, click the three dots, then select Captions preferences and Toggle captions (English only). Google will listen as they present and transcribe their words as they speak. As another example, do they know how to magnify caption size in YouTube? After selecting closed captions, they can simply press the + (plus) key on the keyboard to increase the text size.

Taking it further

Over and above the ever-increasing range of free tech tools, SENCOs will also want to allocate a good part of the SEND budget to buy into more specialist accessibility options – like those from Texthelp, for example, which enable children to open a pdf or web page, hover over a word and get a picture reference or change the font.

Reading/scanning pens are an essential. One SENCO reported how using a reading pen in exams (with the dictionary switched off, as required) saved her school 300 hours of adult time previously spent reading questions to students. Mind-mapping software like iMindMap, Lucidchart, Kidspiration and Mindmeister is also often very useful for students with SEND.

There are many apps available that help children with organisational difficulties – allowing them to manage to-do lists, generate reminders, set goals and organise information. EpicWin, for example, is a tool that helps students stay on task and avoid procrastinating, using gamified role-playing to incentivise task completion. RescueTime is an interesting app focused on time management. It provides visuals to help students analyse how they are using their time and identify wasted time, whilst also showing personal peak times that might be best spent studying.

Audiobooks are useful for dyslexic children and those with visual impairments. The RNIB, the Calibre charity, Learning Ally, OverDrive Education, and Bookshare offer a wide range, but many children prefer to use e-books. The Amazon Kindle app allows them to read Kindle books on their computer, tablet or mobile phone. They can simply upload an e-book on a Kindle app and ask Amazon's Alexa to 'read my latest Kindle book.' The app includes customisation features for improved accessibility and a text-to-speech function. Moon+ Reader is a free e-book reading app which also has many features to customise the viewing experience (including a dictionary add-in) and can handle many e-book formats, including pdf files. Blio is a free-to-download e-reader software platform that preserves typography and is particularly useful for illustrated books.

Finally, there is an ever-growing list of apps to help children with SEMH regulate their emotions – apps like Headspace, Smiling Mind and Stop, Breathe and Think, for example, or, for younger children, Sesame Street's Breathe, Think, Do, which teaches children to keep calm and carry on by introducing three possible strategies for working through problems.

The 'Touch and Learn – Emotions' app is helpful for helping children read body language and develop their vocabulary by looking at photos and matching them with emotion words. A similar app is Avokiddo Emotions, which allows primary children to explore a wide range of feelings through amusing characters and props. Emotionary+ by Funny Feelings is an emotion picture dictionary that guides users through five primary emotions to find the right category of feeling, with all definitions pared back to the essentials and displayed so they can be easily compared. This collection of emotions and funny feelings allows users to draw their own emotionary 'selfie' to show how they are feeling, and has become a popular resource for SEND.

Positive Penguins use CBT principles to challenge negative thinking, and Sōsh Lite is a fun interactive coaching app that helps students (particularly those with autism) to develop social skills and cope with stress or anxiety. Students can browse the emotions gallery, set priorities, shred their emotions in the shredder or pump up the balloon to express their stress level.

Several popular apps, like 'IF . . . The Emotional IQ Game' use a gaming format. With this app, children (recommended ages nine to 11) learn to listen, make friends, and deal with bullying in an adventure story/game format. They navigate adventures and challenges in an imaginary town, while developing their ability to manage emotions like frustration and disappointment, show empathy for others, persist through failure, collaborate, and make good decisions. At intervals, characters encourage the child to stop playing and try out the strategies they've been modelling – such as breathing exercises to calm down, or win-win strategies to resolve conflicts. The game provides a way for parents to be involved too, through a personalized IF . . . app which shows them what and how their children are learning and suggests ways they can provide back-up reinforcement.

Digital learning

The rapid increase in the use of digital learning brought about by the COVID lockdowns has demonstrated the benefits for struggling learners – if they have access to technology at home and in the classroom.

Virtual learning platforms like Google Classroom allow those with organisational difficulties to have lesson agendas, scheduled sessions, work submissions, and resources in one virtual space, with the option of asking the teacher specific questions. Used in an actual physical classroom, pupils can pull up the lesson with embedded links to give just-in-time support.

They might, for example, link to a glossary of key vocabulary, a video demonstration of how to go about a task or to an audio recording of a teacher's explanation of a concept.

Teachers are increasingly developing instructional video libraries – recordings of themselves explaining key concepts and steps for completing complex tasks. Struggling learners tend not to learn concepts the first time they are introduced; 'watch-again' recordings give them a safe space in which to review content at home. In the physical classroom, they can refer to the recordings when they are struggling with a concept or task.

Making videos is now very easy – as easy as pressing the 'Record' button when speaking to a PowerPoint presentation, or when starting a screen-sharing session via Zoom, Google Meet or Microsoft Teams. Home-made videos can be organised into digital playlists based on a unit of work or a topic, alongside student-created videos and relevant videos from YouTube and elsewhere.

Another use of digital tools that is particularly powerful for students with SEND is to record what they have learned – and even better, to produce learning materials for others. A recent meta-analysis (Ribosa and Duran, 2022) concluded that students who used widely available digital tools like Instagram, TikTok and Google Slides to create explanatory videos, animations and games learned significantly more than students who created text-based materials. Unfortunately, the researchers also concluded that creative use of digital tools was 'one of the least frequent uses of media in education.'

Using IT systems to communicate with staff and parents

SENCOs have become skilled in using basic IT and their schools' general MIS systems to communicate quickly and easily. One SENCO puts every child's reading age on the Satchel One software that her school uses, which allows teachers to quickly view their students and class groups and select from a choice of function they need to support their learning. As we saw in Chapter 1, at Castle Academy, which uses the G04Schools MIS, codes for children on the SEND register appear on seating plans and class lists, enabling staff to go to a desktop SEND folder to find out more. Care plans for medical needs are in the same folder, as well as a separate medical folder, thus reducing the number of staff click needs. SENCO Jen Beaton also finds Microsoft's 'Forms' function helpful in gathering information from staff, about a particular pupil or issue, via a quick 'quiz', replacing laborious paper forms.

CASE STUDY

Assistant SENCO Thomas Tillier at Aylesford School in Warwick makes good use of the Synergy communication and information sharing software used by the school. Teachers use the software to take the register, record information about behaviour and set homework. If a pupil has SEND this shows up on their register; one click will take them to that pupil's Individual Pupil Portrait (IPP). These IPPs are developed by support staff with pupils, with the following headings:

- All about me (where the child might be asked 'What are four things about you I'd not be able to guess?')
- What I enjoy
- What I find tricky
- It helps me if . . .

Thomas also adds to Synergy specific 'quick wins' related to the pupil – tips like 'Get them to give out the books', or 'This student – meet and greet'. Sometimes he will add essential safeguarding information like 'Do not give this one sharp scissors or a compass'.

TAs record the progress of pupils they support as 'Track Points' on a spreadsheet Thomas has created: they note whether the pupil is working below/towards/at/exceeding age-related expectations, and whether their attitude to learning is excellent, good, requires improvement or is a cause for concern. The spreadsheet also records the time per fortnight of TA support, whether the child has a TA mentor they meet weekly (those with EHCPs or likely to need an EHCP), whether they have a sixth-form mentor (those with lesser needs), any extra teaching support they receive, lunchtime clubs attended, whether they have specialist teacher support and which, if any, external agencies are involved.

Thomas makes good use of the school's website to communicate with parents, through a dedicated SEND page. He emails parents of children coming to the school with a 'Hello . . . we're from Aylesford and we're here to help' message to introduce the team and let families know how to keep in touch.

Using IT systems to plan, record and evaluate provision across the school

A number of companies provide provision mapping software that has proved a huge timesaver for SENCOs. Examples are SENDit, Arbor, SIMS Provision Map writer and Tes Provision Map (formerly Edukey). The software generally allows a school to record all the provisions it makes along with the pupils and staff involved, the costs and impact/outcomes. Figure 9.1 shows an example of the type of impact data that can be provided.

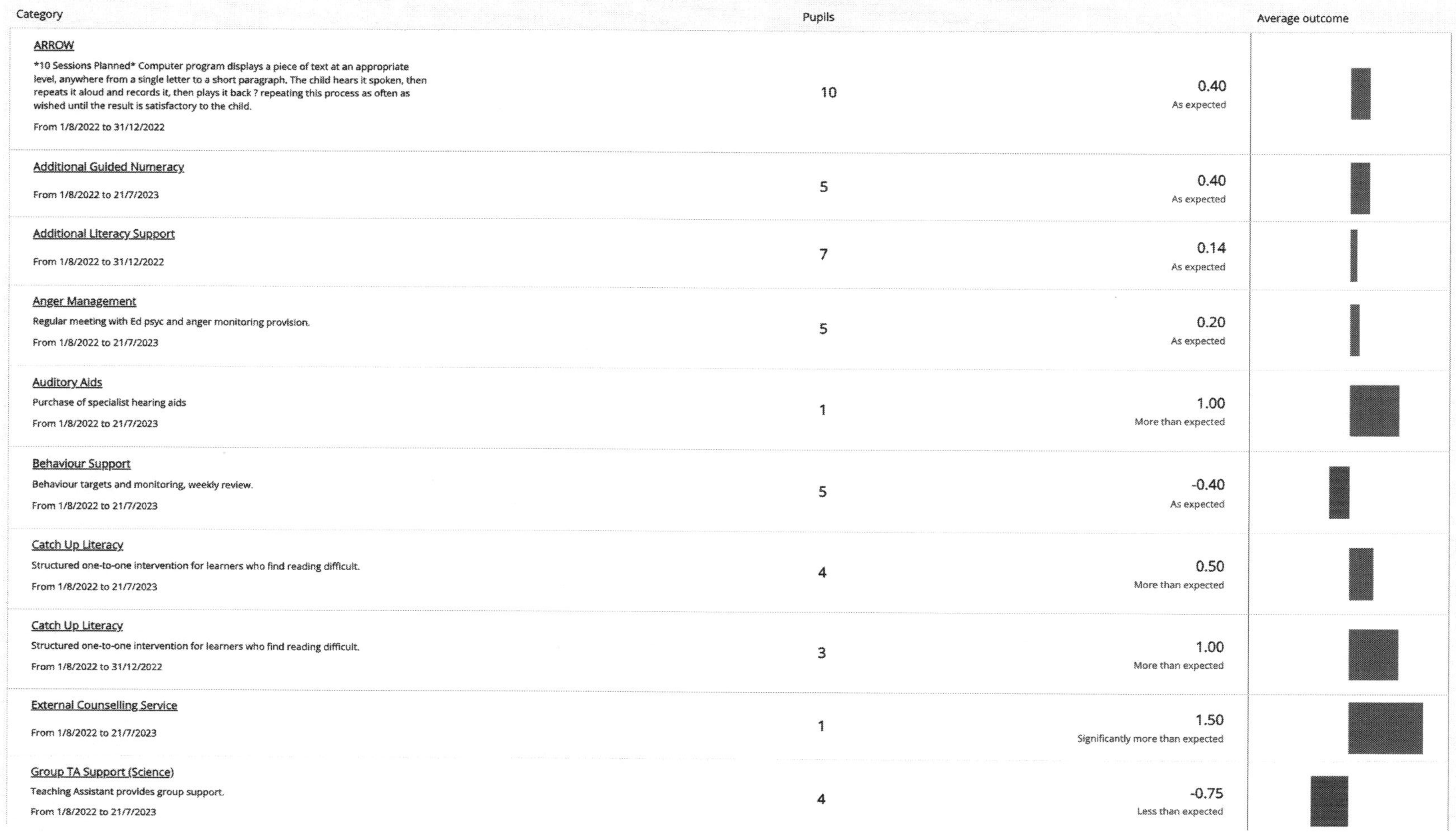

Category	Pupils	Average outcome
<u>ARROW</u> *10 Sessions Planned* Computer program displays a piece of text at an appropriate level, anywhere from a single letter to a short paragraph. The child hears it spoken, then repeats it aloud and records it, then plays it back ? repeating this process as often as wished until the result is satisfactory to the child. From 1/8/2022 to 31/12/2022	10	0.40 As expected
<u>Additional Guided Numeracy</u> From 1/8/2022 to 21/7/2023	5	0.40 As expected
<u>Additional Literacy Support</u> From 1/8/2022 to 31/12/2022	7	0.14 As expected
<u>Anger Management</u> Regular meeting with Ed psyc and anger monitoring provision. From 1/8/2022 to 21/7/2023	5	0.20 As expected
<u>Auditory Aids</u> Purchase of specialist hearing aids From 1/8/2022 to 21/7/2023	1	1.00 More than expected
<u>Behaviour Support</u> Behaviour targets and monitoring, weekly review. From 1/8/2022 to 21/7/2023	5	-0.40 As expected
<u>Catch Up Literacy</u> Structured one-to-one intervention for learners who find reading difficult. From 1/8/2022 to 21/7/2023	4	0.50 More than expected
<u>Catch Up Literacy</u> Structured one-to-one intervention for learners who find reading difficult. From 1/8/2022 to 31/12/2022	3	1.00 More than expected
<u>External Counselling Service</u> From 1/8/2022 to 21/7/2023	1	1.50 Significantly more than expected
<u>Group TA Support (Science)</u> Teaching Assistant provides group support. From 1/8/2022 to 21/7/2023	4	-0.75 Less than expected

FIGURE 9.1 Example of impact data generated by provision mapping software

Source: Reproduced by kind permission of Abigail Hawkins and Tes Provision Map

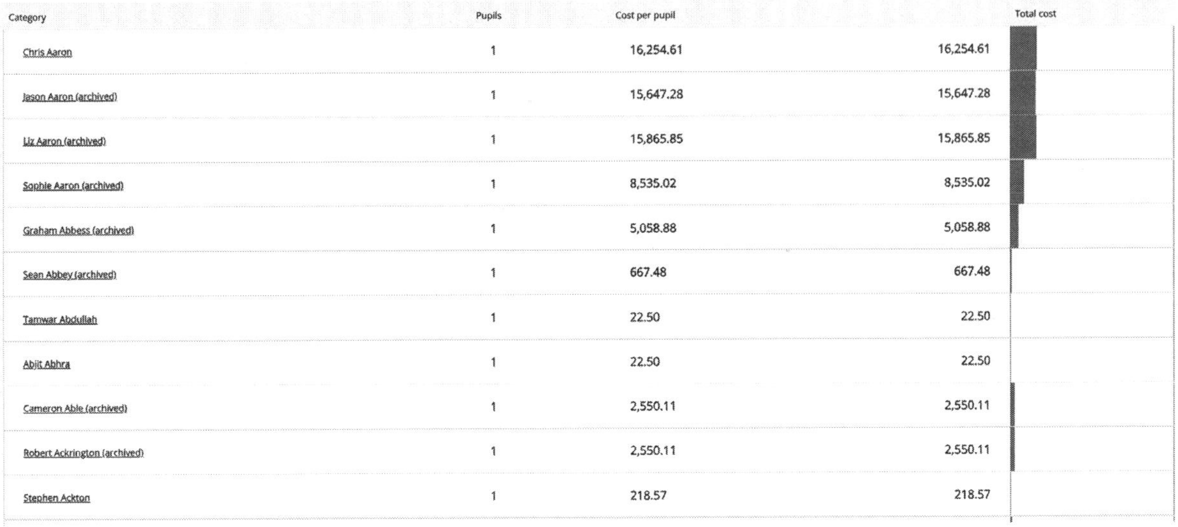

Category	Pupils	Cost per pupil	Total cost
Chris Aaron	1	16,254.61	16,254.61
Jason Aaron (archived)	1	15,647.28	15,647.28
Liz Aaron (archived)	1	15,865.85	15,865.85
Sophie Aaron (archived)	1	8,535.02	8,535.02
Graham Abbess (archived)	1	5,058.88	5,058.88
Sean Abbey (archived)	1	667.48	667.48
Tamwar Abdullah	1	22.50	22.50
Abjit Abhra	1	22.50	22.50
Cameron Able (archived)	1	2,550.11	2,550.11
Robert Ackrington (archived)	1	2,550.11	2,550.11
Stephen Ackton	1	218.57	218.57

Figure 9.2 Costed provision

Source: Reproduced by kind permission of Abigail Hawkins and Tes Provision Map

These IT systems also act as a repository for data on all pupils with additional needs, can hold individual profiles or plans where these are used and allows for information to be shared with parents. Reports on provision made for individual pupils can be pulled off where necessary to make the case for higher-needs funding or an EHCP assessment (Figure 9.2).

CASE STUDY

Henley Bank secondary school uses the Tes Provision Map tool to streamline all records relating to SEND. The system allows for Pupil Passports to be co-produced, with a facility for a school to create its own Passport tiles to customise the format. Parents of children with SEND receive an email with their own log in details so that they can access their child's Passport and dedicated progress page.

Elements of the Passport go onto a Learning Plan, which is more detailed than the Passport and has Area of Need, Target, Desired Outcomes, Strategies and provisions (all Tes Provision Map headings). This level of individual plans is necessary because the local authority insists on all schools using a 'My Plan' or 'My Plan Plus'; Rhian is able to use her Tes Provision Map Learning Plan to fulfil this requirement. When she is applying for an EHCP, Tes Provision Map can create a report showing all the provision the child has received, and the cost.

As we saw in Chapter 7, creating Learning Plans does not feel onerous because responsibility for writing them is distributed.

Plans are reviewed termly, with the responsible member of staff recording whether goals were met. This enables Rhian to use Tes Provision Map to look at the impact of each of the provisions the school makes, from literacy interventions to weekly vocabulary sessions to in-class support, and from speech and language therapy to the 'Positive start in the morning' provision for autistic pupils which we met in Chapter 8.

Tes Provision Map 'talks to' SIMS, Arbor and other school management information systems. This means that pupil data (for example about attendance, Free School Meals and Pupil Premium eligibility) can be quickly imported and routinely updated. It also means that subject teachers at Rhian's school can go from SIMS to the Provision Map home page, enter a year group, then 'pupils I teach', filtered by class and by SEN status. This will take them straight to the Pupil Passports for a particular class.

CASE STUDY

SENCO Margaret Relf at Anglesey Primary has found Tes Provision Map flexible in enabling her to adapt formats to her own needs, and useful in helping her plan, monitor and evaluate the whole range of provision at her school. She uses the 'Waves' model of provision – Wave 1 (for all children), Wave 2 (for some children) and Wave 3 (for a few children). Whilst only those at Wave 3 are on her SEND register, Tes Provision Map allows her to record Wave 2 provision as well – at Anglesey, examples being Lexia literacy groups with a TA, groups with similar needs identified through Speech and Language Link screening and Colourful Semantics groups.

For each named provision, Margaret records the area of concern it meets, the Wave, the start and end date, the session frequency and the session length.

As at Whitefield Primary, whose work on evaluating the impact of provision was described in the last chapter, Anglesey is working on having staff quantify pupil progress over the course of an intervention, using a points system from –2 to +2. For a specific provision like Lexia reading, for example, a 0 would be allocated if a child made two months progress in two months of weekly 40-minute sessions, a +1 if a child made three or four months progress, a

+2 if they made five or more months' progress, a –1 if one month's progress and a –2 if no progress or regression. Tes Provision Map allows Margaret to cost the provision (£74 per pupil in this case), record each child's progress and calculate an average outcome – for example, +1.5. Anglesey's MAT uses standardised tests for reading, English and maths at the start and end of the year for all pupils. Margaret was able to add bespoke sections to Tes Provision Map for scores on each of these.

Another time-saver has been the facility to download Excel files from Tes Provision Map and remove any columns that are not needed. Margaret used this to good effect when setting up whole-school systems for using Speech and Language Link screening software.

At the individual child level, Margaret is able at the press of a button to pull out a complete record for any child. It will contain the usual data about ethnicity, first language, attendance, free school meals status, any medical needs, whether the child is looked after and so on, along with the main SEND area of need. Next come results of standardised texts, then the strategies that are being used in everyday high-quality teaching. Margaret has categorised these under the EEF's 'five-a-day' headings (see Table 9.1 for an example from one child's record). After this come current specific targets, success criteria and strategies or provisions to meet them and a record of discussions with parents/carers. A complete list of all provision the child has received over time can also be easily pulled off, along with a time allocation of current additional provision, which enables her to spot children who may be in 'intervention overload.'

All tech-based SEND systems are, of course, only as good as the staff who input to them. This takes training. Margaret has provided eight CPD sessions for staff on how to develop Personal Learning Plans, record them on Tes Provision Map and share them with parents and review them termly. She has also needed to provide coaching; senior leaders cover staff so that she can work with them individually on the 'I will do one'/'Now you do one' principle.

Strategies – what works and what is going to be put in place   Personal Learning Plan for . . . .

High-quality teaching

EEF 'Five-a-day' strand

Flexible groupings	Cognitive and metacognitive strategies	Explicit instruction	Use of technology	Scaffolding
Purposeful seating arrangements	Tasks link back to earlier (or later) objectives where these are appropriate for the child or group Tasks simplified or extended, for example, short concrete text used by one group or long, abstract text by another, numbers to 100 for one group or to 20 for another Interactive strategies used, for example, children having cards to hold up or own whiteboards or coming to the front to take a role	All children clear about structure of lesson and day, for example, visual timetables	Flash Academy – 15 minutes daily	Children taught strategies which mean they can continue to work without direct teacher help if they are stuck; prompts to remind them are on display Colourful Semantics to support SVO Word mats Sound Mats

Table 9.1 Example of a personal learning plan with strategies categorised under the EEF's 'five-a-day' headings

KEY PRINCIPLES

Key take-aways for SENCOs

- Assistive technology and digital learning tools have the potential to transform learning for pupils with SEND, and are another key way of increasing 'normally available' provision to reduce the need for individual plans
- In many schools, technology has reduced the amount of time SENCOs spend on administrative tasks, by streamlining and analysing pupil records and allowing easy communication with parents and staff

Key questions for the wider school leadership team

- Is there, or could there be, a member of staff in your school who keeps abreast of developments in assistive technology and supports staff and pupils in its use?
- Is your SENCO able to use time-saving software that reduces time spent on SEND administration?

10 Working in partnership

Parents, pupils and outside agencies

Working with parents and carers

Working with parents/carers and pupils themselves is the key to effective provision, and one of the core principles of all recent SEND reforms. Working effectively with parents/carers is also the secret of reducing bureaucracy. If parents are confident about what is being done to support their child, they do not need pieces of paper. They can be your greatest ally in reducing bureaucracy, or – if you get the relationship with them wrong – they can undo all your efforts. Not least, they can exercise their legal right to request a statutory assessment for a possible EHCP that will generate a blizzard of paperwork for you and the local authority.

So it is essential that in making any changes to the way you manage SEND in school, you do this with the full support of parents and carers.

Systems for involving parents/carers

Ideally you will begin by finding out, perhaps through a questionnaire or focus group discussion, how parents/carers feel about your current procedures. They may be happy – but they may not. Parental involvement remains a real challenge for many schools.

> While some parents and carers spoke about participating in decision-making for their child's special educational provision, others felt that they were not given sufficient information about their child's learning and development. Some were not given opportunities to input into support plans by, for example, expressing opinions on targets or provision plans.
>
> Ofsted, *Supporting SEND*, 2021

DOI: 10.4324/9781003313526-10

A study by Lindsay *et al.* (2010), in which parents of children with SEND were interviewed, sums up elegantly what it is that parents really want:

> What gave parents confidence that their child's school could meet their child's needs was very simple: that teachers and/or senior leaders, preferably both, were willing to meet with them and to hear their story and their views about their child; that teachers listened and took seriously what they communicated about their child; that often relatively simple adaptations were made to accommodate their child's learning needs (e.g. alternative ways of recording what they knew); that their child's strengths were recognised and communicated to child, peers and parents; and that the social and emotional impacts of learning difficulties were recognised and addressed.

If your own research shows that parents and carers have concerns about current systems, you will find it easy to explain why you are making changes, such as having individual plans only for children with more complex needs. You might want to invite parents to a meeting to explain any changes; you will certainly want to provide all of them with information in leaflet form. The toolkit section of this book provides a possible model for you to build on.

You will want to make clear the legislative basis for and the advantages of any approach you adopt – for example, the expectation that class or subject teachers build a knowledge of the child's individual needs into their everyday planning. Parents/carers will also be very interested to see the school's provision map, with entry and exit criteria for each additional intervention, so that they know what provision they can expect for their child.

It will be helpful for you to explain your plans for

- involving them, as the experts on their own child, in providing information and feedback to the school;
- making sure all relevant staff are aware of their child's needs;
- setting targets;
- reviewing and reporting on progress;
- making additional provision for the child;
- providing ideas on how they can help their child at home.

In other chapters we have seen how these areas can be addressed in non-bureaucratic ways. Parents can be given a highlighted provision map so that they know exactly what provision their child receives. They should be seen as an invaluable source of information about their child and contribute to pupil-held personal profiles. They should be able to comment on provision, targets and individual plans where pupils have them.

They should also know where their child is in their learning and well-being and what support they can provide at home.

CASE STUDY

At Henley Bank secondary (something of a 'magnet' school of choice for parents of children with SEND), the approach taken by SENCO Rhian Williams at is about making sure parents have easy access to information. Access to their child's pages on Tes Provision Map has proved helpful, and Pupil Passports co-produced with students are sent to parents by email with an invitation to come into school to discuss them if they would like to.

Rhian has organized a half-termly parent workshop programme, with the aim of reaching out to as many families as possible. After COVID lockdowns, she responded to parents' concerns with a workshop on 'Supporting your anxious child'. Parents could join the workshop in person or remotely. 'The gratitude from those attending and enquiries about future sessions made the effort worthwhile', Rhian says, 'and I have since repeated the same workshop in a hybrid format – delivering it live in-school as well as filming it for those who wanted to watch from home.'

Rhian has also set up a 'Behind the mask' forum on understanding autism. The forum recognised that parents are often the real experts here, so they were encouraged to share what they found helpful at home, while staff shared what they do in school to support pupils. The next forum will focus on dyslexia.

But what about face-to-face planning and review meetings? The Code of Practice sets the expectation that where a pupil is receiving SEN support, schools should 'talk to parents regularly to set clear outcomes and review progress towards them, discuss the activities and support that will help achieve them, and identify the responsibilities of the parent, the pupil and the school.' It is expected that these meetings will take place at least three times a year and usually be led by the class teacher or form tutor, supported by the SENCO.

To make this manageable, it is, as we have seen, wise to keep numbers low by ensuring that the SEN label is used appropriately rather than as a catch-all for poor progress, and to build the meetings with parents into regular parents' evenings – with more time allocated to the meeting than might be standard for other pupils. Alternatively, the meetings might take place at special academic tutoring days, where parents, pupil and form tutor meet together on an appointment basis, joined where necessary by specialist colleagues.

Expert SEN leader Gary Aubin (Aubin, 2020) also suggests

- having an 'open-door' policy, making clear to parents they can come in when they need to, and counting these less formal (but often highly productive) meetings as one of the three per year;
- providing a weekly 20-minute appointment slot bookable through the school office;
- building coffee mornings or information events for parents into your calendar;
- piggybacking on other appointments that parents are having with teachers – with a Head of Year or behaviour lead to review a Pastoral Support Plan or on return from a suspension, for example, or to receive a Headteacher's award.

Some schools hold a whole day of SEND reviews. Gary suggests perhaps having these twice a year, with parents' evenings making up the contact in the middle and making the case to senior leaders for administrative support, using the magic words 'statutory duty'. He advises distributing responsibility where possible, to the SENCO's line manager or TA key workers. Meetings for those on SEN support, he writes, should be short and tightly focused on reviewing the child's pupil profile/one-page summary of need. I would add to this that the 20-minute slots he suggests can work if in between the formal meetings parents have had good access to information (for example, through logins to documents held online), and plenty of informal contact with the SEND team on the telephone, over coffee and at drop-ins. Many parents of children with SEND need 'a good listening-to', a chance to offload and find ways to cope and to be connected to sources of support like debt or housing advice, Early Help, domestic violence services, online groups for parents of children with particular types of SEND and so on. It works best to separate discussions about these wider needs from a brisk business meeting focused on the child's needs – which, to my mind, should almost always involve the child or young person themselves.

How we talk and listen to parents is, to me, more important than how often we meet with them. Too many conversations begin (and go on) with teachers and leaders giving information rather than listening. Sadly, too many parents would agree with the mother who told me 'Whenever I go to school, they want to TELL me stuff. They never ask me what I think. They never ask me anything.'

Meetings with parents (conversations in which both partners are often anxious) need not be like this, if we think about seating (always at an angle, never opposite the teacher) and use starters that open up dialogue, like the ones in Table 10.1.

• Has there been anything he's specially enjoyed at school lately?
• How is he feeling about school and her work this term?
• Tell me what he is interested in and likes doing outside school
• What have you noticed is working for him in what we are doing at school?
• Are there things we could be doing differently at school, so he could get on better, do you think?
• Maybe a good target to work at would be for him to. . . . What do you think?
• Maybe a good target for his teachers in school would be. . . . What do you think?
• We're having some trouble getting him interested in reading, and I'm wondering if you could help us? I know you feel you don't know much about how we teach reading, but you do know your boy a lot better than we do!
• From what you say, it sounds as though things are really tough for you just now . . . but you're still managing to cope. Is there something we could be doing in school to help?

Table 10.1 Examples of positive ways of opening up dialogue

Helping parents/carers to help their child – whole-school approaches

As we have seen, the biggest gap in our current SEN procedures is often their failure to support parents/carers in knowing how best to help their child in the areas where they are experiencing difficulty. Equally, we know how fundamental it is for the child's progress that there is home support for learning. Influential research (Desforges and Abouchaar, 2003) has shown that where parents/carers are involved, on average, children's attainment will be 15–17% higher than where they are not involved. John Hattie (2008) estimates that the effect of parental engagement is equivalent to two to three additional years of learning over a pupil's school career.

The type of involvement that brings these gains is not about 'coming into school' – attending school events, turning up at parents' evenings, helping in class and so on. What makes the difference instead is what Desforges calls good at-home parenting. This means the provision of 'a secure and stable environment, intellectual stimulation, parent-child discussion, good models of constructive social and educational values and high aspirations relating to personal fulfilment and good citizenship.' A key element of this is the quality of the early years 'home learning environment' (Sylva *et al.*, 2003): the extent to which parents/carers talk to and play with their child, take them on outings, read to them, teach nursery rhymes and songs, play with numbers and letters and so on. And this is not dependent on the social class or educational level of parents and carers; as Sylva says, 'What you do is more important than who you are.'

How can we help all families provide this sort of good at-home parenting? It is clear that the SENCO cannot achieve this by working on their own. Involving parents/carers of children with SEND, or of EAL learners or other vulnerable groups, needs to build on an existing ethos which conveys to parents/carers that they are valued partners rather than potential troublemakers.

An ethos like this is often tangibly conveyed in some schools, while absent in others. It starts with asking families what their needs are and how the school can help. One school asked this question and introduced drop-in sessions with the school nurse, 'sums for Mums' sessions, workshops on phonics and Family Days Out at weekends. Other schools have provided workshops on how to write a good personal statement/ job application, sessions with a speaker on how to cope with children's sleep problems or tantrums or on how to keep children safe online. It need not be hard to build in 'educational' messages to these sessions, such as the importance of bedtime stories in a workshop on sleep.

EXAMPLE

Netherfield Primary in Nottinghamshire offered the 'Switch On' reading programme to parents who have literacy problems, as well as to children. A father of a Year 5 boy went to see the headteacher to explain that he had two older boys in prison and didn't want the youngest to go the same way. 'Teach me to read', he said. The school did, and the boy came into school one day and said 'My Dad can read now. He read me a bedtime story.'

Netherfield also worked with a local college to bring basic skills and employability courses to the school site and found a local charity willing to use a room in the school for confidential support with domestic violence.

EXAMPLE

Abigail Hawkins, secondary teacher and blogger, was used to sending invitations to parents' evenings and finding no one turned up. But one year, when she found herself with a few free periods in a row, she decided to start a regular two-hour coffee morning for parents, with bacon butties provided. For one session she invited a local company to come and talk about disability benefits; another was about how to set up an e-mail account. The first week, 16 parents representing 11 students turned up; numbers rose, and at one point, 25 students had a parent come in. Parents began to support each other, filling in forms, going with each other to hospital appointments, helping with childcare. They also became much more willing to attend regular parents' evenings once relationships had been built and barriers broken down.

Adapted from Matt Pinkett and Mark Roberts' book *Boys Don't Try?*, 2019

If asking parents how the school can best inform and help them is the foundation of partnership, a parent-friendly ethos can also be conveyed in more subtle ways. An example is the implicit messages given by the school entrance hall, where local radio might be playing (rather than Mozart), where the reading matter on the table in the comfortable waiting area might include *Hello!* magazine as well as the school prospectus. There might be information in community languages and posters inviting parents to join in a range of activities, some of which are deliberately unthreatening to a parent whose own experience of learning may hitherto have been negative – everything from nail art, stress workshops, massage, art and craft and using technology as well as Dads and Lads, Saturday sport and Maths4mums, through to the more 'academic' curriculum workshops.

A backdrop of non-threatening activities is particularly important where children have social, emotional and behavioural difficulties. Research shows that support for parents in developing their parenting skills can have a huge impact on their child's behaviour (Furlong *et al.*, 2012). But the parenting programmes that work, such as those listed in Chapter 8, can easily feel stigmatising and uncomfortable for parents/carers. Very few schools succeed by simply inviting targeted parents to attend a parenting course. There is a potential stigma about such courses, and a feeling amongst most parents that they should somehow automatically know how to bring up a child, that acts as a powerful deterrent. Schools have to work hard to overcome these barriers. Where they are successful, it is usually because they have built up 'parental capital' by offering parents a range of more appealing activities. These help create the climate in which parenting skills courses can be offered as a natural progression for parents/carers who are already confident in coming into school.

In schools with a parent-friendly ethos, care will be taken that parents' and carers' first communications with school are not about any difficulties their child may have. A relationship will have been built up long before this, one that focuses on sharing information about the child as a person and a learner (not a 'special needs child'), and that celebrates strengths and successes, for example, by sending home 'praise postcards' to let parents know when things have gone well, or a short text message at the end of the week.

> Be careful not to define the child by their SEND. For a parent, their child's SEND may be something they disagree with, or deny, or are fearful of, or saddened by; it will certainly only be a description of one aspect of them, rather than the thing that defines them. Show that you know there is much more to their child than a particular area of deficit.
>
> Gary Aubin, 2020

Special efforts may need to be made to reach out to fathers. Fathers' involvement in their child's learning is strongly related to educational attainment and adjustment, particularly for boys and disadvantaged pupils (Flouri and Buchanan, 2002; Blanden, 2006). In the teenage years, one study showed that 90% of boys who felt that their father spent time with them and took an active interest in their progress were confident and successful. By contrast, 72% of those who said their fathers rarely or never did these things fell into the group with the lowest levels of self-confidence and were more likely to dislike school and get in trouble with the police.

CASE STUDY

Cooper's Lane Primary School in Lewisham devised a 'Dads Matter' scheme. A group of fathers and male family figures met once a month in a local pub or restaurant to plan a strategy to encourage fathers to become more involved with their children's learning. Support was particularly targeted at families of children with behaviour difficulties because of the lack of positive male role models many of them had experienced. The group planned trips, home reading activities, fun homework tasks and a 'Bring your dad to school day', when dads would come in and use their talents and interests to work with children. One father, for example, brought in his motorbike to show to the boys. About 60 fathers took part in the scheme, which had a marked impact. Fathers became much more confident to come into the playground and into school, and there has been a reduction in behaviour problems among the target children.

Overcoming barriers

Many parents experience particular barriers to involvement in what the school has to offer. Their own experience of education may make them anxious or angry when coming into school or talking to teachers. They may themselves have low literacy or numeracy levels that make it difficult for them to help their child. Their feelings about their child's difficulties are often those that cause awkwardness in their relationship with the school. They may simply get tired of hearing yet another teacher tell them their child has problems.

But as Klein (2000) puts it, 'Parents don't exist solely as the receptacles of bad news about their children's problem behaviour or poor attainment.' The best SENCOs understand this and go out of their way to overcome barriers and provide extra nurturing for parents as well as pupils – as at Broken Cross, Whitefield and Porters Grange primary schools.

CASE STUDY

Parents of children at Broken Cross primary in Macclesfield tend to be anxious about education and afraid of being judged. Staff have worked successfully to build trust and break down barriers, often by providing practical support for families. 'If they need an emergency dental appointment, we'll book it', says headteacher Donna Lewis. 'Once you can win over those first few families and they trust you, then the message gets out.' Staff are always willing to go the extra mile for children, for example, taking children to speech and language therapy appointments if parents have not managed to get them there.

Support for families starts early. The local Children's Centre closed and the nearest is now a 40-minute walk away, so the school has tried to replicate some of the former provision – training staff in the Triple P parenting programme, for example. The school's nursery is open from 7:30 in the morning till six in the evening and takes children from the age of two. Donna and her husband also run a 7:30 a.m. school breakfast club daily.

The school puts a lot of effort into how it communicates with families. Staff take care to 'speak the language of our parents'; an example is 'book and butty time' when parents get a bacon butty in the school hall when they come in to share a book with their child.

There are clear messages about home learning expectations, which aim to reduce anxiety: 'It is our job to do the teaching; you don't need to worry about that. What you can do is give your child a love of learning.' One successful strategy has been providing parents with 'one-minute guides' on topics such as 'How to talk to your child about a book.'

CASE STUDY

Whitefield Primary keeps parents/carers well informed about groups and activities running in school through social media and frequent face-to-face contact. The school uses the Seesaw Learning Journal for home-school communication, so parents can see what their child is learning and share information from home. Staff are asked to post something interesting about class-based learning every day; through this daily drip-feed, parents get used to looking at the app, just as they would look at Facebook. Seesaw is well used because, SENCO Marie Beale says, 'all parents want to see pictures of their child'. Both Seesaw and the school's website have a language function to ensure parents/carers who speak English as an additional language have equal access to information.

Relationships with parents are warm and enduring, with trauma-informed principles applied to parents as well as children. Marie says, of children with trauma, 'Parents are those children grown up.' There is a lot of listening and empathy: 'We use listening and asking how *they* are. . . . I can see you're feeling. . . . What can we do to help? We're here to work together on this. . . .' Paper communications are avoided. The school helps parents set up an email address if they don't have one, so they can email as well as telephone or text if they need to. Marie notes that 'for some who find face-to-face contact hard, the ability to message the SENCO helps.'

There are regular coffee mornings for families, for example, one with a Local Housing Association and a mental health first aid day, with some curriculum mornings in the pipeline. The inclusion team will make personal phone calls to parents to invite them. The school focuses on the really important things parents can do to support their child's learning, like how to scaffold their child's independent use of technology ready for transition to secondary school.

Now the school is working on a project funded by the SHINE charity, to help parents understand how the school helps children manage their emotions and how they can apply these ideas at home. Parents are learning about the Zones of Regulation approach and taking part in practical activities with their child, like creating a calm-down kit.

CASE STUDY

At Porters Grange Primary in Southend, staff understand that parents experience many difficulties in their lives and have often not had the best experience of school themselves.

SENCO Toni Quinn makes sure parents know that 'the kettle's always on'; there is an open-door policy and parents can always ask 'Has anyone time for a chat?' 'If they want to chat', says Toni, 'we try to get someone to them there and then.' There is constant dialogue with parents; Toni and other inclusion leaders are out on the playground every morning and at pick-up time, having what Toni calls 'pleasant day-to-day conversations that are really important in building trust.'

Parents are on first-name terms with the team. Communication tends to be by phone calls or texting rather than letters or emails. Face-to-face, staff talk with parents in sensitive ways. An example is when they are completing a local authority Early Help assessment. The assessments have many difficult questions, but staff get them done by saying 'You only have to tell us what you want to tell us. We don't want to be bossy but the more honest you can be with us, the more we can help.'

At one secondary school, the SENCO put time and energy into making that all-important first contact with parents/carers. If they would not come to school, she would visit them at home, together with an attendance officer. In the first meeting, she would highlight specific positives about their child and introduce them personally to someone in school (one of the TA team, for example) whom they could contact at any time. After the first meeting she would nurture the relationship by being available in person or on the phone when parents needed to talk, by checking with them when any changes were proposed to the child's pattern of support and by offering practical help. All parents of children with SEND in Year 7 were invited to a coffee morning at the start of the school year. There they heard about the school support systems and could chat informally with the school's educational psychologist, transition worker, Head of Year and SENCO. Through measures like these, the school was able to achieve 100% parental attendance at review meetings.

At a primary school in Bristol that serves one of the most deprived areas of the city, parents' evenings are where initial discussion about a child with SEN takes place, but if parents do not attend, then someone in school will try to catch them later: 'We missed you at parents' evening – how about popping in tomorrow after school?' Teachers stress the positives: 'He did a fantastic piece of work on robots. Why don't you come in and see his books – you'll be pleased.' Class teachers have an informal chat to parents before any sort of formal letter about SEN goes home, and the SENCO follows up with another chat. The school will always telephone a parent who is known to have literacy difficulties, rather than write to them. The SENCO has set up a support group for parents of children with SEND. The group meets once a week for coffee; parents might watch a video on how to help your child at home, borrow reading books or make a game to play with their child.

Practice of this kind challenges our assumptions that some parents will never be able to become involved.

Ongoing support for parents

Having engaged parents, including those who may have been anxious or reluctant, the next challenge is to find ways to provide them with ongoing support. Good ideas from schools include

- inviting a group of parents whose children have the same type of SEND, or are in the same year group, to get together on a one-off or regular basis;
- having a drop-in 'surgery' session at a fixed time each week that is convenient for parents;
- linking a parent or family with another with a child with similar needs in a buddying relationship;
- running a link parent scheme, where a group of parents whose children have already transferred to a secondary school continue to attend activities for Year 6 parents so as to support families over the transition;
- having a room or space specifically for parents of children with SEND, with information leaflets, videos and access to helpful websites and helplines;
- setting up a shared electronic forum where parents can access information such as fact sheets on dyslexia or autism, and comment on local initiatives;
- having staff and families undertake training together, for example, on alternative and augmentative communication;
- identifying a TA or learning mentor as the key contact for a given number of families.

Involving parents in developing your school's SEN information report

The SEN Code of Practice has a long list of information about the implementation of their SEN policy, which schools must place on their website. Rather than simply complying with these headings, some schools have taken the imaginative step of asking parents/carers themselves what questions they want or would have wanted answered about SEN provision for their child and using these to frame their information report. These are some questions that parents have come up with:

- How does the school know if my child might need extra help, and what should I do if I think my child may have SEN?
- Communication – how will the school let parents/carers know about things?
- How will I know how well my child is doing, and how will you help me to support my child's learning?
- How and who do I talk to if my child is not getting the support they need?
- How will the curriculum be matched to my child's needs?
- What support is there for parents/carers?

- How will my child be included in activities outside of the classroom including school trips? What social/out of school activities are there?
- How accessible is the setting environment?
- What specialist services and expertise are available or accessed by the setting?
- What training have the staff supporting children with SEND had or are having?
- How will the school help my child get ready for secondary school/college/work?

The questions will range from the general to the very specific, such as:

- What type and how many complaints did you receive last year, and how were they resolved?
- How flexible is the setting with regards to the average day?
- Can my child's school dinner requirements be accommodated if they have a special diet?
- Do any of the staff speak my child's home language?

The important thing is that (while complying with statutory requirements) you provide information on the questions that really matter for your parents, and provide them in forms that they will find easy to use. This might, for some parents, be a long document, but for others, a PowerPoint with questions and answers in speech bubbles, and lots of pictures. One school, St George's Beneficial in Portsmouth, went as far as to make a film of their 'school offer', showing children with different types of SEND talking about the support and provision they receive.

The same process can be used with children and young people to find out the questions to which they think pupils with SEND would like answers to, and get their views on how the answers should be presented in accessible ways. Young people's questions may be very different from those of adults, for example:

- What's available to help me lead an ordinary life like my mates?
- What's available to help me get qualifications, training or a job, and when?
- How can I get information about what's available?
- How do I get listened to?

Tackling the issue of one-to-one support

A key action in improving your partnership with parents and carers is to give them equal access to the information you use to develop your SEND practices and policies. In-class support from teaching assistants is a case in point. Guided by research, schools have sought to move away from 'Velcro' support for children in class, yet SENCOs often tell me the real problem in implementing this change is strong parental views that this is what works best.

To change this perception, it can help to hold workshops where you share the research findings on TA in-class support – that it does not generally increase attainment, that it can alienate the child from their peers and that it has been shown to lead to dependence rather than independence. In the toolkit section of this book, you will find an information sheet for parents that summarises the issues about TA support in parent-friendly language.

The sheet explores the pros and cons of one-to-one support, alternatives to one-to-one support and how one-to-one support can best be managed when it is necessary. There are also suggestions about questions that parents may want to ask, so schools should ensure they have answers prepared.

Finally, the information sheet contains weblinks and further reading and an entire page of research summaries broken down simply to help parents and SENCOs make the best joint decisions.

You can follow up initial workshops and information by tackling the 'Velcro' issue in meetings with individual families where provision is being discussed. I would begin by exploring the long-term outcomes a parent wants for their child, which are almost always about independence and relationships, then use these as a reality check against short-term plans.

The script might go like this:

> OK so it's really important to you that Dan keeps up with his schoolwork and can take part in all his lessons, and you feel that will happen if he has a one-to-one. But it's also really important to you that he has lots of friends and works towards independence. That will mean we need to plan ways for him to take part in things on his own or with friends. How does that sound to you?

Involving parents in interventions

Having built bridges, forged relationships and provided information about forms of support, the next step for the SENCO is to involve parents in decisions to use a particular intervention or to review its impact. This does is not always happen. As one parent said, 'We had a meeting in January when they asked us what we wanted for Chris. We were not aware of what was available so you can't really ask for something when you don't know if it's available or not.'

This is where the provision map is such a helpful tool, as part of the school's web-based SEND information, particularly if it is combined with clear information about the entry and exit criteria for each provision.

Wherever possible, each intervention should have parental involvement built into its design. Examples of this are

- the take-away home activity book in the Talk Boost language interventions;
- the ideas for home activities included in the 1stclass@number programme;
- the 'Numicon at Home' materials;
- the Incredible Years parenting programme that runs parallel to the Dino Dinosaur social and emotional skills group work intervention programme for children.

The provision planning proformas in the toolkit section of this book signpost the importance of parental engagement within each intervention; if you are developing a planning proforma for an intervention of your own, it will be useful to think about and record this element.

Some interventions ask parents/carers to sign up to a semi-formal contract that sets out what the school will deliver and what the parent is asked to do in return. The well-known Reading Recovery literacy intervention, for example, relies on the child being in school daily for their 12–20-week series of lessons. Where children have attendance problems, there will be a chat with the parents about the investment the school is making in the child for this very intensive intervention and the effects if the child misses sessions. The message is 'If you can get your child to school, we will make sure they get their daily lesson, and they will learn to read really well.' Parents are invited to watch a lesson, and the teacher will spend time with them afterwards to discuss what they saw. Parents also sign up to work with their child every day on the Reading Recovery 'homework'. This is carefully planned so that it does not ask parents/carers to do anything that might cause difficulty. They simply hear their child read one or more short books that the child can already tackle well independently, and help the child reconstruct a cut-up sentence they have written and already reassembled and reread several times in their lesson in school.

Workshops and courses

Finally, the SENCO will want to build on the provision the child receives in school with linked, targeted workshops or courses that will model for the parent the ways in which they can help the child at home. Although IEPs were meant to guide parents on how to help, they do not – according to parents – seem to have succeeded. Often the ideas written on them are too general: 'Hear Jack read every day' can leave the parent wondering how exactly they should do this.

What is more helpful is a practical demonstration. An example for literacy might be a Paired Reading workshop for a group of parents in which they learn how to follow a very simple procedure – first the parent and child read simultaneously out loud until the child signals (for example, by knocking on the table) that he wants to read by himself, then the child reads independently until he gets stuck or makes a mistake, when the parent joins in until the child signals again and so on.

Some schools have also developed Paired Maths schemes, with a stock of games coded according to the maths skill or concept involved and with an accompanying card to highlight the kinds of mathematical language the game could bring out. Parents borrow a game or two each week and record how play went in a home-school book.

Such workshops and courses can be really successful with lower-attaining pupils. Evaluations of Family Literacy and Numeracy courses for parents of three- to six-year-olds, for example (Brooks, 1996, 1998; Brooks and Pahl, 2008), showed that the proportion of children whose low reading level would leave them struggling in school fell from 67% to 9%. Progress in number and mathematical language was also good.

The REAL programme, which involves home visiting and group sessions to develop nursery and Reception children's early literacy skills, also has very good evidence of impact. Randomised trials showed that children showed significant and enduring gains compared with control groups who did not receive the intervention (Nutbrown *et al.*, 2005; Brooks and Pahl, 2008; Hirst *et al.*, 2010).

Equally, parenting skills courses can halve the rate of severe behaviour problems (Furlong *et al.*, 2012 Gardner *et al.*, 2017), with improvements maintained up to ten years later.

A successful import to the UK is the Families and Schools Together (FAST) programme. This eight-week after-school programme is offered to families with three- to eight-year-old children. Families sit at family tables and eat together. Parents are coached by a trained volunteer in how to give instructions and have the child follow them. Children then go off to play while parents discuss issues of their choice in groups. At the end there is a 15-minute special play session in which each parent plays with their child, coached to follow the child's lead. An initial UK evaluation found that the programme reduced teacher-rated emotional and behavioural difficulties in the classroom by 46% and also raised attainment compared with children whose parents just received behavioural parenting pamphlets (Lexmond *et al.*, 2011). A later evaluation for the

Education Endowment Foundation (Lord *et al.*, 2018)) also found an impact on social and emotional outcomes, although not in this case on attainment.

More recently Save the Children have built on FAST and developed an interesting shorter programme called Families Connect, which includes sessions on maths, literacy and social and emotional development. Again, evaluation (Lord *et al.*, 2021) showed it proved easier to impact on children's behaviour and attitude to learning over the short period of the intervention than it did on numeracy, language and literacy measures.

Involving pupils

Pupil involvement was flagged up as a fundamental element of effective SEN practice as long ago as 2001, in the then SEN Code. In the 2011 reforms, ambitions were set even higher: 'We want to give greater control to disabled children and young people themselves – to make them the authors of their own life stories' (DfE, 2011). There has been a great deal of excellent work done since then on how to seek the views of children and young people with learning and communication difficulties, and how to prepare pupils with more complex needs to take an active part in annual and transition reviews.

Yet the involvement of pupils with high-incidence types of SEN is often tokenistic. The volume of individual plans that schools have tried to manage has meant that pupils are often not involved at all, or if they are, the involvement may be no more than putting their signature to targets that the adults have already dictated and reports of progress in which they have had little or no say.

Even for pupils with EHCPs, the situation is far from perfect. A 2019 report (Odell, 2019) explored the views of disabled pupils and found that where reasonable adjustments or extra support were in place, the pupils did not know why or and what the support or adjustments were meant to achieve.

What, then, can the alternative SEND systems suggested in this book, based on intensifying for some pupils the whole-school systems for inclusive learning that are used for all pupils, offer in terms of pupil involvement?

The offer can be significant, where an inclusive school culture encourages *all* children to take responsibility for their own learning, playing a part in assessing their own progress and deciding what they need to learn next. In some schools, pupils actually *lead* reviews with their parents and tutors, contributing their own views on how they are doing before asking others to comment.

CASE STUDY

At one secondary school in a disadvantaged area, parent-teacher meetings are always led by students. They are responsible for writing a letter inviting their parents or guardians to attend, coordinating with the office to schedule a time and putting together a portfolio of their work and answers to self-reflection questions. This all happens about a month ahead, with pupils using a checklist to mark off each of the requirements.

The conferences typically last about 30 minutes, including time for parents to ask questions and for the pupil's tutor to give feedback on the pupil's presentation.

Pupils will lay out samples of their schoolwork, showing a mix of some of their best work and assignments where they struggled. They talk about which subjects are going well, ones where they need to make improvements and what might help that to happen. They also share the results of questionnaires the school uses to help them assess attitudes to school and self, and discuss their social and emotional progress. Then they talk about their long-term goals and plans for the future.

The aim of the conferences is to end up with a plan of action that incorporates the student's goals and fosters parental support. Students appreciate not being talked about in the third person. Their motivation for learning has increased. In the words of one student: 'I get to shape my own life.'

The culture in schools like this one forms a brilliant backdrop for improved participation for pupils with SEND. SENCOs can simply tweak the regular pupil-parent-teacher meetings to make them a little longer, involve a member of the SEND team and address specific SEND-related issues and questions.

Other schools, however, operate on educational models of learners as passive receptacles of subject knowledge imparted by adults, with little opportunity to have their views heard. Here the SENCO's job will be harder, but students with SEND can still be involved in setting their own targets (some personal, some academic), in taking part in SEND-specific review meetings and in contributing to a personal profile or passport that they use to let staff know what their particular needs are and what forms of support they find helpful.

Person-centred planning

Person-centred planning, with its highly visual and engaging techniques, is the key to empowering children and young people. Properly implemented, it involves not only the child and parents but as many as possible of the significant adults in the child's life (Murray and Sanderson, 2007; Department of Health, 2010). Meetings might, for example, involve grandparents, older or younger siblings, neighbours, friends, teachers, support staff, social workers – all those who care about the child and his or her future.

The person who is facilitating the meeting asks everyone to introduce themselves and say what they like, admire or appreciate about the child. These might be qualities, skills or achievements. Next (if this is a review meeting), there will be a progress check on actions: have we all done what we said we would do? What has been achieved since the last meeting? The facilitator asks each person, including the child, about their ambitions for the child. What is it they most want for them? What's important to them and for them now – and in the future?

The facilitator records these and then asks 'Which of these is the most important to you and the child?' There is discussion, and the agreed aspirations can be charted as words or in the form of pictures at the end of a large, long strip of paper on the wall.

Next comes discussion of what is working and not working for the child or young person at the moment. From this discussion might come changes to the child's Personal Passport or One Page Profile, reflecting views on what teachers and other staff need to do to support the child effectively and what the child can do to help themself. The discussion will also generate an action plan about what needs to happen to take the child and family closer to the outcomes they desire. These are recorded in 'what/where/who/when' forms, ready to be reviewed when the group next meet.

The group might then meet three or four times a year to review the plan and evaluate progress. The aim is to reduce dependency on 'agencies' to provide support, by mobilising the energy and commitment of the people around the child – their natural 'circle of support'.

There are a number of useful person-centred tools available to structure and visually record person-centred discussions with young people about their views and feelings (see, for example, the Council for Disabled Children's website and the websites of Helen Sanderson Associates and of Inclusive Solutions). Good ideas include a wall chart with a big horizontal arrow and speech bubbles to record 'What's working', 'What's not working', 'What's important', 'What will a good life look like'? There are 'Circles of Support' maps to record the important people in the child's life, 'Good day, bad day' charts to capture the child's experiences, 'What people like and admire about me' charts, 'Where I want to be' charts and 'Daily routines that are important to me' charts. We can also ask pupils the 'miracle' question: 'If you could wave a magic wand to change things, what would change? What would that look like? What would you be thinking, saying and doing? What would other people be thinking, saying and doing?'

> The professional needs to be the facilitator of the conversation not the leader of the conversation. The child is the expert in what they need.
>
> Hannah, member of FLARE,
> the young person's advisory group for the DfE

Person-centred planning or thinking requires a mind shift that genuinely hands responsibility to the child or young person. Meetings are theirs, not yours. The child or young person is asked where they would prefer people to sit, for example, and what they want recorded, in what colour pen, with whom information can be shared. Often it is they who welcome participants as they arrive, choose the music to play in the background and choose refreshments to be served. They may want to choose an activity (colouring in, modelling, screen game) they can do if they want to stay in the meeting but need something to occupy them for a little while. We should also consider asking them whether they want an in-person meeting, or whether a virtual meeting would be better. Rhian Williams, SENCO at Henley Bank school, found that when she and her team met virtually with the incoming Y6 pupils with SEND during the COVID pandemic, they talked more from the security of their own homes and shared much more information than in normal transition meetings, so this practice has continued.

Really listening to children is a far cry from standard practice in schools, so good training is necessary for all those involved. There is a particular need for support and training in how to engage children and young people with communication and interaction needs. Teachers will need to be skilled in using visuals (real objects, photographs, pictures and symbols) to elicit children's views. For example, they might give a child an image of a particular lesson or event and ask them to place it under a happy face, unhappy face or neutral face picture to indicate how they feel about it. Similarly, different symbols could be used to indicate 'important to me' or 'not important to me'.

Older pupils could complete a mission using a camera to record things that represent 'a good day for me' and 'a bad day for me'; this will help everyone plan what will be needed to make sure the child experiences more good days and fewer bad ones. Pupils might photograph aspects of the school environment that help their learning and make an audio or video recording explaining their choices.

There are more good ideas like this in *Listening to Children and Young People with Speech, Language and Communication Needs*, by Sue Roulstone and Sharynne McLeod (Roulstone and McLeod, 2011), on the Me First website, and in The Communication Trust's *Involving children and young people with SLCN guidance* (https://new.sthelens.gov.uk/media/7522/involving-children-young-people-with-speech-language-and-commuication-needs-toolkit-communication-trust-2017.pdf).

A helpful general guide to what young people want from adults in planning and review meetings (Adams *et al*, 2017) suggests that we should

- consider having the child or young person invite others to the meeting rather than set up a meeting of professionals, then 'invite' the child;
- involve their friends, to give them confidence and encouragement;
- make sure the young person has age-appropriate and accessible information about what will happen when well in advance;
- hold meetings in informal venues rather than in school;
- always include their dreams and aspirations, even if they seem unachievable;
- use accessible language, avoiding jargon;
- build in breaks if at all possible.

When we write profiles, passports, reports and plans, we should avoid putting words into children and young people's mouths – we should only use the first person for something the child has actually said. It is also important when writing or talking about a pupil to use words they would be comfortable with. The check to do is to ask ourselves how we would feel if we were described in the ways we often describe pupils. I was reminded of this when I read an ironic tweet from a senior leader: 'We have two new starters next week. Stephen is socially awkward and finds it difficult to communicate. Emma is a "character". She is brash and loud but has an awful home life. He is Head of Year 8 and she is Assistant Head (Behaviour).'

Like person-centred planning, personal budgets have represented another significant challenge to current practice. Evidence suggest that they have been little used since introduced in the last round of SEND reforms. Many schools have been worried that pupils and their families will make inappropriate choices, misuse public funding and prevent schools from doing what they know to be right for pupils. There is certainly one good way to achieve this – by not fully involving the pupil and family all the way along the line, from the first time the pupil is identified as having SEND. The child and family should be seen from the start as equal partners in decision-making, contributing their essential views on what might work and what might not and being fully aware of the provision available in school, its scientific evidence base, the outcomes each provision should achieve and the entry and exit criteria. Similarly, the family need to know about all the external services with whom the school engages and the benefits for the child of working with therapists and psychologists who have an ongoing relationship with the school. This is crucial because these external professionals, when already working with a school, will be able to influence whole-school approaches and everyday class teaching rather than simply taking the child off for the kind of 'therapy in a cupboard' intervention that will be ineffective unless closely linked to the child's everyday learning diet.

Where the child and family have equal access to all this information, they will be less likely to seek to use a personal budget for their 'own' speech and language therapist, for example, or for unproven interventions. Evidence from local areas who have used personal budgets, moreover, suggests that the choices made by young people and their families who elect for a personal budget have been wise ones. Families tended to choose to spend money on things that would make a big difference to what we in schools often forget – the child's overall quality of life, especially their social life after school, at weekends and in the school holidays. Disabled young people, for example, have asked for part of their budget to be spent on a taxi to pick them up later than usual so that they can attend an after-school club. They have asked for a family friend or older sibling to be paid to take them to the cinema or a restaurant: all activities that make their lives 'more ordinary', which is what matters most to them.

So personal budgets, and person-centred planning, can be powerful tools for positive change. But so are simpler ways of giving children power over their own lives. Choice and control can apply to everyday learning as well as to financial transactions. If pupils are not doing well, we can have an open-ended conversation with them, saying, for example, 'I want to be able to teach you in a more effective way. So what's been going well, what hasn't worked well?' Choice and control can apply, too, to the way we manage behaviour. Schools that emphasise behavioural choices in the language they use with pupils ('What happened when you did xxx? What other choices could you have made?') are giving pupils a share of control. Schools that use restorative approaches are going even further, as they are handing responsibility for making reparation to the pupil after things have gone wrong and hurt or damage has been the result.

Sometimes it is small things that make the difference. In one school, autistic pupils who found it hard to say how they were feeling could simply leave their planner open at a page that showed their mood so that the teacher would know if they were tipping over into meltdown. In another, autistic children were shown photographs of strategies that might help them and asked to say whether or not they would be useful. In another, a child with emotionally based school refusal managed to get back into school by being given the lead in deciding what the next appropriate step for her would be (Figure 10.1).

The key is putting ourselves in the child or young person's shoes and finding a way to give them a voice.

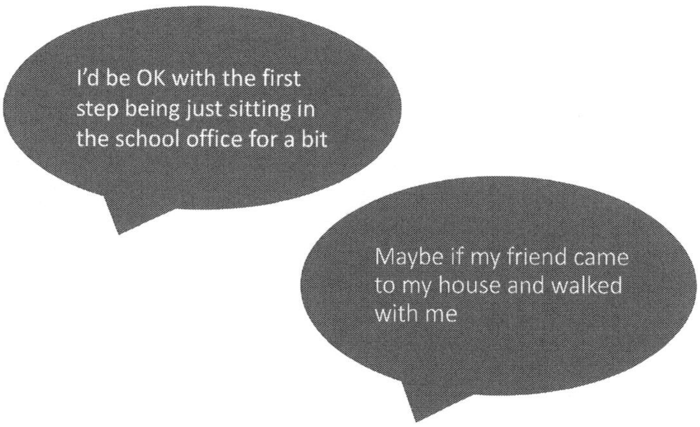

FIGURE 10.1 Pupils taking the lead in their own plans

> Tell a young person what to think and you lose their trust, ask a young person what they think and you empower them for life.
>
> Megan, member of FLARE, the young person's advisory group for the DfE

Children and young people may not, however, respond to efforts to involve them without specific help from SENCOs. Pupils who have, for so long, had the label 'SEN' applied to them by others, rather than being asked how they want to be identified and discussed, are not necessarily ready to hold their own profiles or tell adults what they need in the way of help. A legacy of shame and stigma lies between the children we are now identifying as 'special needs pupils' and those of the future, who may be part of a culture where all pupils are encouraged to identify their strengths and weaknesses and understand that they may all need a little extra help from time to time. The intensification of 'normal' systems used for all pupils is one way of achieving this kind of culture. Another is work with all pupils, and with staff, to promote disability awareness and disability equality and on the effects of stigma, teasing and name-calling.

This can be followed up by specific mentoring of individual pupils by disabled older peers and adults – to help them define themselves confidently as disabled and articulate equally confidently what they need and do not need from those around them. The aim is that all children and young people with SEN or disabilities can be as clear as the autistic young man who manages his difficulty in handling two-way conversations by telling everyone, 'You will have to tell me when I've talked to you long enough because I won't know.' Or the dyslexic girl who told staff, 'If you put diagrams and pictures, then I get it.' And as clear as pupils at The Bromfords Secondary school in Essex, where slots on staff meetings allow them to talk to staff directly about the support they need, and where a boy with cerebral palsy who was about to join the school (and was worried lest staff baby him) walked up on the stage during a staff training event, at the SENCO's suggestion, so that they could all see his capabilities.

At this same school, pupils have a say in when and where they want support from TAs. One young man, for example, was able to ask to book time with a particular TA when he had a difficult piece of homework to complete.

SENCOs' involvement in training pupils in self-advocacy, and creating a climate in which pupils can ask for what they need as their right, is vital in beating bureaucracy. In the end, those who are best positioned to make sure their needs are met are pupils themselves. It is the pupils themselves who are always there, in every teaching and learning situation, with every supply teacher for the class, in every part of the extended school day. If we can help them communicate their needs, many of the elaborate and paper-driven SEN systems that we have designed to fulfil this communication role may become redundant.

> Having worked in schools where students are often reluctant to be seen as needing additional support, I feel true joy when I am reminded by students that they need their coloured exercise books, asked why they did not receive their extra time in an assessment, or asked to check that their teachers are aware of the information on their student passport.
>
> Rhian Williams, SENCO at Henley Bank secondary school

Involving outside agencies

Some of the bureaucracy in SEND is about trying to protect the interests of pupils and parents. As we have seen in this chapter, there may be more effective ways of achieving this than documents that surface from time to time and are then forgotten.

Another function of bureaucracy, however, is one of gatekeeping and rationing limited resources. Psychology services, learning and behaviour support services, speech and language therapists and social services use paperwork to try to manage an open-ended demand for services that they are simply not staffed to meet.

Understandably, these agencies have to ration what they provide, for example, by providing them only when the school itself can show that it has made substantial efforts to understand and help the child from its own resources, before asking for outside help. The result is often a set of complex referral forms, a different one for each agency, accompanied by requests for copies of recent IEP/ISPs. Quite rightly, too, external agencies require information in order to gain a good picture of a child's profile and needs and what has been tried so far to help them. On this they can build their own interventions.

SENCOs are not in control of the systems used by outside agencies, unless their school or MAT is directly commissioning and paying for the service – a growing trend. Where this is not the case, they can seek to influence agencies' systems. Increasingly, groups of professionals work in a locality with a defined group of schools. There is often an opportunity for headteachers and SENCOs to sit on local management groups or panels that help to develop the local systems that will allocate time and manage referrals.

One helpful development that SENCOs can seek to bring about in their own area avoids referral forms altogether by having regular in-school multi-agency meetings. These can take various forms. They may be formal and infrequent, or smaller and more frequent – for example, involving a monthly hour with the school's EP, EWO and school nurse, at which actions for previous meetings are reviewed and four or five children or families discussed in depth. Other agencies can be invited when their presence will be relevant to a particular child to be discussed.

The facility to meet virtually, which took off during the COVID pandemic, is making arrangements like this much easier. If it is still not possible to influence outside agencies' referral systems so that referrals stem from face-to-face contact rather than forms in triplicate, however, SENCOs should try to collectively insist that there is just one multi-purpose form used by all agencies. Fortunately, this is increasingly happening in many local areas as a result of single gateways for Early Help family support.

SENCOs can also circumvent some referral forms by submitting existing paperwork they hold on the child, rather than starting afresh. They might, for example, send

- the latest pupil personal profile;
- a highlighted provision map showing the provision the child receives;
- attainment and progress data.

The only thing they might need to add to this is a very clear description of what they want from the agency. Is it assessment to help clarify needs? Is it training for those working with the child in school? Is it direct therapeutic input that no one in the school has the skills (or could acquire the skills through training) to provide? Is it support for the family? Is it simply extra resources?

Local authority systems for schools to request EHCPs remain, in many cases, extremely cumbersome. Karen Truelove, SENCO at Cathedral School in Essex, told me she spent over three days providing 'evidence for everything' when completing a request to initiate an EHCP assessment. In Southend, in contrast (just over the Essex LA border), Toni Quinn was able to praise her LA's move to a user-friendly single online platform for all matters relating to a child's EHCP.

Schools also have to fall in with the local requirements of Early Help assessments. These are shorter than the Common Assessment Framework (CAF) they replaced, more strengths-based and conversational. The jury is still out on whether the bureaucracy involved is worthwhile. It may be that the Early Help process will achieve its aim of making sure that no child falls through the net, but equally we should not be surprised if there are delays in accessing services and minimal progress towards interagency working, or if overstretched and fallible human beings still fail to communicate, despite various forms and databases to help them do so. Meanwhile, a suggestion to SENCOs might be that they avoid being seduced by an elegantly designed Early Help template into spending hours and hours inputting information that may not ever be used. The basics may be enough.

Finally, it must be acknowledged that some external agencies, particularly in the health service, are still having to work with antiquated and largely paper-based systems that in turn impose bureaucratic burdens on SENCOs. Margaret Relf, SENCO at Anglesey Primary, told me how, on the day I interviewed her for this book, she received a huge pile of speech and language therapy programmes, all sent by post, that she then had to distribute to teachers and scan into Tes Provision Map. It took her a whole day. I had no advice to give other than perhaps documenting that time and seeking a meeting with this particular SLT service, who may not fully understand school systems and the implications of their approach in terms of workload, and might also need a nudge to move to the more productive and modern ways of working developed by other SLT services.

An example of this, demonstrating how hard-pressed external agencies can work effectively with equally hard-pressed schools, is the Hackney SLT service. They work in schools rather than clinics, modelling to teachers and TAs how to deliver SLC programmes and provide communication-supportive classroom environments. After COVID, when numbers of children needing help increased and waiting lists grew, they proactively developed Verbo (verboapp.co.uk), an online speech and language therapy toolkit for education staff. The app provides screening tools, interventions with video modelling and resources, target trackers, staff training, robust impact measures and outcome reports, the opportunity to communicate directly with a therapist and the facility to share information with parents. It is all aimed at building long-term capacity in schools to support children themselves, and all achieved without a single piece of paper.

A model to share with your external agencies, perhaps?

KEY PRINCIPLES

Key take-aways for SENCOs

- Working in partnership with pupils and their parents/carers is based on putting ourselves in their shoes, and listening rather than always 'telling'
- Meeting parents/carers of children with SEND three times a year can be achieved by using informal contacts and building meetings into regular school systems
- How we talk with and listen to parents is as important as how often we meet them
- The most effective SEND systems for involving pupils build on a whole-school ethos where pupils are able to take the lead in their own learning, and on support for those with SEND so they can confidently give their views

Key questions for the wider school leadership team

- Have you asked your parents what the school can do for them, or just told them what they need to do for the school?
- Have all staff had training in how to work with parents?
- Does your SENCO have the administrative support they need to coordinate meetings with parents?
- Do you as a leader of SEND have at least a basic understanding of person-centred planning?

11 Making the change

It will be clear by now to those reading this book that its theme is not only a reduction in bureaucracy but also a fundamental re-think in the way we manage SEND in schools.

The subsequent case study illustrates how one school has managed this re-think, completely overhauling their SEND systems.

CASE STUDY

Leanne Pasdari, SENCO at St James' Primary in Gorton, Manchester, set out in collaboration with her senior leadership team to use the ideas in this book to change the way SEND was managed in school. Previously, large numbers of children were placed on the SEN register. Teachers tended to depend on teaching assistants to support these children, and in some cohorts with significant needs, children had become reliant on having a TA sitting with them at all times.

In addition, children with SEND were supported by a SEND TA whose original role was to work one-to-one, out of class, for 30 minutes twice a week with each individual. She supported 25 children, taking their IEPs and using them to set work for them. There was very little dialogue between the teachers and the TA and almost no input from the teachers into the work she carried out.

Leanne began by working with colleagues to seek their views on the current system and collecting evidence about the impact of support. Staff expressed doubts about how far in-class support from TAs was effective, where their curriculum knowledge was weak. The SEND TA felt that her workload was unmanageable and leading to high stress levels. Data showed that children with SEND were making limited progress across the curriculum.

The school also identified exceptions to this general pattern; for example, in one Year 5 class where the children with SEN were making better than expected progress in all areas of the curriculum. In this class there was consistent collaborative working between the class teacher and the TA, including weekly

DOI: 10.4324/9781003313526-11

planning meetings, daily feedback between all adults working in class and the consistent sharing of information relating to each individual pupil.

Leanne was able to share the outcomes of her SEND self-evaluation with colleagues, so that they became aware there was a problem with the status quo. Next, she undertook a pilot to trial a new role for the SEND TA, which, if successful, would send a wider message to the school that children with SEND did not need one person assigned to them in order to succeed.

A new small group literacy intervention was introduced for 30 minutes a day, led by the SEND TA working collaboratively with the class teacher in order to set targets for the children and plan sessions, which the class teacher reinforced within the mainstream classroom. The results were impressive, and the pilot became part of the school's new systematic provision map.

This kind of evidence helped staff to consider new ways of working. As SENCO, Leanne recognised that they would need a blend of pressure and support if they were to take on the challenges of assuming a greater responsibility for children with SEND. The pressure in part came from the 2014 SEN reforms, which make it clear that the class teacher is responsible and accountable for progress of all pupils, even those receiving specialist support. It also came from performance management.

There is now regular monitoring to ensure that accountability lies with teachers for all groups of children's progress. Teachers and TAs plan together, and information about pupils is shared with all adults working with them; in most classes, children identified as having the most challenging need are now fully included in class teachers' planning and consistently work in small groups within the classroom rather than outside. New performance management targets incorporating SEND are in place for those cohorts where this is not the case. Performance management for all staff now includes judgements on how well they plan for and teach pupils with SEND.

Leanne ran a staff meeting on SEND, explaining

- that taking part in an intervention programme would not of itself constitute SEN Support as it is an extension of the school's curriculum and is part of the core offer – thus reducing the numbers of children on the SEN register;
- the expectations for children who do need SEN Support, for whom staff should set out interventions and expected outcomes, and review progress, each term;

- her availability to help with differentiation where children are working significantly below expected levels;
- the absolute importance of ensuring that any additional support is outcome-focused: 'What are the outcomes of this support? How will this support benefit the pupil? What do the parents expect the outcomes to be? Timed, recorded, assessed half termly.';
- the use of the school's provision map as the most important tool for tracking interventions, and for any intervention taking place to have a specification, a timescale and register of attendance – all in a file kept by the class teacher;
- the plan for phase leaders to look at these files in their fortnightly monitoring;
- the need for all teachers to plan lessons so as to remove barriers to learning;
- the need to put children and parents at the centre of discussions about the support offered, to ask parents to share their knowledge about their children and their development and help work out what is best for their child.

To support staff, the school's leadership team made it their priority to develop everyone's confidence in understanding the varying needs of children with SEND and how to meet those needs. Staff training was provided in the first term, followed in the second term by monitoring and feedback from the SENCO, literacy and numeracy leaders. Leanne also provided fortnightly planning and differentiation workshops after school, and drop-in sessions every other week for class teachers to come and discuss any concerns.

In order to improve communication with all parents and ensure consistency of target-setting for children, the school has reshaped the way in which targets are set and in the way in which parents are involved in this process. Parents are now invited to attend a 'pupil conferencing' session with the class teacher, in which they set the targets in collaboration with their children. The expected outcome of this is that parents will have a clearer idea on how to support their children and therefore increase academic progress. Where teachers have very significant concerns about pupils, Leanne, as SENCO, attends the meetings. From this, a plan for additional provision is drawn up and further meetings scheduled.

The challenge

The kind of re-think involved at St James' Primary, and many schools like it, involves a lot of people in school in changing the way they do things. It means changing SEND from a bolt-on activity undertaken by a few, to an integral aspect of whole-school systems for all pupils.

SEN/D as bolt-on activity	⇨	SEND as an integrated aspect of whole-school systems
Conceptualisation: task of SEN viewed as the preserve of specialists		Conceptualisation: task of SEND viewed as whole-school
Values: individual values and the emergence of subcultures		Values: a shared commitment to inclusion
Approaches to teaching and learning: individual problem-solving approaches used to support the achievement of students with SEND		Approaches to teaching and learning: collaborative problem-solving approaches used to support the achievement of students with SEND
Resources for support: used to strengthen SEND discrete provision		Resources for support: potentially available to all pupils and used for flexible provision and individual planning
Specialist leadership roles: a few staff take on formal and informal leadership activities to support the learning of students with SEND		Specialist leadership roles: highly distributed, with staff taking on formal and informal leadership activities to support the learning of all students
Approaches to integrated services: problems are referred to specialist services outside the school		Approaches to integrated services: services beyond the school are used to enhance the flexibility of provision

Table 11.1 Moving to a whole-school approach

Source: Chapman *et al.*, 2011, National College of School Leadership

The difference between these two approaches is brilliantly captured in a National College of School Leadership publication (Chapman *et al.*, 2011) on leadership that promotes the achievement of pupils with SEND (Table 11.1).

It will not be enough, however, for the SENCO to announce to colleagues that in the future there will be a whole-school approach with fewer IEPs/ISPs, a greater focus on outcomes, reduced reliance on 'hours' of TA support and that they will be expected to take more responsibility for the targets, progress monitoring and strategies used to support pupils with SEND. Change, alas, is not that easy.

Everard and Morris (1990) divide those involved in change into four groups:

- Those who are ready to oppose the change
- Those who are willing to let it happen
- Those who are willing to help it happen
- Those who are willing to make it happen

For the SENCO this means making sure that you enlist those who you think will really want the change to happen as allies from the start – for example, key members of each subject department in a secondary school, or key parents who have influence on others. It also means you need to think carefully about who might be worried about your new ideas, how you can respond to their worries and how you can make sure you involve them actively in the planning. The chart in Table 11.2 may help.

Concern	Possible strategies
Class teachers: • The more children I have with IEPs/ISPs, the more TA support I will get in my class • Doing all this brings more resources through external agencies and ECHPs • It will mean more work for me	• Show how the audit of needs and provision map provides the fairest match of resources to need • Point out the realities of local funding arrangements and the emphasis on provision that must be made from schools' own budgets • Offer to work alongside the teacher to help with planning and target-setting • Show how time will be provided to support this • Work in stages; try out the new system with just one willing year group or faculty, for example, and get them to report back
Parents: • The teachers won't know my child has SEND • My child won't get the help they need • I won't know what is happening for my child and how they are doing • I won't be involved in helping my child at home	• Involve parents and pupils in devising a format for a personal profile for pupils with additional needs • Show how the provision map works • Ask parents to comment on your planned systems and formats for tracking and monitoring progress • Tell parents about arrangements for drop-in times, conversations and review meetings • Provide information on the workshops and courses provided in school
SENCO: • Without the security of IEP/ISPs, I won't have a handle any more on what is happening, and staff won't use strategies/make an effort to meet SEND	• I can monitor what is happening by looking at teachers' planning and through classroom observation and talking to pupils
All • It may not work	• Build in an abort button – we will try the new system till x and then review it – if we aren't happy, we can go back to the old system

Table 11.2 Strategies to address concerns

It will also be important to ask staff, at the stage when you are working together to agree a new system, to identify the resources they will need to make the change work. The resource identified will most likely be time, for staff INSET and for staff to take a new look at scaffolding and adaptive teaching within their medium- and short-term planning. Time will also be needed for you to work alongside colleagues to support improved practice.

These are some ways in which schools have created time:

- In one school, the head instituted a curriculum day when she brought in a team from outside the school to work with the children on creative projects. This freed up staff to work in phase teams on curriculum and lesson planning.

- In another school, twice-termly staff meetings are set aside for phase-based curriculum planning
- Another school established a buddy system for planning. Foundation Stage and Key Stage 1 teachers were paired with Key Stage 2 teachers so that they could help them plan work for older children working significantly below age-related expectations.
- Another school reduced the SENCO's teaching load for one year so as to free him to work with subject colleagues in a cycle that involved joint planning, teaching and review

Effective support for change means not expecting staff to become experts in inclusive teaching overnight. The ideas in this book ask a lot of them. They will need to use scaffolding to help students achieve class learning objectives, sometimes plan for a small number of children to work on learning objectives closely linked to the work of the class but taken from earlier in progression frameworks, use varied, inclusive teaching approaches and help pupils set and review both academic and personal targets. It will work best if you start small, perhaps getting to grips with tracking backwards and forwards in objectives frameworks to identify appropriate learning objectives, before asking staff to think about access strategies. And the SENCO can help staff use simple systems to change their practice, as in this example:

> One SENCO suggested to colleagues that they identify two or three inclusive teaching strategies for lower attaining children, and for their highest attainers, that they wanted to use more often. They then put these up on post-its on the wall, so as to remind themselves throughout the day. 'Make it personal' (e.g. link an explanation to pupils' own real-life experience), 'Chunk my instructions', 'Teach the key vocabulary I'm using' were examples of strategies staff chose for themselves. They also decided that to stretch higher attainers they wanted to ask more higher order questions using words like 'deduce', 'predict', 'infer', so put these up on post-its too and set themselves a target of asking at least one or two in each session.

Another great idea is to support teachers in making changes by identifying a small pot of money that they can bid into, for resources they feel they need in order to develop their practice. At Hampstead School in London, staff were asked to identify a key performance indicator that could be monitored, then to bid for relevant support. Some staff bid for cover time to enable them to plan with specialists, others chose to go to conferences or buy books to extend their learning about SEND, others bid for teaching resources or to make a video for new teachers in their department.

Once you have made a plan for introducing, implementing and embedding changes to your current SEND system, it will be useful to run a final check using the chart in Table 11.3.

	+	SKILLS	+	INCENTIVES	+	RESOURCES	=	CHANGE
	+	SKILLS	+	INCENTIVES	+	RESOURCES	=	CONFUSION
	+		+	INCENTIVES	+	RESOURCES	=	ANXIETY
	+	SKILLS	+		+	RESOURCES	=	RESISTANCE
…ISION	+	SKILLS	+	INCENTIVES	+		=	FRUSTRATION

TABLE 11.3 Managing complex change
Source: Adapted by Richard Vila, Bayridge Consortium Inc. from Knoster, 1991

The chart identifies four key elements that need to be in place if a complex change is to be successful – vision, skills, incentives and resources.

Where there is no clear vision for what needs to change, and what the new system will look like, the result for all involved (staff, parents, pupils) will be confusion. This points to the need to spend time on self-evaluation, sharing the outcomes and identifying with all stakeholders how they want things to be in the future. People need 'the big picture' – the background and context for the proposed change and how things will improve as a result.

Where there is a vision, incentives and resources but those who will have to implement a change do not have the skills they need, there will be high levels of anxiety. This points to the need for a really good plan for any INSET which staff will need. It also means thinking about the skills that pupils will need, and any necessary development work to help them become confident partners in setting and reviewing targets for their personal and academic development, and communicating to others what their needs are and what forms of support they find helpful.

Where there is vision, and professional development, and resources but no incentives, there will be resistance (often subtle but nevertheless powerful) amongst parents and colleagues in school. The way round this is to highlight very clearly what everyone has to gain from the new system.

For parents, this will be better progress for their child – with teachers really having to think about how to teach them rather than handing responsibility over to support staff – and clarity about what extra provision their child can access, over and above the all-important inclusive class and subject teaching. You will need to provide many parents with the evidence, summarised in this book, that the ways of managing things that they have come to expect (attaching TAs to children as if by Velcro, and working on three or four SMART targets) have not, according to national data and Ofsted, led to improved outcomes for pupils with SEND – indeed, rather the reverse.

The same arguments can be used to provide staff with incentives to make the change: new systems will mean improved outcomes for children, reflected in the school's self-evaluation and evident to Ofsted, and linked to rewards inherent in the performance management system. There may be other incentives, too, that a creative staff group can come up with as a way of celebrating the effort everyone has put in to make the new system work.

Finally, where there are incentives, coupled with vision and skills, but not enough resources (time or money), the result will be frustration – a familiar scenario for the education staff who have been asked to implement a thousand new initiatives over the last ten years, not all of them adequately funded. As we have seen, proper discussions with senior leaders in school about what time and resources will realistically be required, for the initial preparation period and when the change is implemented, will help reduce staff frustration.

Change and the role of teaching assistants

One change that presents particular challenges is helping class and subject teachers deploy extra adults within their lessons so as to maximise pupil participation, independence and achievement. To engage colleagues, SENCOs will first need to enable them to reflect on whether there might be a problem in the way they currently work with their TAs.

The first step might be to share key findings from the DISS (Deployment and Impact of Support Staff) research, which provides national statistics on patterns of within-class deployment. In this study (Blatchford *et al.*, 2012), researchers sat in classrooms observing pupils every ten seconds and coding their interactions. The results, covering thousands of pupils, are shown in Table 11.4.

The table shows that pupils with SEN had fewer interactions with their class and subject teachers than did pupils without SEN. This evidence may help explain the DISS study's finding, which we touched on in earlier chapters, of a negative relationship between pupil progress and the amount of TA support that they received, after controlling for other factors that might explain this relationship.

A wise HMI once said, 'The DISS study does not show that the more time TAs spend with pupils, the less progress they make – it shows that the less time they spend with

Interaction by type of SEN	Teacher	TA
Non-SEN	55%	27%
School Action	24%	32%
SA+ or Statement	21%	41%

Table 11.4 Children's interactions

their teachers, the less progress they make.' SENCOs can share this interpretation with colleagues and ask them whether in their classrooms it could be true that the most skilled and qualified adults are often spending the least time with children who most need their help.

To find out whether the national patterns apply in school, SENCOs could, if time allows, even set up some classroom observations, as part of school self-evaluation. The observer might focus on five pupils with SEND and five without SEND in a class, to work out the percentage of interactions with teachers and TAs for each group, then look at the results together with the teacher.

Experience suggests that once teachers become aware of any discrepancy between the time they personally spend with children with and without SEND, they rapidly change the way they work.

At this point, it will be important to explain to colleagues that even though overall deployment of TA support across the school may be based on allocating more time to challenging classes, this does not mean that the class or subject teacher has to deploy that support exclusively or even particularly to the individual pupils who present learning or behaviour challenges. The only exception to this would be where a child has an EHCP that specifies a prescribed role for a TA, and/or where a child has physical or medical needs that mean they must have personal support for health or care reasons.

You can provide staff with information on alternatives to individual support, such as:

- rotation by group;
- support at the point of need;
- room management.

In rotation by group, the teacher and TA alternate from lesson to lesson. In one lesson, the TA works with middle- or high-attaining groups, while the teacher works with the lower-attaining. In another, the roles might reverse.

Support at the point of need can be used where the teacher sets tasks at different levels of challenge and enables children (with support) to choose the appropriate task. The children then ask for help when they feel they need it, for example, by holding up traffic light cards (green for confident, amber for not quite sure, red for not confident at all) or using the thumbs system (up for confident, sideways for so-so, down if they need help and further explanation).

Room management is a system often used in special schools. Here, one adult (the 'individual helper') will work in a focused way with a selected group or a series of individuals, while the other (the 'activity manager') deals with the rest of the class. If there is a third adult (perhaps a parent volunteer), s/he can take the role of 'mover', who aims to maintain the flow of activity in the class by dealing with minor distractions as they arise. Roles are pre-planned and can change from lesson to lesson; obviously it is important that the class or subject teacher primarily takes the individual helper role, providing specific and detailed teaching.

Room management is particularly relevant given the DISS findings that teachers spend the bulk of their time, other than whole-class teaching, on what the researchers call roving the classroom. Given the right training in behaviour management, this 'patrolling' role is clearly one that might be taken by support staff, 'flipping' the support and leaving the teacher free to teach.

Staff might also want to reflect on how they deploy TAs during whole-class teaching and whether any changes might be needed. How much time do TAs spend idle? When they are occupied, is it often in what the DISS team call 'stereo teaching' – relaying back to a pupil what the teacher has said but in slightly different words. It is worth teachers shadowing a pupil with SEND to experience this for themselves; they will find it almost impossible to follow the teacher.

In some circumstances, it might be better not to attempt whole-class teaching at all but instead to split the class so that some pupils engage in carefully planned activities supported by the TA while others experience the from-the-front teaching, then swap. Pre-teaching or review of key topic vocabulary can be a particularly useful activity for the TA to undertake here in their support role.

There are many other roles that TAs can profitably take (Table 11.5). It can be useful to share this table at a whole-staff meeting, opening a discussion with teachers and TAs on which models might be further developed in school and which might be reconsidered.

Finally, you might want to move the discussion on to ways in which class and subject teachers can reduce the need for TA support altogether.

Role	Advantages	Disadvantages
Running small group or 1:1 intervention programmes	Likely to have high impact if intervention is proven and TA is well trained and supported.	Less effective if poorly linked to class work, or if pupil misses essential aspects of curriculum.
	TAs can develop expertise, for example, ELKLAN-trained language specialist, Emotional Literacy (ELSA) specialist.	Teachers can become de-skilled if all the specialist expertise sits with TA.

Table 11.5 Roles for TAs

Role	Advantages	Disadvantages
Class-based in-class support	Can be effective if presence of TA enables teacher to work with lower attaining groups.	Little evidence of impact on attainment, progress and attitudes to learning. Can distance pupil from class/subject teacher and from peers. Can lead to over-dependence.
Faculty or department-based in-class support	Enables TAs to develop subject knowledge. More likely to promote independence as TAs not attached to individual pupils.	Little evidence of impact on attainment, progress and attitudes to learning.
Pre-teaching of concepts and vocabulary to prepare pupils for later class work	Some evidence of impact on vocabulary development. Promotes independence.	Can be difficult to timetable.
Personal assistant (PA) support for physical care	Essential for some pupils with medical or physical needs.	Risk of cotton-wool effect if overused. Can promote dependence.
Preparation of resources for children to use in class	Where directed by the teacher, helps them differentiate effectively. Promotes independence.	Risk that teachers leave all the differentiation to the TA.
Observation and assessment of pupils to inform teacher planning	Helpful where used to improve the quality of teaching and learning for pupils with SEND.	Can go wrong if TAs not trained in assessment techniques.
Working with pupils to develop their one-page profiles/Pupil Passports	Supports pupil engagement and person-centred planning. Likely to improve quality of teaching experienced by pupil.	Not useful if staff fail to make use of the information in the profile/Passport.
Setting pupils up with assistive technology	Supports pupil independence and curriculum access.	Not useful if teachers do not build use of appropriate technology into their planning.
Support in unstructured times, which some children with SEND find less easy to manage than the classroom	Useful if TA sets up activities for all and supports child to join in.	Can reduce peer interaction if TA works only with child.
Key worker, acting as link between family, pupil, school staff and outside agencies	Highly valued by families in schools that have developed this role.	Time-intensive Risk of over-focus on care at the expense of academic learning.

Table 11.5 (Continued)

EXAMPLE

TAs often say they have to repeat the teacher's instructions to children because they don't remember them. Ask your colleagues to come up with all the ways teachers can improve the clarity of their instructions and scaffold children's comprehension and recall.

Take feedback and add any ideas they did not come up with. Teachers could, for example, give instructions in the order in which they should be followed, 'chunk' them and simplify the syntax. They could supplement verbal instructions with visuals. They could ask the child to repeat back an instruction, encourage children to ask for clarification or repetition if they have not understood, leave instructions on the board or on a laptop in the corner of the room or tell children they can start if they are ready/wait to have the instructions explained again if they would like to.

Make the point that good teacher scaffolding can take away the need for an additional adult on whom the child comes to rely.

Ultimately, bringing staff on board with changes to the way TAs work may require a 'suck it and see' approach, in which new approaches are tried out and evaluated, with the promise that the status quo can be reinstated if they do not work. This is particularly the case where teachers are being asked to manage with less in-class TA support so that more time can be devoted to evidence-based intervention programmes, as in the subsequent case study school.

CASE STUDY

Arbourthorne Primary school in Sheffield made a conscious decision some years ago to review the deployment of TAs. Plans were put in place to develop them as highly skilled intervention specialists, delivering one-to-one and small group programmes. A well-equipped intervention suite was constructed to accommodate this new way of working. Class teachers, after some initial disquiet, soon came on board with the change. 'Once teachers saw the impact,' say the school, 'they began to ask for more of what was clearly working.' TAs can also see the effects of their work and have become very aware of the difference they are making to children's lives. They value being treated as expert professionals, both through training and regular observation and feedback on their work.

Staff now work collectively to analyse data and make decisions about which individuals will benefit from in-class support and which will benefit from additional, targeted literacy and numeracy intervention programmes delivered by TAs. Data are regularly gathered to evaluate the impact of interventions. As a result of both interventions and high-quality in-class support from teachers, TAs and one-to-one tutors, the percentage of children achieving the expected standard in English and maths combined rose from 35% to 76% over a period of three years.

Change and the SENCO

In all the work you may do with parents, pupils and colleagues to bring about changes in the way SEND is managed in your school, it is important to remember also that a new system may represent considerable change for you too, as SENCO.

Fundamentally, what you will become is less of a manager of paper and meetings, and more of a strategic manager and a leader of inclusive teaching and learning in your school.

You might want to reflect on what proportion of your time you currently spend on each of these broad activity headings:

- SEND Code of Practice procedures – individual plans, reviews, records, reports, meetings
- Contributing to year group/subject curriculum planning
- Monitoring – observing lessons and providing feedback
- Managing TAs or other staff
- Supporting school-based staff professional development and work with parents to help them support their child's learning
- Strategic management of SEND – school self-evaluation (including analysing data on the progress and participation of children with SEND), planning and evaluating additional provision, contributing to the school improvement plan
- Teaching children with SEND
- Linking with outside agencies
- Organising resources

If you record the proportion of time spent on each of these as a chart, it might, perhaps, look like the one in Figure 11.1, with by far the most time spent on processes that research has shown to have the least impact on children's progress. If so, share this with your headteacher, and ask them to consider this question:

> Your SENCO knows about SEND. Your subject leads for English and maths know about teaching English and maths. Your Science Head of Department knows about teaching science. Your Heads of Year/pastoral leads know about children's behaviour and well-being. Would you be happy if they all spent most of their time on paperwork and chasing funding?

Returning the ownership of pupils with SEND to their class and subject teachers should enable you to shift the emphasis, so that your chart might look more like the one in Figure 11.2. Alternatively, if strategic management is really not your thing, and someone else in school carries out that role for inclusion, you could shift the time pattern so that

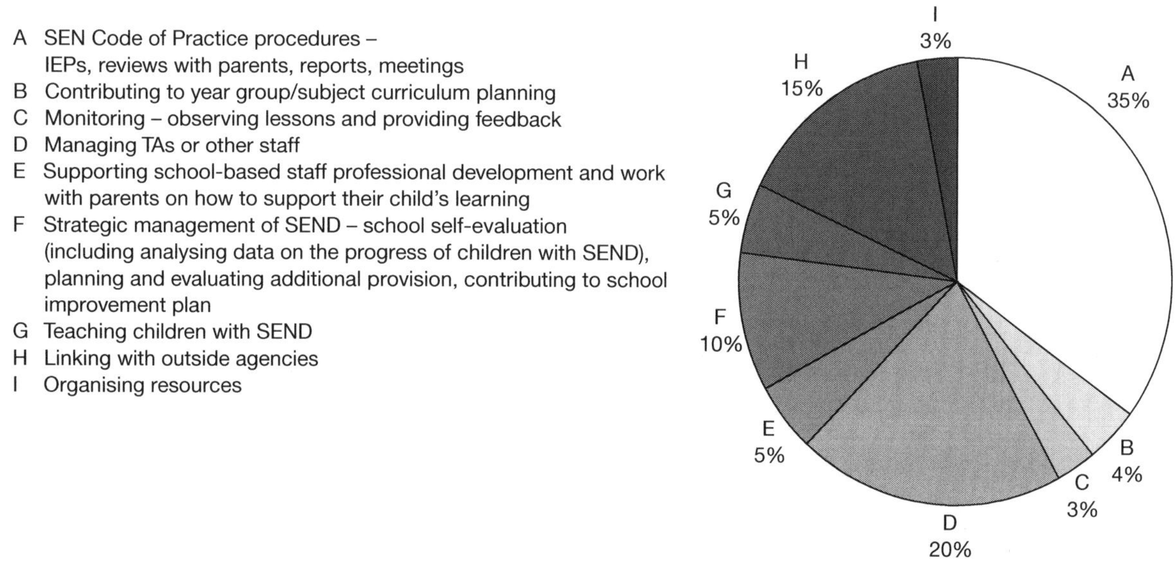

FIGURE 11.1 How do I spend my SENCO time?

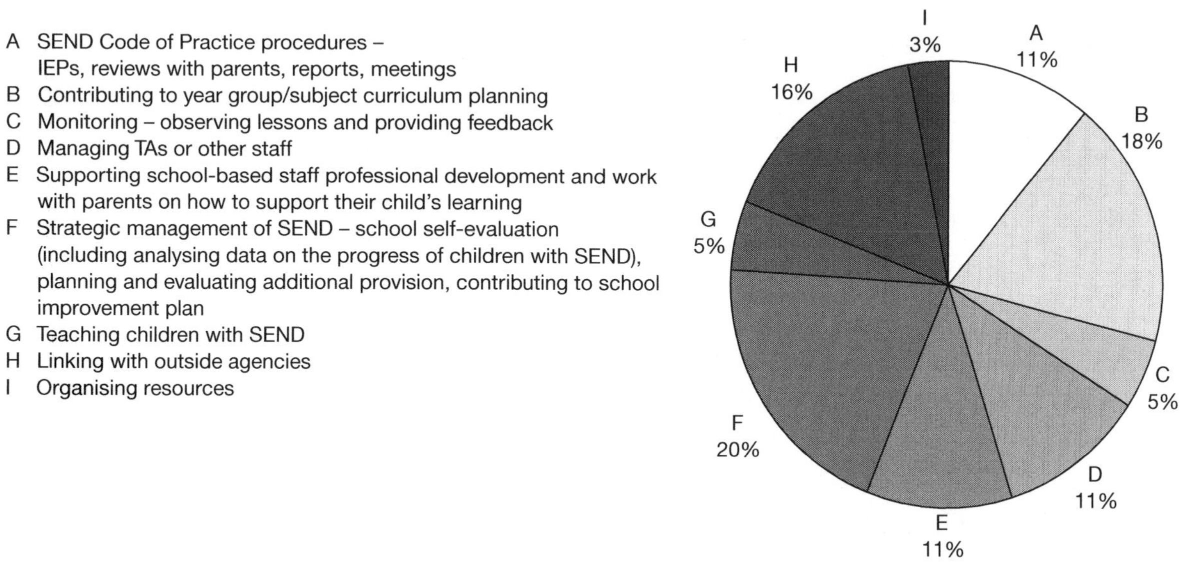

FIGURE 11.2 How do I spend my SENCO time?

you spend more time teaching children with SEND directly, using some of the evidence-based intervention programmes described in Chapter 8, or more time supporting family learning and parenting groups or workshops, as described in Chapter 10.

Managing inclusion is a team job, not the role of a single individual. It is up to you and your school to determine how the various roles in relation to SEND are fulfilled and what your part will be. But shifting away from bureaucratic processes to focus on teaching and learning will have big implications for you, whatever the new pattern of your time. It represents a change, and the same conditions that apply to whole-school change apply also to you. You may have a vision for how you want your role to develop in the future, but it is useful to reflect also on what you need in terms of skills, incentives and resources. The incentive of reducing fruitless paperwork may be sufficient, but you may also want to have the effort involved in managing that change recognised and rewarded through your own performance management. You will perhaps be able to articulate to senior leaders the differences you see in your future role, and enter into discussions about how they will be reflected in management structures and pay scales.

Resource implications for your changed role should not be excessive. A reduction in bureaucracy is intended to change the way you use existing time rather than require lots more. But you will need resources in the form of time at staff meetings or INSET days to introduce staff to new systems, and time identified in their timetables to work with you as you support them in developing their inclusive teaching practice.

Finally, there are likely to be substantial skills implications in a change of role for you. Table 11.6 provides a skills audit to guide you in planning your own professional development. Courses or school-based support on all of this should be available from your MAT, your local authority, from independent providers, from organisations like nasen, from research and good practice Hub schools or from higher education institutions.

✓ Tick the column that best fits you			
Knowledge, skills, understanding	**I need to learn more about this**	**I feel pretty confident in this**	**I can support other SENCOS in this**
Inclusive classroom planning and teaching			
Interpreting and using data on pupil progress			
Provision mapping			
The evidence base for different intervention programmes			
Evaluating the quality and impact of intervention programmes in school			
Providing support to other adults (TAs, learning mentors) delivering intervention programmes			

Table 11.6 Skills audit for SENCOs

✓ Tick the column that best fits you			
Knowledge, skills, understanding	**I need to learn more about this**	**I feel pretty confident in this**	**I can support other SENCOS in this**
Undertaking classroom observations and feeding back to staff			
Monitoring planning			
Coaching colleagues			
Providing INSET			
Person-centred planning			
Training pupils in self-advocacy			
Providing workshops and running groups for parents to help them support their children's language, literacy or mathematics learning, or their social and emotional development			

Table 11.6 (Continued)

KEY PRINCIPLES

Key take-aways for SENCOs

- Changing practice in school, so that class and subject teachers take more responsibility for meeting SEND, needs careful planning, to ensure ownership by colleagues and senior leaders, sufficient resources and a blend of pressure and support
- It is important to help staff reflect on how they work with TAs and the match to evidence on what works
- It is important to reflect on your own role as SENCO and the balance of time you spend on different types of activity, to establish whether you need to shift the emphasis to one of strategic management or direct work with children and families

Key questions for the wider school leadership team

- Is SEND a bolt-on activity in your school (seen as the preserve of specialists, with resources allocated to discrete SEND provision and pupils 'referred on' to outside agencies), or is it an integrated aspect of whole-school systems (seen as the preserve of all staff, with resources for support potentially available to all pupils, leadership roles distributed and outside agencies asked to enhance the school's continued efforts to meet pupils' needs)?
- Is your SENCO able to act as a leader of inclusive teaching and learning, or do they spend most of their time on paperwork and chasing funding?
- In your classrooms, is it ever the case that the most skilled and qualified staff are spending the least time with the children who most need their help?

Conclusion

Making change happen is difficult. So, however, is the everyday job of SENCOs and classroom teachers as they struggle to support children with SEN or disabilities and find that their progress remains limited. Because of this, change is essential.

Readers of this book will by now understand how fundamental are the changes proposed in the way we manage SEND in schools. The theme may have been how to beat bureaucracy – but it has also been how we might get a better deal for children with SEND through the changes we make to our systems. It has been about recognising that from the learner's point of view, if educational change does not happen in classrooms then it does not happen.

It has been about shifting effort away from documents and meetings that happen outside the classroom and have little impact on what happens inside it, onto placing more of the responsibility for meeting individual needs back with the class or subject teacher.

This will only work if we make it easy for these teachers to take on this shift of responsibility. It will only be manageable if the systems we ask them to use for pupils with SEND are the *same* as they use for all the class – embedded in their regular target-setting, assessment and curriculum planning processes.

Taken to the limit, these new systems may eventually mean that, while retaining the concept of disability, we can dispense with the more nebulous concept of 'special educational needs' altogether and simply think about how learning can be personalised for a whole range of children who from time to time require extra responsiveness from us, for all sorts of reasons linked to the experiences they are going through. So far, the notion of special educational needs and the elaborate and separate bureaucracy around it have only served on the whole to marginalise pupils and make them 'someone else's problem'. Integrated, personalised systems will mean they make better progress.

Bureaucracy, it is interesting to reflect, is what others ask of you. *Systems*, however, are what you devise for yourself and your own setting. Schools like the ones in our case studies show us that more effective systems are possible. Such schools would not claim to have beaten bureaucracy, but they do feel they have held it at bay. Where there is paperwork, it is paperwork that the school sees as meeting the particular needs of their children – not paperwork done for its own sake with little impact on learning. Staff may be working just as hard as ever, but they feel that the actions they take now make sense and will make a difference. As one SENCO put it, 'It's how you *feel* about the time not the actual time that matters.'

The schools described in this book have found new meaning in what they do, as a result of changing the way that key people, particularly the SENCO, spend their time. Scaffolding learning, adaptive teaching, provision mapping and national SEND reforms have created the context that makes this possible. It is up to us all now to follow their lead.

Beating bureaucracy toolkit

The materials in this section are available to download from

www.routledge.com/cw/gross

Information for Ofsted and other outside agencies

We agree with Ofsted that what makes most difference to higher outcomes for pupils with SEND is a curriculum that works for all learners, and high-quality teaching by class and subject teachers who understand pupils' needs, adapt their teaching accordingly and carefully monitor pupils' progress.

We have therefore focused our SEND strategy on making sure all staff understand the needs of pupils they teach, through information they access electronically, and on staff CPD on inclusive teaching. We do not rely on individual education/support plans since the evidence suggests that these are not always successful in influencing day-to-day teaching. It is our policy to write and review separate individual education/support plans only for children with lower-incidence, complex learning difficulties or disabilities, where a number of different agencies are involved.

There are many children in our school with needs that could be called 'special' who are not on the SEN register. That is because we have worked hard to extend the range and quality of provision that is 'normally available', thus reducing the numbers of children who need provision that is additional or different. The children we place on our SEND register are again those with more complex needs and external agency involvement.

Much of the evidence of the impact of our support for pupils with SEND, and the systems that support that impact, is located within regular school systems for all:

- Tracking data on pupil academic progress
- Inclusive curriculum planning
- Pupil-held personal and academic targets
- Provision map of all our interventions for pupils with SEND/eligible for the pupil premium/eligible for catch-up tuition
- Evaluations of the interventions in our provision map

In addition, evidence can be found in the following SEND-specific systems:

- Data on the attainment and progress of pupils with SEND
- Data on overall participation of pupils with SEND in extracurricular activities
- Data on the destinations of pupils with SEND on leaving our school
- Data on the overall exclusions, suspensions and attendance of pupils with SEND, and their experience of bullying
- Personal Profiles/Passports for individual pupils on the SEND register
- Records of conversations with parents/carers of pupils on the SEND register
- Parent/carer workshops listed on our website
- SEND self-evaluation audit and action plan (including current Accessibility Plan and whole-school CPD plan). Our self-evaluation includes summary of progress data, information from work scrutiny and classroom observation, information from pupil and parent surveys, information from evaluation of interventions.
- Details of performance management and professional development of teaching assistants, linked to pupil outcomes
- Governors' monitoring and evaluation programme for SEND

Our systems to ensure the progress and well-being of pupils with SEND are set out subsequently.

Purpose of an effective send system	How the purposes are achieved in our school
Identification – ensuring that children's needs are identified.	Class and subject teachers track pupil progress closely and identify pupils requiring support. Parental concerns expressed to teacher or SENCO are followed up. Class/subject teachers use checklists to screen pupils with weak reading or spelling for dyslexia. We screen all pupils with literacy difficulties or behavioural/emotional difficulties for speech, language and communication needs.
Assessment – ensuring that assessment takes place, to better understand the barriers to learning and how they might be overcome.	SENCO trains/coaches colleagues in involving the pupil in identifying strengths, difficulties and what helps. SENCO uses appropriate tools to assess pupils with literacy, numeracy or social and emotional difficulties. SENCO uses information from outside agencies' assessments to develop strategies for pupils with low-incidence/complex needs.
Communication – making sure that all relevant staff and outside agencies know what the child's needs are and what should be done to support them.	We use pupil-held Personal Profiles/Passports that record strengths, difficulties and what helps. SENCO provides training for pupils in how to communicate their needs.
Identifying priorities and setting targets for learning or behaviour involving pupils.	We use pupil-owned targets set together by the class or subject teacher and the pupil.

Purpose of an effective send system	How the purposes are achieved in our school
Identifying strategies, in the classroom and elsewhere, to help the child achieve targets.	SENCO provides strategy suggestions for staff. SENCO and school-based social and emotional learning specialist act as consultant to colleagues on what works for lower-attaining pupils, pupils with SEND and those with social, emotional and mental health difficulties.
Tracking, monitoring and reviewing progress.	Standardised assessments are used before and after an intervention. Standard school attainment tracking systems are used, with SENCO support for colleagues in tracking the progress of pupils working outside pre-key stage standards
Engaging parents and carers – agreeing priorities and targets with them, making sure they know what is being done to help their child and to what effect, suggesting ways in which they can support their child's progress.	Our school's online SEND 'offer' has been developed by asking parents what their key questions are about provision for their children. It contains a clear provision map showing the extra provision and what entry levels entitle a child to access that provision. We hold termly conversations with the parents of pupils on the SEND register and the pupils themselves to agree on goals and review progress. SENCO and curriculum specialists run workshops for parents/families and implement projects (such as paired reading) for specified groups.
Engaging pupils – seeking their views and agreeing priorities and targets with them.	We use varied and often visual ways to elicit pupils' views and work with them to prepare them to lead their own review meetings.
Coordinating the actions to be taken by the school and outside agencies and evaluating their impact.	Internal provision and external agency involvement are recorded on a cumulative overview/record of progress tracking sheet for each pupil on the SEND register, alongside progress tracking data and data on behaviour and attendance. The impact of interventions on our provision map is evaluated through before and after measures.
Informing decisions about the allocation of resources – extra adult time and/or physical resources.	We use a detailed whole-school provision map to plan additional provision.
Supporting transition – making sure that information about the child's needs is passed on as they move from one class or setting to another.	We pass on pupil personal profiles and record of additional provision (highlighted, dated provision maps and cumulative overview/record of progress tracking sheet).

Information for parents and carers

Dear Parent,

This letter is for parents and carers of children with special educational needs or disabilities. It explains how we will help your child at X school.

We want to make sure that everyone in school understands your child's needs. So we will work with you and your child to write a Personal Passport/Profile that will go to everyone who teaches Y. The Passport/Profile will say what Y is good at, what s/he finds difficult and what helps him/her to learn.

When teachers plan their lessons, they will think about what exactly your child needs to know and learn, what teaching approaches will work best and what they need to do to overcome any barriers that will stop your child from learning. You are very welcome to look at examples of teachers' planning. We will also make sure you know about your child's individual targets, which they set with their teachers.

If you would like to help your child reach these targets through home activities, we can suggest ideas. Sometimes we organise special events in school – like how to help your child with literacy or social and emotional learning – that we hope you will come to and find useful.

Y may also have extra one-to-one or small group help with language, literacy, maths, social and emotional or coordination skills. Our school 'provision map' shows what help we provide in each year group. We would like you to see this map. If your child needs this extra help, it will be for a fixed period of time. We will assess progress before and after this extra teaching so that we can tell you what difference it has made.

Some children may also have long-term one-to-one support in class for some or part of the day. In general, though, this will be where they need physical care. National research has shown that for other children, too much one-to-one support may mean they see less of the most qualified person in the class – their teacher – and as a result, they do less well with their learning. Too much one-to-one support for a child with SEND can also mean that other children tend to ignore them, so their social development is affected. Lastly, it can make them depend on their teaching assistant for help, when we really want them to learn to be independent.

That's why we want the class or subject teacher to plan carefully other ways of overcoming any barriers to learning your child may experience, such as using technology, rather than just relying on a teaching assistant.

Class/subject teachers assess each child's overall progress once a term. Progress will be discussed at parents' evenings twice a year and at an extra meeting in the spring term. At these meetings, we want you to tell us about anything that will help us do a better job to help your child.

But please don't wait for parents' evenings if there is anything you would like to discuss. Just get in touch – your contact person is Z, tel:

With best wishes,

Information for parents on support in the classroom

Because your child has special educational needs or a disability, you will be planning with us the best way to help your child in school. We've written this information sheet to tell you about 'what works' in classroom support. The information is based on research. If you would like to know more about the research, we've given some weblinks and reading later in the sheet.

One-to-one support

Most parents want one-to-one support for their child either from a teaching assistant (TA) or learning support assistant (LSA). Ideally, they would like full-time one-to-one support.

BUT did you know that

- too much one-to-one support from a TA or LSA may mean the child sees less of the most qualified person in the class (their teacher) and as a result they do less well with their learning?
- too much one-to-one support for a child with special educational needs or a disability (SEND) can also mean that other children tend to ignore them, so their social development is affected?
- support can make them depend on their TA to help them, when we really want them to learn to be independent?

> He's in my class but not on my radar
>
> Teacher describing a child with special needs with his own TA

That's why in our school we want the class or subject teacher to carefully plan ways of overcoming any barriers to learning a child may experience, such as using technology, rather than simply relying on a TA/LSA.

> I'm in the bottom table group and we can't do anything by ourselves so we always have to have an adult working with us
>
> A child to an Ofsted inspector

What are the alternatives to one-to-one TA/LSA support?

Some children absolutely do need a TA or LSA with them a good deal of the time if they have physical or medical needs which mean they must have personal support for health or care reasons. For many other children, it can sometimes be more effective to spend at least some of any available money on other options such as specialist advice from teachers or therapists, funded time for class and subject teachers to meet and plan with these specialists, training for staff supporting the child, time-limited one-to-one or small group intervention programmes or resources to enable the child to work independently in class.

What works best where it is necessary for a TA or LSA to support my child in class?

If a TA or LSA is supporting your child in class, it often works best if the TA or LSA sometimes works with another group so that the class or subject teacher can themselves work with your child. Or the TA/LSA might move round the classroom answering children's questions and dealing with minor distractions so that the teacher can work in a focused way with a particular group or a series of individuals.

Another idea is for the TA/LSA to take a group of children with SEN to teach key concepts and vocabulary for the topic that is going to come up next in class so that they come to it with a head start. Alternatively, the TA/LSA might help a child with SEN or a disability to get set up with any technology they are going to use to help them communicate, read text or record their ideas.

Whatever the role assigned to a TA or LSA, it is vital that the teacher lets them know in advance what children will be learning in a lesson and what they should be doing to help children succeed in the lesson.

> Can you make sure you listen to this 'cos you're going to have to tell me again in a few minutes?
>
> A boy to his TA, while the teacher was giving instructions

Questions to ask us

What are you doing in school to adapt classroom and subject teaching to meet my child's needs?

Is there any technology that they could use in class to help overcome barriers to their learning?

When do the teacher and TA/LSA talk to each other about how my child is doing and how best to support them?

Does the TA supporting my child see the teacher's lesson plans in advance?

What training have teachers had on how to get the best from TA support?

What training has the TA supporting my child had?

What are you doing to help my child become more independent?

What are you doing to help my child fit in with the others in their class and make friends?

Weblinks and further reading

https://educationendowmentfoundation.org.uk/education-evidence/teaching-learning-toolkit/teaching-assistant-interventions

Blatchford, P. et al (2011) Reassessing the Impact of Teaching Assistants: How Research Challenges Practice and Policy. London: Routledge

Klassen, R. (2001) 'After the statement: reading progress made by secondary students with specific literacy difficulty provision', Educational Psychology in Practice,17(2): 121–133

Reynolds, D. and Muijs, D. (2003) 'The effectiveness of the use of learning support assistants in improving the mathematics achievement of low achieving pupils in primary school', Educational Research, 45(3): 219–2

Giangreco, M., Edelman, S., Luisellu, T. and Macfarland, S. (1997) Helping or hovering? Effects of instructional assistant proximity on students with disabilities, Exceptional children, 64, 7–18

Giangreco, M. F. (2010) 'One-to-one paraprofessionals for students with disabilities in inclusive classrooms: Is conventional wisdom wrong?' Intellectual & Developmental Disabilities, 48, 1–13

MENCAP (1999) On a Wing and a Prayer. London: MENCAP

Webster, R. and Blatchford, P. (2013) The Making a Statement project final report. A study of the teaching and support experienced by pupils with a statement of special educational needs in mainstream primary schools. London: Institute of Education

Webster, R. et al (2012) Maximising the impact of teaching assistants. London: Routledge

Research into TA deployment

Decreased independence

Professor Michael Giangreco, in an article called 'Helping or hovering?' observed that when an assistant was nearby, children were more likely to seek help and less likely to work independently.

This same study found that the presence of a TA/LSA also sometimes prevented the child from interacting with other children in the class.

Another study of children with Statements of SEN (EHCPs) found that where they had a TA with them, they had half as many interactions with their classmates as other pupils.

Lack of teacher interaction

The charity MENCAP studied schools which were thought to have good practice in inclusion. They found that, even in these schools, the TA was often the child's main teacher, doing all the planning, with few opportunities to liaise with the class teacher.

The presence of a TA, they observed, tended to prevent the class teacher from considering their own role in adapting the curriculum to ensure their pupils' access and participation.

The researchers also noted many cases where the teacher more or less ignored the child, or where the presence of the TA prevented other children from seeking to interact with him or her.

The DISS study

The DISS study was a large research project on the characteristics, impact and deployment of support staff. It was funded by the Department for Children, Schools and Families (DCSF) and the Welsh Assembly Government (WAG) and took place from 2003 to 2008.

Researchers sat in classrooms observing pupils every ten seconds and noting down who they were talking and working with. The results, covering thousands of pupils, showed that children with SEN who had TA support were half as likely to be talking and working with the class teacher than children without SEN. The greater their level of SEN, the less likely they were to be spending time with the teacher.

The DISS study also found that the more TA/LSA support children had, the less academic and social progress they made. This was not because those supported by TAs had SEN or were low achievers to start with. The researchers compared similar children – children with similar academic levels or levels of SEN – so were able to rule out this explanation.

The difference in progress made by children with a lot of TA support was large: as much as a whole year's school progress.

The researchers also looked at the effect of TA support on children's approach to learning (confidence, motivation, relationships with other children, completing work, following instructions, not distracted and not being disruptive). They found a good effect for pupils in Year 9 (13–14-year-olds) but not in any other age group.

Positive impact of TA support

On the other hand, other research shows that some kinds of TA support do lead to very good academic progress. This tends to be when TAs are taking an individual child or group to follow a specific programme to improve literacy, language, maths or social and emotional skills.

The programme may last six weeks to a term – sometimes longer – but it will have a definite beginning and end. The TA will have been well trained to follow the programme, and the class or subject teacher will have had some training too so that they know about the content of the extra sessions and can follow up in class.

Turning the dial: information for school leaders

Schools and settings that 'turn the dial' on SEND are able to turn the dial on a number of key improvement priorities, from raising attainment to narrowing the disadvantage gap and improving behaviour. This is because of strong evidence about the links between SEND and these priorities.

Turning the dial on school attainment

Nationally, the attainment gap between pupils with SEND and their peers is twice as big as the gap between pupils eligible for free school meals and their peers.

In 2019, only 22% of pupils with SEND reached the expected standard in reading, writing and maths at the end of KS2. In 2021, the Attainment 8 score for these pupils was 31.1, compared to 54.5 for pupils without SEND.

Turning the dial on narrowing the gap between disadvantaged children and their peers

Narrowing the attainment gap between less well-off children and their peers is another key priority for schools. It is unlikely that this will be possible without paying attention to SEND. This is because of the considerable overlap between SEN and disadvantage – the percentage of pupils in England with SEN support who were eligible for free school meals in 2019/20 was 29.9%, nearly double that for pupils with no SEN (14.9%).

Turning the dial on attendance

Attendance is a current priority nationally and locally. The absence rate for pupils with an EHC plan was 13.1% over 2020/21, and 6.5% for those with SEN support, compared to 3.9% for pupils with no SEN. Whilst absences for some children with EHCPs can be expected to be higher because of associated medical or mental health needs, the majority of absences for all pupils with SEND cannot be explained in this way and can be tackled.

Turning the dial on behaviour and mental health

The Timpson Review of school exclusions (2019) found that children with SEND accounted for 46% of all permanent exclusions and 44.9% of suspensions. Some of these are related to social, emotional and mental health needs, but others are not. It has been found that two-thirds of pupils at risk of exclusion from school have speech, language and communication needs (SLCN) (Clegg, 2004). Eighty-one percent of children with emotional and behavioural disorders are found to have previously unidentified language disorders. Mental health needs also very often arise from unmet speech, language and communication needs: young people referred to mental health services are three times more likely to have SLCN than those who have not been referred.

Turning the dial on destinations

Pupils with special educational needs are less likely to have any sustained destination than those with no identified SEN: 89.3% of pupils with SEN go on to education, employment or apprenticeships on leaving school, compared to 94.7% of those with no identified SEN.

The numbers

Nationally, pupils with SEND make up 16.6% of the school population. By the end of Year 7, almost one in three pupils have been classified as SEN at least once in school census. Given these numbers, and the current gaps between pupils with SEND and their peers, it will not be possible to increase overall school attainment and attendance, or decrease behaviour and mental health difficulties, without focusing on how the school can improve SEND practice in every classroom and every aspect of school life.

Reflection points

- Is SEND leadership reflected adequately in membership of your senior leadership team?
- Where does SEND figure in your school improvement plans?
- How much CPD time do you invest in SEND?
- Does your SENCO have a voice in planning the curriculum, improving and monitoring classroom teaching and learning and in whole-school strategies for behaviour and attendance, mental health and well-being?
- Do they have enough time for roles like these, or are they totally occupied with matters relating to individual pupils?

Your SENCO knows about SEND. Your subject leads for English and maths know about teaching English and maths. Your Science Head of Department knows about teaching science. Your Heads of Year/pastoral leads know about children's behaviour and well-being. Would you be happy if they all spent most of their time on paperwork and chasing funding?

Personal passport

CHILD'S PHOTOGRAPH

NAME:

D.O.B.:

SEN Support/EHCP:

SEN support began:

Areas of concern:

WHAT AM I GOOD AT?

WHAT DO I FIND HARD?

WHAT SHOULD TEACHERS AND OTHER PEOPLE IN SCHOOL DO TO HELP ME?

One Page Profile/Personal Passport

Who I am		**What helps me**		
Photo/name/class or form				
My gifts	Things I find hard	What teachers can do to help me	What I can do to help myself	Resources I need
		e.g. • Talk to me in short sentences • Explain words to me	e.g. Tell the teacher when I haven't understood	e.g. Visual timetables

Progress review meetings with parents and pupils (SEN or disability)

Pre-meeting information for class teacher or form tutor to gather

- ✓ Notes of last meeting
- ✓ Academic progress
- ✓ Achievement of curricular and personal targets
- ✓ Progress in relevant social/emotional, organisational, study and 'learning-to-learn' skills
- ✓ 'Before' and 'after' assessments showing impact of any interventions used (literacy, language, mathematics, social and emotional, motor coordination, other)

Agenda

- What does everyone really like and admire about x right now?
- How is x's progress – at school, at home and in the community?
- Have we all done what we said we would do at the last meeting?
- What has been the impact – is it taking x closer to reaching his/her goals?
- What's working? What's not working?
- What's important now to x/what's important now for x?
- What do we need to do now?

Notes

Actions agreed

Date: Signed:

Cumulative tracking and intervention record

Name:

Attainment[1]																		
			+	*+														
		#+	#	#														
	#+*	*	*															
	Term 1	Term 2	Term 3	Term 1	Term 2	Term 3	Term 1	Term 2	Term 3	Term 1	Term 2	Term 3	Term 1	Term 2	Term 3	Term 1	Term 2	Term 3
	Year 1			Year 2			Year 3			Year 4			Year 5			Year 6		
Provision in place																		

* Child's reading attainment

Writing attainment

+ Maths attainment

1 In this column, the school enters the numbers or letter codes it uses to track small-steps progress towards age-related expectations, with the code for exceeding Year 6 age-related expectations at the top of the column and codes for working at pre-key stage standards at the bottom.

Inclusive planning format

Unit: ______________ **Date:** ______________ **Year group:** ______________

Key learning objectives: ____

Learning outcome for unit: ____

Planning for inclusion – note here the teaching approaches and access strategies you will use to overcome barriers to learning for all pupils, and any differentiated learning outcomes for 'outliers' – pupils working well below age-related expectations.

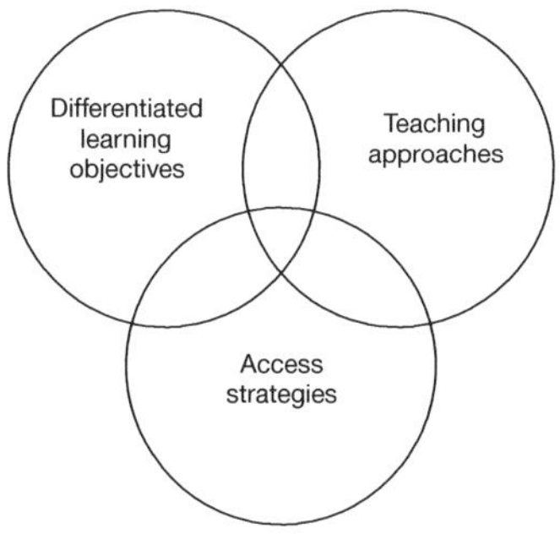

End of Unit Review of inclusive strategies used

What went well?

Even better if …

Session/lesson	Whole class learning and teaching	Independent learning	Guided learning	Assessment criteria	Plenary
1					
2					
3					
4					
5					

Medium-term plan

Year: Term:

HIGHLIGHT THE INCLUSIVE TEACHING STRATEGIES RELEVANT TO THE CLASS CHOOSE THREE OF THESE STRATEGIES TO FOCUS ON AS PART OF YOUR PROFESSIONAL DEVELOPMENT	
Plan seating taking into account needs of pupils with sensory impairment, distractible pupils, anxious pupils needing to be near door. Avoid background noise. Check light source in front of me, not behind. Face pupils when speaking. Cue pupils in to what I am going to talk about, and cue again when the topic changes. Clarify, display and refer back to new or difficult vocabulary. Break long instructions down into chunks and say one at a time. Check for understanding of instructions – ask pupil to explain them in their own words. Jot instructions down on post-it notes, or ask a pupil to do this for a study buddy. Use visual supports – pictures, concrete objects, visual timetable. Pitch questions so they are relevant for different learner levels. Give time/support before responses are required – thinking time, partner talk, persisting with progressively more scaffolding until child can answer. Use buddying for seating and paired/partner work – more settled pupil paired with a child who finds concentration difficult, more able with less able. Plan pre-tutoring by TA for individuals/groups, where this will help them to access the lesson. Make sure TA knows learning objective for any pupil(s) they will be supporting.	Make tasks more open/closed for different individuals and groups, according to need. Plan tasks as extended or short for different individuals and groups, according to need. Clearly explain and model tasks – check for understanding, task cards or boards as reminders, make time available and expected outcomes clear. Provide resources to help pupils be independent – write down and leave up instructions after saying them, keep relevant material from whole-class session on display, provide word lists or mats, dictionaries of terms, glossaries, maths resources such as number lines. Vary pupil groupings according to purpose and learning objective. Use buddying, text-to-speech technology where necessary to ensure that pupils can access written text/instructions. Plan alternatives to written recording for those who find this difficult – role-play, drama, making posters, video recording, audio recording, dictating to a study buddy, speech-to-print technology, annotating print-outs of IWB pages, mind mapping, card sorts, matching labels to diagrams or pictures. Use large print worksheets (12–14 point Arial), cream/buff paper. Use alternatives to copying notes from the board, for example, photocopy transcript of another pupil's notes. Provide scaffolding for writing – writing frames, clue cards, choice of words to fill in blanks. Give pupils opportunity to feed back in plenary in variety of media. Give pupils time to copy down homework or provide it on a sheet or school app. Model the homework in class time.

	UNIT **(Weeks)**	**LEARNING OBJECTIVES** **(for all pupils and 'outliers' working well below age-related expectations)**
1		
2		
3		
4		
5		

Review of key strategies used as part of your professional development What went well? What did you notice about the impact? Even better if . . . .

Task Management Board

Task management board	
Task:	**Equipment/tools needed:**
1.	
2.	
3.	
4.	
I will be finished when:	I can now:

Reproduced by kind permission of Thomas Tillier, Assistant SENCO

Strategy sheet: attention deficit hyperactivity disorder (ADHD)

Please use the highlighted strategies with . . . (pupil) in . . . (form).

Take child to unfamiliar classroom before lesson so that they can familiarise themselves with it and discuss where they should sit.

Discuss seating pupil near front with their back to the class, between two good role models and well away from areas other pupils need to walk through.

Establish a quiet place where pupil can go to work.

Keep one wall plain if you have lots of displays so the pupil can sit facing that to avoid overstimulation.

Provide a 'settling in' task the pupil can get on with on entering the classroom, such as a word search.

Allow pupil to fiddle with a piece of Blu-Tack, rubber band, squeeze ball or another chosen object.

Have them use a mini-whiteboard to record their ideas, to stop them shouting out.

Make tasks short, with frequent breaks and opportunities to move around and use up energy – putting post-its up on the wall, cleaning the whiteboard or tables, etc.

Give instructions simply and clearly. Make sure the pupil is looking at you first. Check that he or she has understood them.

Aim for a ratio of four positive comments to one negative, and teach pupil how to reward themselves: 'You managed to concentrate on your work very well just then; give yourself a pat on the back.'

Devise a private signal system to let the pupil know when they are off-task or behaving inappropriately.

Use a planned reward system.

Teach/use clear classroom routines, for example, have all pupils hold an object when it is their turn to talk. Display classroom rules and routines for pupil to refer to. Illustrate them visually – for example, use a traffic-light system to indicate whether pupils can talk or not, or symbols for different noise levels (partner voices, group voices, classroom voice, playground voices).

When pupil is misbehaving,

- say what you want him or her to do, rather than what you don't – 'N, I want you to keep your hands in your lap' instead of 'N, stop bothering P';
- label the behaviour but not the pupil – not 'You big bully' but 'N, bullying is not allowed in our school';
- remind pupil of a rule, rather than telling them off – 'N, our rule is we put up our hand to answer', or make a point of praising a pupil who is keeping the rule – 'A, I like the way you put your hand up when you knew the answer';
- use the language of choice, reminding pupils of the consequences of the various behavioural choices open to them.

Give frequent time warnings so pupils know when they will be expected to have finished a task.

Use a kitchen or sand timer to help pupil complete a task in a specified period of time.

Strategy sheet: attention deficit hyperactivity disorder (ADHD)

Continued

To help pupil work independently,

- actively teach core routines for certain tasks, having pupil practise them with progressively less help until they can quickly tell you and show you what they have to do if you ask them to do that type of task;
- give independent tasks that have previously been modelled for the whole class;
- give clear guidelines: 'I expect you to have produced at least three lines by ten past ten; I will be asking you then to share these with your writing partner.';
- use task cards/checklists for them to tick off as they complete each element of a task;
- provide support in the form of writing frames, word mats, relevant classroom displays, and prompts such as a card with ideas for 'Five things to do if you are stuck with your work'.

Ask another pupil or a small group to buddy the pupil who is having difficulties, praising them when they achieve easily reachable behavioural targets.

Strategy sheet: autism

Please use the highlighted strategies with . . . (pupil) in . . . (form).

Take child to unfamiliar classroom before lesson so that they can familiarise themselves with it and discuss lighting, position of teacher, where they should sit, for example, near the door or away from busy displays and distractions.
Keep one wall plain if you have lots of displays so the pupil can sit facing that to avoid sensory overload.
Allow pupil to use ear defenders and a 'noiseometer' on the wall to show classmates when noise levels get too high.
Set up an individual workstation with propped box files as screeners.
Prepare the pupil before the session/lesson by outlining what it will be about.
Provide a 'settling in' task the pupil can get on with on entering the classroom, such as a word search.
Support oral presentations/explanations with charts, diagrams, pictures, real objects or mime.
Set tasks with clear goals, and write worksheets in step-by-step form.
If pupil becomes anxious, allow him/her to remove self to an agreed calm-down area.
If pupil becomes upset, try asking him to take a pile of books or other 'heavy load' to another room.
Teach a relaxation strategy like slow breathing, and cue pupil when they need to use it.
Teach/use clear classroom routines, for example, have all pupils hold an object when it is their turn to talk. Display classroom rules and routines, illustrated by pictures, for pupil to refer to. Illustrate them visually – for example, use a traffic-light system to indicate whether pupils can talk or not, or symbols for different noise levels (partner voices, group voices, classroom voice, playground voices).
Use a visual way of showing the pupil what they/the class will be doing, such as a sequenced series of pictures (a visual timetable), clockface divided into sections or written list.
Use timeline of events →→ that branches ↕ to show where pupil will have to make choices.
Where visual timetables with cards are used, choose autistic children be the ones to put up the cards on the timetable.
Where visual timetables are used, include an 'oops' card to add any unexpected changes to the regular routine.
Put the next day's visual timetable up before children leave at the end of the day.
Use pictures or symbols to show pupils what they will be doing 'Now' and 'Next'. Use 'If' and 'Then' pictures/symbols to show what the pupil will be able to do if they first complete a certain task.
Use pictures to flag up a change in activity in advance, such as a round table to show pupils are going to move into groups.
If the pupil has sensory issues, provide gloves or other means of handling tactile materials (tongs, etc.).

Strategy sheet: autism

Continued

Use short, simple instructions. Give one at a time and check for understanding. Repeat instructions in same words rather than different ones. Write instructions down or ask a TA to record them on a mini-whiteboard the pupil can slip under their work as a checklist for the pupil to follow and tick off when completed.

Use pupil's name before asking a question or giving an instruction.

Avoid or explain metaphorical language and idiom like 'pull your socks up', 'it's raining cats and dogs', 'in a minute'.

Explain any changes of routine to the pupil in advance.

Give time warnings: for example, 'in five minutes it will be time to . . .'

Involve the pupil by asking direct, concrete questions at their level of understanding.

Support writing with writing frames, templates (e.g. writing up a science experiment), mind maps, gapped handouts.

Allow pupil to work alone rather than in a group where possible. If in a group, give clear roles within the group, and put the rules and roles into writing.

Use visual prompts on cards or photos, or consistent non-verbal signs (sit, look, listen, hand up, wait, quiet) to show pupil the social behaviours expected.

Prevent repetitive questioning by giving pupil a set number of question cards to give you each time they ask a question – when cards are gone, no more questions.

Don't ask the pupil to talk or write about imagined experiences.

Teach a single method for the pupil to follow rather than expect them to choose from multiple methods, for example, when completing calculations.

Avoid tasks which depend on empathy (e.g. in literature, history, geography, PSHE and citizenship).

Set explicit and clear expectations, for example, how many lines to write, how many questions to answer, how long to listen (use timer).

Put a green 'start' dot on the pupil's book and a line to show where to finish. Use in and out boxes for work to be done and work that is finished.

Provide pupil with a symbol card to display when he or she wants help.

Expect to teach pupil social skills, for example, what to say/do when praised, how to ask for help. Always tell the pupil what to do rather than what not to do.

Provide a structure for unstructured time, for example, chess club rather than break time outside.

Model to the pupil that making mistakes is OK and a part of the learning process.

Use incentives base on pupil's interests, for example, a pause every hour to focus on their interest or obsession, once they have completed their work.

If pupil goes off at a tangent, direct conversation back to the topic in hand: 'Right now we are talking about volcanoes.'

Use immediate and individualised reward systems, for example, collecting a number of stickers.

Strategy sheet: social, emotional and mental health needs

Please use the highlighted strategies with . . . (pupil) in . . . (form).

Consult pupil about where they should sit, for example, by the door if anxious, or next to a more settled peer.

If pupil becomes wound up/anxious, allow him/her to remove self to an agreed calm-down area.

Model talking about how you are feeling, reflect back how you think the pupil might be feeling, help pupil connect their actions to the underlying feelings. Reiterate that all feelings are OK – it's what we do with them (behaviour) that might not be.

Support pupil to use planned strategies to regulate their emotions, for example, personal calm-down box, deep breathing.

Make tasks short, with frequent breaks and opportunities to move around.

Remember that children (and adults) who are stressed find it hard to take in and remember complex information; make instructions short and clear. When pupil is experiencing emotional turbulence or anxiety, provide low-key tasks and increased structure and predictability in the classroom environment.

Set tasks with clear goals, outputs and timescales.

Make explicit the relevance of any task to the pupil's goals.

Teach/use clear classroom routines, for example, have all pupils hold an object when it is their turn to talk. Display classroom rules and routines for pupil to refer to. Illustrate them visually – for example, use a traffic-light system to indicate whether pupils can talk or not, or symbols for different noise levels (partner voices, group voices, classroom voice, playground voices).

Expect to teach pupil specific behavioural skills, for example, how to ask for help.

When pupil is misbehaving:

- say what you want him or her to do, rather than what you don't – 'N, I want you to keep your hands in your lap' instead of 'N, stop bothering P';
- label the behaviour but not the pupil – not 'You big bully' but 'N, bullying is not allowed in our school';
- remind pupils of a rule, rather than telling them off – 'N, our rule is we put up our hand to answer', or make a point of praising a pupil who is keeping the rule – 'A, I like the way you put your hand up when you knew the answer';
- use the language of choice, reminding pupils of the consequences of the various behavioural choices open to them.

Reframe their actions and attribute positive reasons for their behaviour: 'I can see you're not joining in the group discussion, but that's probably because you need some extra thinking time.'

Make an effort to 'catch the pupil being good' and praise them. Aim for a ratio of four positive comments to one negative, and teach pupil how to reward themselves: 'You managed to concentrate on your work very well just then; give yourself a pat on the back.'

Use proximal praise – praise a nearby pupil who is behaving appropriately.

Devise a private signal system to let the pupil know when they are off-task or behaving inappropriately.

Use a planned reward system for appropriate behaviour.

Strategy sheet: social, emotional and mental health needs

Continued

Identify at least one success each day/lesson.

Enhance access to technology – use of the internet to research a topic, access to predictive word processing software and onscreen word grids to support writing, opportunities to create presentations.

To help pupil work independently:

- actively teach core routines for certain tasks, having pupil practise them with progressively less help until they can quickly tell you and show you what they have to do if you ask them to do that type of task;
- set independent tasks that have previously been modelled for the whole class;
- give clear guidelines: 'I expect you to have produced at least three lines by ten past ten; I will be asking you then to share these with your writing partner.';
- use visual prompts in the form of pictorial task cards;
- provide support in the form of writing frames, word mats, relevant classroom displays and prompts such as a card with ideas for 'Five things to do if you are stuck with your work'.

Take steps to build pupil's self-confidence:

- Find out what they know about or are good at, and have them share this with the rest of the class or school.
- Give them responsibilities, for example, organising a lunchtime or after-school club, being a playground buddy, helping those who are new to the school.
- Have them keep records of new things they learn and can do.
- Ask them to tutor another pupil with their work.
- Photocopy or photograph good pieces of work for them to take home.

Take special steps to build the relationship with the pupil:

- Take extra care to greet the pupil each day, and say a word or two individually to them.
- Have lunch with the pupil from time to time. Try to involve them in a lunchtime or after-school club that you run.
- Invite them to help you with daily tasks.
- Listen without giving advice or opinions; show that you understand how the pupil feels: *'That must have made you very angry/upset.'*
- When things go wrong, reject the behaviour, not the pupil: *'This is not the behaviour I expect to see from someone as kind and helpful as you.'*
- Don't be afraid to tell the pupil you like them and that what happens to them matters to you: *'You really matter to me, and it's important to me that you do well this year.'*

Organise time – perhaps during registration – for a teaching assistant to chat with the pupil, giving them a chance to talk about anything that may be troubling them and get themselves ready for learning.

Ask another pupil or a small group to buddy the pupil who is having difficulties, praising them when they achieve easily reachable behavioural targets.

Deploy a teaching assistant to model, coach and reinforce group work skills when the pupil is working collaboratively with other pupils.

Strategy sheet: dyspraxia, motor coordination and associated difficulties*

Please use the highlighted strategies with . . . (pupil) in . . . (form).

Minimise need for extensive handwritten recording – use technology (predictive word processor, onscreen word banks, graphics packages), bullet points, mind mapping, flow charts, gapped handouts, buddy acting as scribe, pre-prepared post-its with information the pupil can pick up and place on the page, print-off of IWB page for pupil to annotate.
Avoid asking pupil to copy from board – quickly jot things down for them, provide a slip with date/title/learning objective that they can stick in their book or use a photocopy transcript of another pupil's notes
Allow pupil to choose writing tools that are most comfortable for them – pencil, pen, felt pen.
Design worksheets so that the layout is uncluttered. Use buff or cream paper, large print (12–14 point) and a clear font such as Arial. Set information out in panels. Signpost sections with key words, symbols and pictures. Put important information in bold or colour.
Check seating – desktop should be at elbow height, pupil should be able to sit right back in their chair with knees bending back at right angles and feet flat on the floor. Put box or large book under feet if necessary.
Use aids supplied – portable writing slope, clipboards to attach paper to, non-slip mats, repositional glue sticks used to anchor paper or other materials, ruler and paper backed with Dycem, small tray for equipment, triangular and thick-barrelled pencils/pens/paintbrushes or smooth-flowing rollerball pens, two handled/loop handled/spring-loaded scissors, handled ruler, transparent pencil case, templates and stencils (e.g. map outlines) for drawing.
Use a reminder handwriting alphabet and numeral formation guide at top of desk.
Use larger-lined book or paper, columns or boxes to place numbers in, squared paper. Attach paper to desk with Blu-Tack.
Provide the pupil with study packs – everything they need for each subject/lesson in a separate folder, plus pack of highlighter pens, post-it notes, a line tracker for following text, various-sized card 'windows' to limit vision to one area of page, sticky labels to use to correct or conceal.
Teach pupil strategies to improve organisation, such as diaries, workplans, checklists of equipment they have to bring to school each day, use of organiser functions on laptop or mobile phone.
Help pupil follow text on board or IWB by writing/highlighting alternate lines in different colours.
Enlarge pages from textbooks, cut out the particular exercise needed and then mount it on a separate page.
If the pupil needs to work through a series of questions, help them keep their place by using a paper clip or blob of Blu-Tack to indicate which question they are on.
Pair pupil with a more coordinated study buddy for practical work.
Provide additional time for practical tasks, changing for PE, putting on coat, etc.
Provide pre-prepared formats (diagrams, charts and graphs) on which pupil can record information.

Strategy sheet: dyspraxia, motor coordination and associated difficulties*

Continued

Teach pupil to talk themselves through visual and spatial tasks – for example, learn verbal model for letter formation ('b – start at top, down, up, round'), translate maths calculations into verbal problems.
Seat pupil away from distractions with plenty of space on each side of them – pupil should have writing arm on the outside edge of shared table. Pupil should be able to see the teacher without turning their body.
Avoid criticism if pupil looks untidy.
Choose resources that don't require manipulation (for example, number line rather than counters in maths).
Colour-code spatially confusable items, for example, minus sign in one colour, plus sign in another.
Allow ample rest periods as concentration and motor effort is demanding and pupil is easily fatigued.
Write down homework for pupil, post it on the school's app or give it on a sheet or pre-printed sticky label they can put in their book. Accept homework written down by parents.

* See also speech and language – expression – if speech articulation is a problem.

Strategy sheet: dyslexia

Please use the highlighted strategies with . . . (pupil) in . . . (form).

Have pupils work in pairs – dyslexic pupil who has good ideas but difficulty with spelling and handwriting with a pupil who is good at writing but not so strong on ideas.

Design worksheets so that the layout is uncluttered. Use buff or cream paper, large print (12–14 point) and a clear font such as Arial. Set information out in panels. Signpost sections with key words, symbols and pictures. Put important information in bold or colour.

Have any text that the pupil will struggle with read to them by a 'study buddy' or TA or appropriate assistive technology.

Avoid asking pupil to copy from board – quickly jot things down for them, provide a slip with date/title/learning objective that they can stick in their book or use a photocopy transcript of another pupil's notes.

Be aware that the pupil may find it hard to hold questions, information or instructions in their head for long enough to act on them, and:

- repeat instructions/questions;
- 'chunk' them rather than saying in one long string;
- jot them down on a sticky note, or encourage the pupil to do so;
- allow time for processing (for example, paired discussion with a partner before putting hands up).

Be aware that dyslexic pupils may know something one day and forget it the next, may lose or forget equipment they need or may forget what they are supposed to be doing in the course of a lesson. Avoid criticism when this happens; instead, talk with them about strategies they can use to help them remember things.

Use technology supports – laptop, predictive word processing, grids of useful words, sound files attached to information/instructions, sound files of key texts/revision notes, portable electronic phonetic dictionaries, Siri/Alexa support for spellings, speech-supported texts, text-to-speech applications, spellcheckers, mind mapping software, reading pens, digital audio recorders/phones.

Mark for content rather than presentation. When marking, praise for two correct spellings, target two incorrect spellings and use these errors as teaching points. Suggest a way of avoiding the mistake in the future – for example, the similarity of the spelling to other known words, or 'the tricky bit' that has to be learned.

Give pupil a checklist to help them edit their work.

Enable pupils to record their ideas using alternatives to writing: PowerPoint presentations, making videos or posters, oral presentations, dramatic reconstructions, mind maps, matching labels to pictures/diagrams/maps, sorting statements or pictures into categories.

Scaffold writing:

- Provide writing frames and templates (e.g. writing up a science experiment) to help structure thinking.

Strategy sheet: dyslexia

Continued

- Provide prompt sheets: questions to answer, key words to build each section or paragraph around, sentences or paragraphs to put in correct order, paragraph openings.
- Provide clue cards.
- Use cloze procedure (where the pupil fills in missing words in text).
- Print off an IWB page used in whole-class session and have pupils add to it/annotate.

Do not expect pupils to easily remember sequences such as days of the week, months of the year, the alphabet, times tables, number facts. Provide aids (for example, a pocket alphabet or calendar, table squares, calculator).

Avoid embarrassing pupils by asking them to read aloud in front of others, unless they volunteer.

Overcome problems in learning by rote by helping pupils recognise patterns, use mnemonics or use memory strategies that create relationships between items in a list in order to aid recall.

Allow extra time to complete tasks, and be aware of the fatigue the pupil may experience because of the amount of effort they have to put in to learning.

Teach pupil strategies to improve organisation, such as diaries, workplans, checklists of equipment they have to bring to school each day, use of organiser functions on mobile phone/laptop.

Provide the pupil with a study pack – spellchecker, highlighter pens, glue sticks, post-it notes, a line tracker for following text, audio recorder, reading pen, index cards for subject vocabulary or spelling mnemonics, sheet of high-frequency words, alphabet strip, memory jogger card for b/d confusion, sticky labels to use to correct or conceal, a tables square, a calendar, a calculator.

Write down homework for pupils, or give it on a pre-printed sticky label or sheet they can stick into their book, post it on the school app, or record your instructions on a mobile phone or tablet. Model the homework in class time. Allocate a homework buddy they can ring if they have forgotten what to do ('phone a friend').

Strategy sheet: hearing impairment

Please use the highlighted strategies with . . . (pupil) in . . . (form).

Use TA for pre-tutoring – preparing pupil for lesson, for example, explaining new words and concepts.
Take child to unfamiliar classroom before lesson so that they can discuss lighting, position of teacher, where they sit.
Seat pupil at front where able to read text, hear and lip-read.
Position sign supporters alongside teacher where pupil can see both.
Ensure light is on teacher's face, that is, light source behind pupil – don't stand with your back to a window.
Face pupil when speaking to facilitate lip-reading; repeat any instructions that have been given when the pupil could not see the speaker; avoid writing on board or IWB while speaking as you will not be facing pupil.
Don't make the pupil concentrate on lip-reading for too long without a break.
When other pupils contribute, ensure that they speak one at a time. Paraphrase their contributions back to the class.
Speak clearly, naturally and at a normal rate – shouting or exaggerated 'mouthing' distorts normal lip patterns.
Minimise background noise, for example, noisy heater, buzzing light. Make other pupils aware of need for a quiet working environment.
Use short simple instructions. Give one at a time and check for understanding. Repeat instructions first in same words, but then if the pupil does not understand a word, use a different one.
Support oral presentations/explanations with charts, diagrams, pictures, real objects or mime.
Write topics or headings on the board as you introduce them.
Prepare the pupil before the session/lesson by outlining what it will be about.
Use pupil's name before asking a question or giving an instruction.
Cue pupil in to a change of topic of conversation/presentation – say 'now we are going to talk about . . .'.
Question pupil after some other pupils have given examples of what is required.
Accept pupil's spoken utterances, but rephrase and give them back in a grammatically correct version.
Be aware that independent writing will reflect the pupil's spoken language levels and will not necessarily be grammatically correct.
Support writing with writing frames and lists of vocabulary to choose from.
Put up a list of key vocabulary for a particular topic or lesson, and teach the meaning of each word.

Strategy sheet: hearing impairment

Continued

<table>
<tr><td>Use a range of ways of recording so that learning is not limited by the pupil's ability to write full English sentences:

• Bullet points and mind maps
• Ordering tasks – for example, ordering cut-out words to make a sentence, or sentences to make a sequence of instructions
• Matching tasks, such as matching labels to pictures/diagrams/maps
• Cloze procedure, where they fill in missing words in text
• Annotating a printout of IWB page
• PowerPoint presentations
• Making posters, oral presentations, videos, dramatic reconstructions</td></tr>
<tr><td>Agree private signal that pupil can use to show you when they have not understood.</td></tr>
<tr><td>Try to use video with subtitles; if not available, ensure pupil can access video material after lesson to go through it again. Don't ask pupil to make notes while watching a video.</td></tr>
<tr><td>Allow extra time to complete tasks, and be aware of the fatigue the pupil may experience because of the amount of effort they have to put in to listening.</td></tr>
</table>

Strategy sheet: learning difficulties

Please use the highlighted strategies with . . . (pupil) in . . . (form).

Use TA for pre-tutoring – preparing pupil for a task so that they come to it already knowing the key vocabulary and concepts.

Link new learning to what pupil already knows – for example, start lesson with class mind map of what they already know about a subject.

Tell pupils the three key points of the lesson, teach them and recap on them at the end.

Break new learning down into small steps.

Provide multiple examples of new concepts, and take these examples from children's own real-life experience rather than talking in the abstract.

Use visual and kinaesthetic learning – learning from pictures, diagrams, mind maps, using practical equipment, handling objects, moving and doing rather than sitting.

Use scaffolding – having a peer or adult work alongside the pupil at first, then gradually withdraw as confidence grows, or having pupil finish a task that has already been part-done for them.

Use short, simple instructions. Give one at a time and check for understanding. Write down and leave up instructions after saying them.

Question pupil after some other pupils have given examples of what is required.

Give pupil time to think or to talk to a partner before answering a question, or say 'I'm going to come back to you in a minute to ask you xxxx'.

If pupil can't answer a question, scaffold/support till they can rather than saying, 'Can anyone help x?'; echo back the pupil's answers in expanded form.

Buddy the pupil with a more able peer.

Have any text that the pupil will struggle with read to them by a 'study buddy' or TA or appropriate assistive technology.

Put up a list of key vocabulary for a particular topic or lesson and teach the meaning of each word.

To help pupil extract the salient points from information that they are given, use highlighter pens, or provide cards telling them what they have to look out for on a visit, in a text or from sources such as film.

Make learning strategies explicit by 'thinking aloud' yourself.

Help pupil develop and generalise effective learning strategies – when successful, ask them to identify what they did to solve the problem/find the information.

Model to the pupil that making mistakes is OK and a part of the learning process.

Agree a private signal that the pupil can use to show you when they have not understood.

Pair higher-attaining with lower-attaining pupils, and provide a range of collaborative activities so that they can help one another.

Strategy sheet: learning difficulties

Continued

Prepare pupils for writing – have them work in a group with you or a TA to rehearse orally what they want to say, then plan the writing together.
Enable pupil to record their ideas using alternatives to writing: PowerPoint presentations, making posters, oral presentations, videos, dramatic reconstructions, mind maps, matching labels to pictures/diagrams/maps, sorting statements or pictures into categories.
Use software that supports writing, with onscreen word grids from which they can choose the words they need.
Scaffold writing: • Provide writing frames and templates (e.g. writing up a science experiment) to help structure thinking. • Supply prompt sheets: questions to answer, key words to build each section or paragraph around, sentences or paragraphs to put in correct order, paragraph openings. • Provide clue cards. • Use cloze procedure (where the pupil fills in missing words in text). • Print off an IWB page used in whole-class session and have pupils add to it/annotate.
Give homework instructions on a sheet and make time to explain them. Record them on mobile phone or tablet or post on the school's app. Model the homework in class time. Allocate a homework buddy to ring if they need help ('phone a friend').

Strategy sheet: speech, language and communication needs

Please use the highlighted strategies with . . . (pupil) in . . . (form).

Use TA for pre-tutoring – preparing pupil for a task so that they come to it already knowing the key vocabulary and concepts.
Begin work on a new topic with pupils' existing knowledge and experiences – make a mind map or other visual representation of what they already know.
When you start a new topic, develop a class chart of the vocabulary that pupils will find useful or need to learn. Teach each word by helping children build a web of associations – what it sounds like, what it means, words it goes with, how it fits in a sentence.
Use cued listening – give pupil a small number of questions that they will have to answer after listening to teacher presentation or video input.
Use pupil's name before asking a question or giving an instruction.
Give directions before an activity, not during it.
Keep verbal instructions simple and in the order you want them carried out. Be aware of how many 'information-carrying' words you are using: 'Get your maths book from the pile on **my desk**; on a **clean page**, write the **date** and then **copy down** the **calculations on the board**' has more information-carrying words than many adults will be able to remember.
Check for understanding – ask the pupil to tell you what they have to do.
Agree a private signal pupil can use to show you they have not understood, or teach them to say 'Sorry, I didn't understand that – can you say it again, please?' Praise them for asking for clarification.
Support your oral presentations/explanations with pictures, real objects or mime. Use visuals (real objects, photographs, symbols) appropriate to pupil's developmental level rather than chronological age. Use visual timetables.
Display classroom rules and routines, illustrated by pictures, for pupil to refer to. Illustrate them visually – for example, use a traffic light system to indicate whether pupils can talk or not, or symbols for different noise levels (partner voices, group voices, classroom voice, playground voices).
Use symbols to support spoken language and text (www.widgit.com).
Use visual summaries of discussions – mind maps, flow charts, diagrams, comic strip format, graphic organisers.
Cue pupil in to a change of topic of conversation/presentation: say 'Now we are going to talk about . . . '.
When you ask a question, give pupil time (at least ten seconds) to respond and then, if necessary, repeat what you said. Use the same words unless you think the vocabulary was too difficult to understand.
Question pupil after some other pupils have given examples of what is required.
Give pupil time to talk to a partner before answering a question, or say 'I'm going to come back to you in a minute to ask you xxxx. But first I'm going to ask y a question'.

Strategy sheet: speech, language and communication needs

Continued

If pupil can't answer a question, scaffold/support till they can rather than saying, 'Can anyone help x?'
Use a hierarchy of questions – start with an open question ('What do you think might happen next?'), then if support is needed, frame the question as alternatives ('Do you think x or y?').
Use question prompt card to help pupils know how to respond, for example, 'Where?' question requires a place.
Pair pupil with a study buddy to repeat instructions and demonstrate tasks.
Accept pupil's spoken utterances, but rephrase and give them back in a grammatically correct and expanded version.
Support oral work with talk frames/key phrases ('First . . . next . . . finally', 'I think . . . but on the other hand').
Provide topic-related role-play/drama opportunities and model the language to be used.
Talk aloud about what you are doing using statements which give children examples of the language they might use.
Support writing with writing frames and lists of vocabulary to choose from.
Use a range of ways of recording so that learning is not limited by the pupil's ability to write full English sentences: • Bullet points and mind maps; • Ordering tasks – for example, ordering cut-out words to make a sentence, or sentences to make a sequence of instructions; • Matching tasks, such as matching labels to pictures/diagrams/maps; • Cloze procedure, where they fill in missing words in text; • Annotating a print-off of IWB page; • Powerpoint presentations; • Making posters, oral presentations, videos, dramatic reconstructions.
Provide the pupil with a study pack – glossaries of key subject vocabulary, highlighter pens, glue stick, post-it notes, index cards to make their own mind maps/cartoon strips/key word lists, templates for writing up science experiments, etc.
Allow extra time to complete tasks, and be aware of the fatigue the pupil may experience because of the amount of effort they have to put in to learning.
Write down homework for pupil, put it on the school's app, give it on a pre-printed sticky label or sheet they can stick into their book or record your instructions on a mobile phone or tablet. Model the homework in class time. Allocate a homework buddy they can ring if they have forgotten what to do ('phone a friend').

Strategy sheet: visual impairment

Please use the highlighted strategies with . . . (pupil) in . . . (form).

Use TA for pre-tutoring – preparing pupil for lesson, for example, explaining concepts that rely on vision for understanding.
Don't ask pupil if they can see what is on board/IWB, etc. (they may not know) – check by using symbols that pupil knows, then use same-size font/background/colour as the symbols you have checked.
Take child to unfamiliar classroom before lesson so that they can discuss lighting, where they sit.
Avoid pupil having to look directly into a light source – do not sit or stand with the light behind you.
Use clear, well-spaced print that is suitably contrasted with the background according to individual pupil's needs (for x, y colour on z background). Use non-glossy, non-reflective paper. Use photocopies of masters, not of faint blurred versions.
Give verbal information to replace/supplement information from pictures, questions, facial expression.
Use tactile experience to replace/supplement visual input (for example, if class is watching sugar cubes dissolve in a beaker, pupil can put their hand in beaker and feel it dissolve).
Ensure pupil has an individual copy of print material being read, in the appropriate format (e.g. large print, Braille). This applies to information on classroom walls too (posters, key vocabulary lists).
Say pupil's name before asking a question or giving an instruction, and indicate who is talking in a class discussion.
Provide pupil with own copy of materials to be written on board or IWB; read aloud what you or other pupils are writing up.
Use larger-lined paper, columns or boxes to place numbers in, squared paper. Have pupil use dark pen instead of pencil.
When alerting pupils to an action, artefact, illustration or example, don't just point – describe what you want the pupils to take notice of, and if necessary describe what it is.
Ensure pupil uses aids supplied – such as CCTV, hand-held and portable video magnifiers, book stands, speech output software, digital accessible information system.
Ensure pupil has access to the most appropriate medium for recording work (heavily lined paper, laptop, Braille machine, tape recorder, headphones, digital accessible information system). Access to power supply or space for Braille machine may be required.
Ensure pupil has all the curriculum materials and equipment required to hand and that the materials are organised and contained consistently and securely (use Dycem non-slip mat, a high-sided tray or container with compartments).
Raise position of text (e.g. use sloping desk, reading stands).

Strategy sheet: visual impairment

Continued

Minimise need for extensive handwritten recording – use technology (predictive word processor, onscreen word banks, speech to print applications, graphics packages), bullet points, mind mapping, flow charts, gapped handouts, buddy acting as scribe, photocopied transcripts of notes, printout of IWB page for pupil to annotate.
Use tactile indicators – Blu-Tack, paper clips – to help pupil find information, locate where they need to be on page, keep track of which question they are on in a series.
Allow extra time to complete tasks, and be aware of the fatigue the pupil may experience because of the amount of effort they have to put into learning.
Record your homework instructions on a mobile phone or tablet. Allocate a homework buddy they can ring if they have forgotten what to do ('phone a friend').

Provision map (primary)

PROVISION	YR	Y1	Y2	Y3	Y4	Y5	Y6
Language intervention							
Literacy intervention							
Maths intervention							
Motor coordination programme							
EAL provision							
1–1 counselling							
Small group social and emotional work							
In-class support for individuals							
Attendance and extra-curricular provision							
More able provision							
Other							

Provision map (secondary)

PROVISION	Y7	Y8	Y9	Y10	Y11
Literacy intervention					
Maths intervention					
Oral language intervention					
EAL provision					
1:1 social/emotional/mental health work (counselling/CBT)					
Focus group work to develop social and emotional skills					
In-class support for individuals					
Out of school/extra-curricular provision					
More able provision					
Other					
Other					

Intervention plan: nurture group

Name of provision	NURTURE GROUP
Aims of the programme	To develop the skills young children need in order to learn: the ability to settle, listen, concentrate, share and make friends.
Description of programme	Small class of up to 12 children taught by a teacher and a TA. Children register with their mainstream class and spend some time there each week but spend most of the day in the nurture group room. This is designed to replicate a nurturing home, with areas themed around home, kitchen, work and play.
Target group	Children who are unable to respond in a mainstream class, are seriously disruptive or withdrawn and failing to learn because their basic emotional and social needs have not been met in their early years. Usually Reception age.
Entry level	Scores on Boxall Profile that indicate developmental levels well below those expected of competently functioning children, or behaviours which are preventing the child making progress both academically and socially.
Exit level	Teacher judgement based on changes to Boxall Profile or use of Nurture Group Reintegration Readiness Scale (Doyle, 2001) – numerical score 218 (70%) or above.
Length of intervention	Two to five terms.
Frequency	Daily.
Delivered by	Teacher and TA or nursery nurse.
Suggested start date	Anytime.
Groupings	Group of up to 12.
Assessment method	Boxall Profile.
Monitoring arrangements	HT/Deputy HT observation using checklist of criteria for effective nurture groups from Nurture Group Network.
Arrangements for parental involvement	Parents invited to join nurture group regularly for breakfast; staff discuss and model strategies for promoting social and emotional development.
Arrangements for linking intervention to class teaching	Joint medium-term planning by nurture group and class teacher. Class teacher to notice and praise specific behaviours as advised by nurture group teacher.

Task	Date/Information	Checklist (tick when completed)
Identify children to be assessed on Boxall Profile	Names:	
Set a date for assessment	Date:	
Select children for the group	Names:	
Set a date for a parent meeting	Date:	
Set a date for the intervention programme to begin	Date:	
Set a date for HT/Deputy HT observation	Date:	
Set a date for post-programme assessments	Date:	
Set dates for three- and six-month follow-up assessments	Dates:	
Complete evaluation and disseminate outcomes to SLT	Date:	

Intervention plan: SEAL focus group

https://sealcommunity.org/national-resources?resources%5B0%5D=category%3ASmall%20group%20work

Name of provision	SEAL FOCUS GROUP – MANAGING STRONG FEELINGS
Aims of the programme	To accelerate pupil progress towards SEAL learning outcomes. 'I understand why feelings sometimes "take over" or get out of control and know what makes me angry or upset', 'I have a range of strategies for managing impulses and strong emotions so they do not lead me to behave in ways that would have negative consequences for me or for other people.'
Description of programme	Six two-hour small group sessions in school followed by one day off-site team challenge activities.
Target group	Year 8 pupils who have difficulty in managing strong feelings.
Entry level	High per-week rate of behaviour incidents
Exit level	
Length of intervention	Seven weeks.
Frequency	Weekly.
Delivered by	Learning Support Base teacher and learning mentor (LM).
Suggested start date	Spring term.
Groupings	Maximum eight with a balance of pupils – some impulsive, some easily upset, no more than four who are often angry.
Assessment method	Pupils who might benefit from the scheme are identified using self and tutor referral. Evaluation is via changes to per-week behaviour incidents and reductions in number of times per month pupil is placed in detention or referred to Head of Year.
Arrangements for parental involvement	Parent meeting to discuss intervention/contribute to initial and final assessment.
Arrangements for linking intervention to class teaching	All staff briefed to model, notice and praise appropriate management of strong feelings.

Task	Date/Information	Checklist (tick when completed)
Identify pupils who might benefit	Names:	
Set a date for pupil meetings (to secure sign-up and complete self-rating scales)	Date:	
Set a date for parent contacts	Date:	
Select pupils for the group	Names:	
Fix a timetable for the sessions each week	Times:	
Fix dates for initial planning (half day) and post-session reviews/forward planning for the teacher and LM	Dates:	
Decide where the sessions will take place	Location:	
Set a date for the intervention programme to begin	Date:	
Set a date for SENCO to monitor	Date:	
Set a date for end of intervention post-programme assessments	Date:	
Set dates for three- and six-month follow-up assessments	Dates:	
Complete evaluation and disseminate outcomes to SLT	Date:	

Intervention plan: Language for Behaviour and Emotions

http://thinkingtalking.co.uk/lfbe/

Name of provision	**LANGUAGE FOR BEHAVIOUR AND EMOTIONS**
Aims of the programme	To develop the language children need for positive behaviour.
Description of programme	Focuses on children's language, emotional and thinking skills. Covers language comprehension monitoring, understanding words, figurative language, emotional literacy, narrative and solving people problems.
Target group	Pupils in upper KS2 and KS3 with SEMH and SLCN including developmental language disorder (DLD) and autism.
Entry level	High per-week rate of behaviour incidents.
Exit level	-
Length of intervention	Minimum 12 weeks.
Frequency	Flexible.
Delivered by	TA, learning mentor (LM) or teacher.
Suggested start date	-
Groupings	Small group or individual.
Assessment method	The programme has its own LFBE assessment tool to use pre- and post-intervention.
Arrangements for parental involvement	Parents informed child will be taking part and what they can be expected to learn.
Arrangements for linking intervention to class teaching	Class teacher/tutor oversight of programme.

Task	**Date/Information**	**Checklist (tick when completed)**
Identify pupils who might benefit	Names:	
Carry out initial assessments	Names:	
Fix a timetable for the sessions each week	Times:	
Decide where the sessions will take place	Location:	
Set a date for the intervention programme to begin	Date:	
Set a date for SENCO to monitor	Date:	
Set a date for end of intervention post-programme assessments	Date:	
Set dates for three- and six-month follow-up assessments	Dates:	
Complete evaluation and disseminate outcomes to SLT	Date:	

Intervention plan: Nuffield Early Language Intervention (NELI)

Name of provision	**NUFFIELD EARLY LANGUAGE INTERVENTION**
Aims of the programme	To improve communication, language and literacy skills.
Description of programme	The programme provides structured activities to develop pupils' oral language skills in a variety of situations. In the second half of the programme, there are also activities to develop phonological awareness and early letter-sound knowledge.
Target group	Reception – the five or six children who score lowest on LanguageScreen compared to their peers.
Entry level	Low scores on LanguageScreen app.
Exit level	-
Length of intervention	20 weeks.
Frequency	Three small group sessions and two individual sessions weekly.
Delivered by	TA, who has been trained to deliver the programme.
Suggested start date	Early in autumn term
Groupings	Three–six pupils
Assessment method	Pre and post LanguageScreen scores
Monitoring arrangements	Class teacher to observe TA twice during the 20-week programme
Arrangements for linking intervention to class teaching	Support for TA from class teachers trained in NELI
Arrangements for parental involvement	Introductory information letter and newsletters

Task	**Date/Information**	**Checklist (tick when completed)**
Set a date for screening YR classes	Date	
Seek parental consent for screening		
Select children for the group	Names:	
Fix a timetable for the sessions each week	Times:	
Allocate half a day of preparation time for the TA	Date:	
Decide where the sessions will take place	Location:	
Fix a time for a weekly teacher/ TA review session	Time:	
Set a date for the intervention programme to begin	Date:	
Set dates for class teacher to observe session	Dates:	
Set a date for post-programme assessments	Date:	
Complete evaluation and disseminate outcomes to SLT	Date:	

Intervention plan: Talk Boost

Name of provision	TALK BOOST
Aims of the programme	To narrow the gap in speaking and listening skills between four- to seven-year-olds with language delay and their peers.
Description of programme	The programme provides structured activities to develop pupils' oral language skills in a variety of situations.
Target group	Year R to Year 2.
Entry level	Teacher assessment of language delay using the Progression Tools in the pack.
Exit level	
Length of intervention	Ten weeks.
Frequency	Three × 30–40 mins weekly.
Delivered by	TA, who has been trained to deliver the programme.
Suggested start date	Flexible.
Groupings	Four in group.
Assessment method	Progression Tools.
Monitoring arrangements	Class teacher to observe TA twice during the ten-week programme.
Arrangements for parental involvement	Programme has Children's Activity Books – activities for children to take home and share with parents and carers.
Arrangements for linking intervention to class teaching	Programme has weekly activities linking small group activities to the class and supporting whole-class speaking and listening skills.

Task	Date/Information	Checklist (tick when completed)
Identify children to be screened	Names:	
Set a date for screening	Date:	
Select children for the group	Names:	
Fix a timetable for the sessions each week	Times:	
Allocate half a day of preparation time for the TA	Date:	
Decide where the sessions will take place	Location:	
Fix a time for the weekly teacher/ TA review session	Time:	
Set a date for the intervention programme to begin	Date:	
Set a date for the parent meeting	Date:	
Set a date for the progress checks during the programme	Date:	
Set dates for class teacher to observe session	Dates:	
Set a date for post-programme assessments	Date:	
Complete evaluation and disseminate outcomes to SLT	Date:	

Intervention plan: Reading Recovery

Name of provision	READING RECOVERY
Aims of the programme	To generate accelerated learning back to age-appropriate reading and writing levels.
Description of programme	Reading Recovery is an intervention programme for children who have made very little progress in reading and writing during their first year in school. It involves a daily one-to-one lesson with a highly trained teacher.
Target group	Year 1/Year 2.
Entry level	Lowest-attaining pupils.
Exit level	Age-appropriate attainment in reading and writing.
Length of intervention	12 to 20 weeks.
Frequency	30 mins daily.
Delivered by	Teacher with Reading Recovery teaching qualification.
Suggested start date	After the child has been in school for three terms.
Groupings	One-to-one
Assessment method	Book band level/running record. Writing sample. BAS reading test. Reading Recovery Observation Survey.
Monitoring arrangements	Reading Recovery teacher to be observed teaching by qualified RR Teacher Leader.
Arrangements for parental involvement	Contract with parents, parents invited to observe lessons, daily homework tasks for children to complete with parent.
Arrangements for linking intervention to class teaching	Class teacher observes session early on and towards end of child's programme.

Task	Date/Information	Checklist (tick when completed)
Identify children to be assessed	Names:	
Set a date for assessments	Date:	
Select children to take part	Names:	
Fix a timetable for the sessions each week	Times:	
Decide where the sessions will take place	Location:	
Fix date for Teacher Leader to monitor teaching	Date:	
Set a date for the intervention programme to begin	Date:	
Set times for liaison with class teacher	Times:	
Set dates for post-programme assessments	Dates:	
Set dates for three- and six-month follow-up assessments	Dates:	
Complete evaluation and disseminate outcomes to SLT	Dates:	

Intervention plan: Catch Up Literacy

Name of provision	CATCH UP LITERACY
Aims of the programme	To address the problem of underachievement rooted in literacy difficulties.
Description of programme	Book-based intervention for struggling readers. It uses Catch Up Literacy assessments for learning to determine what the learner can do and where their needs lie, and to set Catch Up Literacy targets. These help to inform individualised, one-to-one sessions.
Target group	Learners who are struggling readers rather than beginner readers.
Entry level	
Exit level	Reaches age-related expectations.
Length of intervention	An average of six to 12 months (depending on need).
Frequency	Two × 15 minutes a week
Delivered by	TA who has completed recognised training.
Suggested start date	Flexible
Groupings	One-to-one.
Assessment method	Catch Up Literacy assessments for learning Standardised tests Tracking through Catch Up Literacy levels
Monitoring arrangements	Catch Up Coordinator undertakes 'Delivering Catch Up Literacy' and 'Managing Catch Up Literacy' training and uses the Catch Up Coordinator Action Plan to support/monitor/observe TA.

Task	Date/Information	Checklist (tick when completed)
Select children to take part	Names:	
Catch Up Literacy-trained TA assesses children using Catch Up Literacy assessments for learning	Date:	
Fix a timetable for the sessions each week	Times:	
Decide where the sessions will take place	Location:	
TA/Catch Up Coordinator implement Action Plan	Date:	
Set a date for the intervention to begin	Date:	
Set a date for parent meetings	Date:	
Set times for liaison with class teacher	Times:	
Set a date for post-intervention assessments	Date:	
Set dates for three- and six-month follow-up assessments	Dates:	
Complete evaluation and disseminate outcomes to SLT	Date:	

Intervention plan: 1stClass@Number

Name of provision	**1STCLASS@NUMBER**
Aims of the programme	To enable children to reach age-related expectations in numeracy.
Description of programme	Early intervention programme for children who have fallen behind their peers in numeracy.
Target group	1stClass@Number 1 – for children who need further support at the level of the Year 1 curriculum. 1stClass@Number 2 – for children who need further support at the level of the Year 2 curriculum.
Entry level	Working below age-related expectations, lowest scores on Sandwell test
Exit level	Age related expectations in numeracy
Length of intervention	Up to 30, 30-minute sessions
Frequency	Three × 30 minutes a week.
Delivered by	Trained TA.
Suggested start date	Flexible.
Groupings	Up to four children in a group.
Assessment method	Sandwell Numeracy Test. Teacher assessment.
Monitoring arrangements	TA to be observed teaching by class teacher or (where available) Numbers Count teacher.
Arrangements for parental involvement	Games@Home, a pack of five mathematical games linked to 1stClass@Number 1 that parents can play with their children
Arrangements for linking intervention to class teaching	Class teacher observes sessions.

Task	**Date/Information**	**Checklist (tick when completed)**
Select children to take part	Names:	
SENCO assesses children using Sandwell test	Date:	
Fix a timetable for the sessions each week	Times:	
Decide where the sessions will take place	Location:	
Fix a date when class teacher will monitor teaching	Date:	
Set a date for the intervention programme to begin	Date:	
Set a date for parent meetings	Date:	
Set times for liaison with class teacher	Times:	
Set a date for post-programme assessments	Date:	
Set dates for three- and six-month follow-up assessments	Dates:	
Complete evaluation and disseminate outcomes to SLT	Date:	

Intervention plan: Success@Arithmetic

Name of provision	SUCCESS@ARITHMETIC
Aims of the programme	Success@Arithmetic: Number Sense For pupils in Years 3 to 5 who need support to understand the number system and develop fluency with number facts. Success@Arithmetic: Calculation For pupils in Years 5 to 8 who need support to understand and develop fluency with formal written methods.
Description of programme	Tailored calculation-based small group programme based on an initial detailed assessment.
Target group	Pupils who have difficulties with arithmetic proficiency and need support to improve their understanding of number and written calculation skills.
Entry level	Teacher assessment.
Exit level	-
Length of intervention	Up to 24 sessions.
Frequency	Flexible – short teaching sessions several times a week.
Delivered by	TA working with teacher.
Suggested start date	Flexible.
Groupings	Group of up to three.
Assessment method	Success@Arithmetic trains a lead teacher and one or two TAs together. The lead teacher conducts a diagnostic assessment and selects a series of Success@ Arithmetic steps to form a tailored programme of detailed plans.
Monitoring arrangements	Lead teacher to observe TA once during the intervention.
Arrangements for parental involvement	-
Arrangements for linking intervention to class teaching	Lead teacher devises child's programme.

Task	Date/Information	Checklist (tick when completed)
Select children to take part	Names:	
Teacher assesses children	Date:	
Fix a timetable for the sessions each week	Times:	
Allocate half a day of preparation time for the TA	Date:	
Decide where the sessions will take place	Location:	
Fix a date when teacher will monitor teaching	Date:	
Fix a time for a weekly teacher/ TA review session	Time:	
Set a date for the intervention programme to begin	Date:	
Set a date for post-programme assessments	Date:	
Set dates for three- and six-month follow-up assessments	Dates:	
Complete evaluation and disseminate outcomes to SLT	Date:	

Intervention plan: tutoring

Name of provision	TUTORING UNDER THE NATIONAL TUTORING PROGRAMME
Aims of the programme	To help pupils who have fallen behind to catch up with their learning – for primary pupils in maths, English and science, and for secondary school pupils in maths, English, science, humanities and modern foreign languages.
Description of programme	Flexible sessions, face-to-face or online, from trained external or internal tuition partner or member of school staff, normally a qualified teacher.
Target group	Pupils in Years 1 to 11 who have fallen behind, particularly those who are FSM-eligible.
Entry level	Working below age-related expectations.
Exit level	
Length of intervention	12 to 15 hours.
Frequency	Flexible.
Delivered by	Trained external tuition partners or school staff.
Suggested start date	Flexible.
Groupings	Small groups of 1:3 are recommended but can be up to six pupils, with group sizes of 1:1 or 1:2 for pupils with SEND.
Assessment method	Teacher assessment.
Monitoring arrangements	Tutoring lead within school to observe sample of sessions.

Task	Date/Information	Checklist (tick when completed)
Select children to take part	Names:	
Fix a timetable for the sessions each week	Times:	
Decide where the sessions will take place	Location:	
Set a date for the intervention to begin	Date:	
Set times for liaison with class/subject teacher	Times:	
Set a date for post-intervention assessments	Date:	
Complete evaluation and disseminate outcomes to SLT	Date:	

Record of intervention programme

WEEK COMMENCED												
Names	Pre-intervention assessment outcomes	Wk 1	Wk 2	Wk 3	Wk 4	Wk 5	Wk 6	Wk 7	Wk 8	Wk 9	Wk 10	Post-intervention assessment outcomes
Sessions run												
Weekly meeting with teacher												
Evaluation												

Notes:
Write in all dates in advance where possible.
Tick in the weekly box if the child attended the session.
Continue on further sheet where programmes last longer than 10 weeks.
If assessments are on another sheet, write 'see attached sheet' and staple to the record sheets.

Monitoring the quality of intervention sessions

QUALITY FEATURES	✓	EVIDENCE
The right pupils have been targeted.		
The location is appropriate.		
The frequency of the intervention is as specified.		
The session length is as specified.		
The session content matches that specified in the programme.		
Resources have been pre-prepared and are well managed.		
The adult and the pupils know what the learning objectives are.		
The adult has sufficient subject knowledge to promote learning.		
The session is planned and adjusted on the basis of assessment and pupils are helped to identify their own learning targets and to assess their own progress.		
Key instructions and learning points are given concisely and clearly and repeated as necessary.		
Behaviour is well managed and the adult promotes interaction between the pupils in the group.		
The adult promotes pupils' independence as learners, helping them recognise what strategies they are using successfully and apply them in other situations.		
The adult creates a secure and supportive learning environment where there is safety to have a go and make mistakes.		
The adult challenges pupils and expects the most from them.		
Teaching styles and approaches are active, lively and multisensory; the session is well paced.		
Class or subject teacher and additional adult plan and review the intervention jointly.		
There are opportunities for pupils to apply their learning and have it reinforced in class/across the school.		
Parental involvement is secured as specified in the programme.		

Actions:

References

Adams, L., Tindle, A., Basran, S. *et al.* (2017) *Education, health and care plans: A survey of parents and young people*. London: DfE.

Andrä, C., Mathias, B., Schwager, A. *et al.* (2020) Learning foreign language vocabulary with gestures and pictures enhances vocabulary memory for several months post-learning in eight-year-old school children. *Educational Psychology Review*, 32, 815–50.

Anti-Bullying Alliance (2021) *Reducing bullying in school: A summary of findings from the independent evaluation of the all together programme 2017–2021*. London: Anti-Bullying Alliance.

Aubin, G. (2020) Practical ways to meet parents/carers 3 times per year. *SEND Matters Blog*, 6 July.

Aubin, G. (2021) Seeing without observing: How to be a visible SENDCO without adding to school scrutiny. *SEND Matters Blog*, 4 November.

Baumeister, R., Campbell, J., Krueger, J. *et al.* (2003) Does high self-esteem cause better performance, interpersonal success, happiness, or healthier lifestyles? *Psychological Science in the Public Interest*, 4 (1), 1–44.

Blanden, J. (2006) *Bucking the trend: What enables those who are disadvantaged in childhood to succeed later in life?* London: Department for Work and Pensions.

Blatchford, P., Russell, A. and Webster, R. (2012) *Reassessing the impact of teaching assistants: How research challenges practice and policy*. London: Routledge.

Boddison, A., Curran, H. and Moloney, H. (2020) *National SENCO workforce survey 2020: Time to review 2018–20*. Bath: Bath Spa University.

Branagan, A., Cross, M. and Parsons, P. (2020) *Language for behaviour and emotions*. London: Routledge.

Bromley, M. (2021) Adaptive teaching explained: What, why and how? *SecEd*, 8 December.

Brooks, G. (1996) *Family literacy works*. London: NFER/BSA.

Brooks, G. (1998) *Family numeracy adds up*. London: NFER/BSA.

Brooks, G. and Pahl, K. (2008) *Effective and inclusive practices in early literacy, language and numeracy: A review of programmes and practice in the UK and internationally*. London: CfBT Education Trust.

Campbell, T. (2021) *Special educational needs and disabilities within the English primary school system: What can disproportionalities by season of birth contribute to understanding processes behind attributions and (lack of) provisions?* London: LSE Centre for Analysis of Social Exclusion (CASE).

Chapman, C., Ainscow, M., Miles, S. and West, M. (2011) *Leadership that promotes the achievement of students with special educational needs and disabilities*. Nottingham: National College for School Leadership.

Chatzitheochari, S., Parsons, S., and Platt, L. (2016) Doubly disadvantaged? Bullying experiences among disabled children and young people in England. *Sociology*, 50 (4), 695–713.

Clegg, J. (2004) Language and Behaviour: an exploratory study of pupils in an exclusion unit *Proceedings of the British Psychological Society Developmental Section Annual Conference*, Leeds, September.

Cochrane, S. (2006) *Putting the pieces together: A guide to provision management*. London: London Regional Partnership.

Cosgrove, R. (2021) *Inclusive teaching in a nutshell*. London: Routledge.

Damsgaard, L., Nielsen, A., Gejl, A. *et al.* (2022) Effects of 8 weeks with embodied learning on 5–6-year-old Danish children's pre-reading skills and word reading skills: The PLAYMORE project, DK. *Educational Psychology Review*, 34, 1709–37.

DCSF (2007) *Social and emotional aspects of learning for secondary schools*. London: DCSF.

Dempsey, N. (2021) *The current approach is based on the fairly arbitrary notion of there being distinct SEND and non-SEND learners*. https://inco14.wordpress.com/2021/05/08/the-current-approach-is-based-on-the-fairly-arbitrary-notion-of-there-being-distinct-send-and-non-send-learners/comment-page-1/.

Den Heijer, A. (2018) *Nothing you don't already know*. Scotts Valley, California: CreateSpace.

Desforges, C. and Abouchaar, A. (2003) *The impact of parental involvement, parental support and family education on pupil achievement and adjustment: A review of the literature*. London: DfES.

DfE (2011) *Support and aspiration: A new approach to special educational needs and disability*. London: DfE.

DfE (2022) *Special educational needs in England, January 2022*. London: DfE.

DfE and DH (2014) *Special educational needs and disability code of practice: 0 to 25 years*. London: DfE and DH.

DfES (2005a) *Excellence and enjoyment: Social and emotional aspects of learning*. London: DfES.

DfES (2005b) *Higher standards, better schools for all*. London: DfES.

Department of Health (2010) *Person centred planning: Advice for using person-centred thinking, planning and reviews in schools and transition*. London: Department of Health.

Doyle, R. (2001) Using a readiness scale for reintegrating pupils with social, emotional and behavioural difficulties from a Nurture Group into their mainstream classroom: A pilot study. *British Journal of Special Education*, 28 (3), 126–32.

Education Endowment Foundation (2015) *Making best use of teaching assistants*. London: Education Endowment Foundation.

Education Endowment Foundation (2021) *Special educational needs in mainstream schools*. London: Education Endowment Foundation.

Education Endowment Foundation (2022) *Education Endowment Foundation teaching and learning toolkit*. London: Education Endowment Foundation.

Elley, D. (2020) Beyond the tick list: The ice cream sundae approach to explaining autism. *The Optimus Blog*, 16 July.

Ellis, S., Tod, J. and Graham-Matheson, L. (2012) *Special educational needs: Reflection, renewal and reality*. Birmingham: NASUWT.

Everard, B. and Morris, G. (1990) *Effective school management*. London: PCP.

Every Child a Chance Trust (2009) *The long term costs of literacy difficulties* (2nd edn.). London: Every Child a Chance Trust.

Feinstein, L. (2000) *The relative importance of academic, psychological and behavioural attributes developed in childhood*. London: London School of Economics.

Fernandes, M., Wammes, J. and Meade, M. (2018) The surprisingly powerful influence of drawing on memory. *Current Directions in Psychological Science*, 27 (5), 302–8.

Fitzgibbon, G. and O'Connor, B. (2002) *Adult dyslexia: A guide for the workplace*. London: Wiley and Sons.

Flouri, E. and Buchanan, A. (2002) What predicts good relationships with parents in adolescence and partners in adult life. *Journal of Family Psychology*, 16, 186–98.

Francis, B., Taylor, B. and Tereshchenko, A. (2019) *Reassessing 'ability' grouping: Improving practice for equity and attainment*. London: Routledge.

Furlong, M., McGilloway, S., Bywater, T. *et al.* (2012) Behavioural and cognitive-behavioural group-based parenting programmes for early-onset conduct problems in children aged 3 to 12 years. *The Cochrane Library*, (2).

Gardner, F., Leijten, P., Mann, J. *et al.* (2017) *Could scale-up of parenting programmes improve child disruptive behaviour and reduce social inequalities? Using individual participant data meta-analysis to establish for whom programmes are effective and cost-effective*. Southampton (UK): NIHR Journals Library, December. PMID: 29227603.

Gerber, S., Finn, J., Achilles, C. and Boyd-Zaharias, J. (2001) Teacher aides and students' academic achievement. *Educational Evaluation and Policy Analysis*, 23 (2), 123–43.

Giangreco, M., Cloninger, C. and Iverson, V. (1993) *Choosing Options and Accommodations for Children (COACH): A guide to planning inclusive education*. Baltimore: Paul H Brookes.

Giangreco, M., Edelman, S., Luisellu, T. and Macfarland, S. (1997) Helping or hovering? Effects of instructional assistant proximity on students with disabilities. *Exceptional Children*, 64, 7–18.

Gross, J. (1994) Asperger syndrome: A label worth having? *Educational Psychology in Practice*, 10 (2).

Gross, J. (1996) The weight of the evidence. *Support for Learning*, 11 (1), 3–8.

Gross, J. (2002) *Special educational needs in the primary school: A practical guide* (3rd edn.). Buckingham: Open University Press.

Gross, J. (2013) Who really has special educational needs? *Special Children*, autumn issue (213).

Gross, J. (2018) *Time to talk* (2nd edn.). London: Routledge.

Gross, J. (2021) *Reaching the unseen children: Practical strategies for closing stubborn attainment gaps in disadvantaged groups*. London: Routledge.

Gross, J. and White, A. (2003) *Special educational needs and school improvement*. London: David Fulton.

Gutman, L. and Schoon, I. (2013) *The impact of non-cognitive skills on outcomes for young people: Literature Review*. London: Education Endowment Foundation/Cabinet Office.

Hattie, J. (2008) *Visible learning*. London and New York: Routledge.

Hirst, K., Hannon, P., and Nutbrown, C. (2010) Effects of a preschool bilingual family literacy programme. *Journal of Early Childhood Literacy*, 10, 183–208.

House of Commons Education and Skills Select Committee (2006) *Special educational needs: Third report of session 2005–6*. London: HMSO.

Howes, A. (2003) Teaching reforms and the impact of paid adult support on participation in learning in mainstream schools. *Support for Learning*, 18 (4), 147–53.

Hutchinson, J. (2021) *Identifying pupils with special educational needs and disabilities*. London: Education Policy Institute.

Independent Review Unit (2006) *IRU statement for 2006*. London: DfES.

Jay, T., Willis, B., Thomas, P. *et al.* (2017) *Dialogic teaching evaluation report and executive summary*. London: Education Endowment Foundation.

Karpicke, J. and Roediger, H. (2010) Is expanding retrieval a superior method for learning text materials? *Memory & Cognition*, 38, 116–24.

Klein, R. (2000) *Defying disaffection*. London: Trentham Books.

Knight, C. (2021) The impact of the dyslexia label on academic outlook and aspirations: An analysis using propensity score matching. *British Journal of Educational Psychology*, 91, 1110–26.

Knight, C. and Crick, T. (2021) The assignment and distribution of the dyslexia label: Using the UK Millennium Cohort Study to investigate the sociodemographic predictors of dyslexia in England and Wales. *PLoS One*, 0256114.

Knight, S. (2022) *The chronicles of a therapeutic classroom: Ten low-cost ideas*. www.headteacher-update.com/best-practice-article/the-chronicles-of-a-therapeutic-classroom-ten-low-cost-ideas-well-being-vulnerable-pupils-attachment-mental-health/246320/.

Knightsmith, P. (2022) Practical strategies for building self-esteem in pupils with ADHD. *SecEd*, 5 April.

Knoster, T. (1991) Factors in managing complex change. *Material presentation at TASH conference*. Washington DC: The Association for People with Severe Disabilities.

Lamb, B. (2009) *Lamb inquiry: Special educational needs and parental confidence*. London: DCSF.

Lepkowska, D. (2021) *An inclusive school playground: Six key criteria*. www.headteacher-update.com/knowledge-bank/an-inclusive-school-playground-six-key-criteria-send-inclusion-outdoor-education-primary-reception-nursery-play-equipment/241759/.

Lexmond, J., Bazalgette, L. and Margo, J. (2011) *The home front*. London: Demos.

Lindsay, G., Cullen, M., Cullen, S. *et al.* (2010) *Evaluation of impact of DfE investment in initiatives designed to improve teacher workforce skills in relation to SEN and disabilities*. London: DfE.

Lord, P., Rennie, C., Smith, R. *et al.* (2021) *Randomised controlled trial evaluation of families connect*. Slough: National Foundation for Educational Research.

Lord, P., Styles, B., Morrison, J. *et al.* (2018) *Families and Schools Together (FAST): Evaluation report*. Slough: NFER.

Maloney, H. (2022) How to be a great SENCO. *The SecEd Podcast*, 2 February. www.sec-ed.co.uk/knowledge-bank/the-seced-podcast-how-to-be-a-great-senco-schools-send-inclusion-special-needs-students-children-headteacher-leadership-teaching-education-learning/.

Massonnié, J. (2020) Understanding the impact of classroom noise on children's learning and well-being, and its modulation by executive functions. *Conference Paper: Birkbeck College*, University of London. www.researchgate.net/publication/351867759_Understanding_the_impact_of_classroom_noise_on_children's_learning_and_well-being_and_its_modulation_by_executive_functions.

Morewood, G., Humphrey, N. and Symes, W. (2011) Mainstreaming autism: Making it work. *Psychology*, 1 December.

Moyles, J. and Suschitzky, W. (1997) *Jills of all trades: Classroom assistants in KS1 classes*. London: University of Leicester/ATL.

Murray, P. and Sanderson, H. (2007) *Developing person-centred approaches in schools*. Stockport: HSA Press.

Nutbrown, C., Hannon, P. and Morgan, A. (2005) *Early literacy work with families*. London: SAGE Publications.

Odell, E. (2019) *Special or unique: Young people's attitudes to disability*. London: Disability Rights UK.

Ofsted (2004) *Special educational needs and disability: Towards inclusive schools*. London: Ofsted.

Ofsted (2006) *Inclusion: Does it matter where pupils are taught?* London: Ofsted.

Ofsted (2010) *The special educational needs and disability review*. London: Ofsted.

Ofsted (2021) *Supporting SEND*. London: Ofsted.

Oredipe, T., Kofner, B., Riccio, A. *et al.* (2022) Does learning you are autistic at a younger age lead to better adult outcomes? A participatory exploration of the perspectives of autistic university students. *Autism*. https://doi.org/10.1177/13623613221086700.

Papps, I. and Dyson, A. (2004) *The costs and benefits of earlier identification and effective intervention*. London: DfES.

Parr, C. (2019) Social inequality. *Times Educational Supplement*, 8 November.

Pegram, J., Watkins, R., Hoerger, M. *et al.* (2022) Assessing the range and evidence-base of interventions in a typical school cluster. *Review of Education*, 10 (1).

Perry, B. (2009) *Dr Bruce Perry Pt 3 video*. www.youtube.com/watch?v=ZVRO7PdYRnM.

Pinkett, M. and Roberts, M. (2019) *Boys don't try?* London: Routledge.

Pinney, A. (2004) *Reducing reliance on Statements: An investigation into local authority practice and outcomes*. London: DfES.

Rattan, A., Good, C. and Dweck, C. (2012) 'It's OK: Not everyone can be good at math': Instructors with an entity theory comfort (and demotivate) students. *Journal of Experimental Social Psychology*, 48, 731–7.

Ribosa, J. and Duran, D. (2022) Do students learn what they teach when generating teaching materials for others? A meta-analysis through the lens of learning by teaching. *Educational Research Review*, 37.

Roulstone, S. and McLeod, S. (Eds.). (2011) *Listening to children and young people with speech, language and communication needs*. Guildford: J&R Press.

RSA (2022) *The inclusive and nurturing schools toolkit*. London: RSA.

Runeckles, C. (2022) Making the most of metacognition. *Research Schools Network Blog*, 9 May. https://researchschool.org.uk/news/making-the-most-of-metacognition.

Schunk, D., Hanson, A. and Cox, P. (1987) Peer-model attributes and children's achievement behaviors. *Journal of Educational Psychology*, 79, 54–61.

Sherrington, T. (2021) Five ways to: Scaffold classroom dialogue. *Blog Post*. December 1. https://teacherhead.com/2021/12/01/five-ways-to-scaffold-classroom-dialogue/.

Sherrington, T. (2022) Rehearsal first: Retrieval practice later: An important distinction. *Blog Post*. January 16. https://teacherhead.com/2022/01/16/rehearsal-first-retrieval-practice-later-an-important-distinction/.

Shield, B. and Dockrell, J. (2008) The effects of classroom and environmental noise on children's academic performance. *Proceedings of the 9th International Congress on Noise as a Public Health Problem*. ICBEN, Foxwoods, CT.

Shifrer, D. (2013) Stigma of a label: Educational expectations for high school students labeled with learning disabilities. *Journal of Health and Social Behavior*, 54 (4), 462–80.

Sobel, D. and Alston, S. (2021) *The inclusive classroom: A new approach to differentiation*. London: Bloomsbury.

Stalvey, S. and Brasell, H. (2006) Using stress balls to focus the attention of sixth-grade learners. *Journal of At-Risk Issues*, 12, 7–16.

Sylva, K., Melhuish, E., Sammons, P. *et al.* (2003) *The Effective Provision of Pre-School Education (EPPE) project: Findings from the pre-school period*. London: Institute of Education, University of London.

Thiede, K., Wright, K., Hagenah, S. *et al.* (2022) Drawing to improve metacomprehension accuracy. *Learning and Instruction*, 77.

Timpson, E. (2019) *The Timpson review of school exclusion*. London: DfE.

Tymms, P. and Merrell, C. (2006) Screening and interventions for inattentive, hyperactive and impulsive children. *European Journal of Special Needs Education*, 21 (3), 321–37.

Tyner, A. and Kabourek, S. (2020) *Social studies instruction and reading comprehension: Evidence from the early childhood longitudinal study*. Washington, DC: Thomas B. Fordham Institute.

van Poortvliet, M., Clarke, A. and Gross, J. (2019) *Improving social and emotional learning in primary schools*. London: Education Endowment Foundation.

Wang, X., Mayer, R., Zhou, P. *et al.* (2021) Benefits of interactive graphic organizers in online learning: Evidence for generative learning theory. *Journal of Educational Psychology*, 113 (5), 1024–37.

Index

Note: Numbers in **bold** indicate a table, schedule, or template. Numbers in *italics* indicate a figure on the corresponding page.

Printed in Great Britain
by Amazon

29286877R00170